# THE
# EINSATZGRUPPEN
# R E P O R T S

# THE
# EINSATZGRUPPEN
# REPORTS

Selections from the Dispatches
of the Nazi Death Squads'
Campaign Against the Jews
July 1941 - January 1943

*Edited by*

Yitzhak Arad
Shmuel Krakowski
Shmuel Spector

HOLOCAUST LIBRARY
NEW YORK, NEW YORK

Translated by Stella Schossberger

Library of Congress Cataloging-in-Publication Data

The Einsatzgruppen reports
1. Holocaust, Jewish (1939-1945) — Sources. I. Arad, Yitzhak,
1926-      II. Krakowski, Shmuel. III. Spector, Shmuel.
IV. Germany. Reichsfuhrer-SS.
D804.3.E46   1989   940.53'18      87-81220
ISBN: 0-89604-057-7 (Cloth)
ISBN: 0-89604-058-5 (Paperback)
Library of Congress Catalogue Card Number 87-81220

THE EINSATZGRUPPEN REPORTS is published by Holocaust Library
in cooperation with Yad Vashem in Jerusalem, Israel.
Printed in the United States of America

# HOLOCAUST LIBRARY

## STATEMENT OF PURPOSE

The Holocaust spread across the face of Europe just a few decades ago. The brutality then unleashed is still nearly beyond comprehension. Millions of innocents — men, women and children — were consumed by its flames.

The goal of Holocaust Publications, a non-profit organization founded by survivors, is to publish and disseminate works on the Holocaust. These will include survivors' accounts, testimonies and memoirs, historical and regional analyses, anthologies, archival and source documents and other relevant materials that will help shed light on this cataclysmic era.

These books and studies will be made available to the general public, scholars, researchers, historians, teachers and students. They will be used in Holocaust Resource Centers, libraries and schools, synagogues and churches. They will help foster an increased awareness of the Holocaust and its implications. They will help to preserve the memory for posterity and to enable this awesome time to be better understood and comprehended.

**Holocaust Library**
216 West 18th Street
New York, NY 10011
212-463-7988

# TABLE OF COMPARABLE RANKS

| U.S. Army | Wehrmacht | SS |
|---|---|---|
| 2nd Lieutenant | Leutnant | Untersturmführer |
| 1st Lieutenant | Oberleutnant | Obersturmführer |
| Captain | Hauptmann | Hauptsturmführer |
| Major | Major | Sturmbannführer |
| Lieutenant Colonel | Obersteutnant | Obersturmbannführer |
| Colonel | Oberst | Standartenführer |
| | | * Oberführer |
| Brigadier General | Generalmajor | Brigadeführer |
| Major General | Generalleutnant | Gruppenführer |
| Lieutenant General | General der Infanterie, der Artillerie, etc. | Obergruppenführer |
| General | Generaloberst | Oberstgruppenführer |
| General of the Army | Generalfeldmarschall | Reichsführer |

* approximate equivalent to a senior colonel

Der Chef der Sicherheitspolizei          Berlin, den 11. Juli 1941.
    und   des SD
- IV A 1 - B.Nr. 1 B/41g.Rs. -

                                          32 Ausfertigungen
                                          19. Ausfertigung

## Geheime Reichsfache!

Ereignismeldung UdSSR.Nr.19.

I) Politische Übersicht.

Im Reich und in den besetzten Gebieten.
Es liegen keine besonderen Meldungen vor.

II) Meldungen der Einsatzgruppen und -kommandos.

Aus organisatorischen Gründen ist ab sofort folgende Änderung in der Bezeichnung der Einsatzgruppen eingetreten:

Einsatzgruppe Dr.Stahlecker = Einsatzgruppe A
Einsatzgruppe Nebe          = Einsatzgruppe B bisher C
Einsatzgruppe Dr.Dr.Rasch   = Einsatzgruppe C bisher B
Einsatzgruppe Ohlendorf     = Einsatzgruppe D.

Die Bezeichnungen der Einsatzkommandos bleiben aus technischen Gründen unverändert.

Gemeinsam mit dem SD-Abschnitt Tilsit wurden im litauischen Grenzgebiet seitens der Stapo Tilsit weitere Großaktionen durchgeführt. So wurden am 2.Juli in Tauroggen 133 Personen, am 3.Juli in Georgenburg 322 Personen (darunter 5 Frauen), in Augustowo 316 Personen (darunter 10 Frauen) und in Mariampol 68 Personen erschossen.

Ferner wurden noch folgende Exekutionen durchgeführt:

Reg.Rat Paefgen-oViA-

---

*The above and following are exact photocopies of several of the original documents from which our selections were made. Each was stamped with "Geheime Reichsfache!" — Secret Affair of the Reich. Some were also stamped "Lagezimmer" indicating that they were to be stored in a safe or strongbox, requiring special permission for access.*

Im übrigen sei die Lage im Raume von
K o w n o ruhig. Nur ganz vereinzelt werden Truppen-
teile von versprengten Rotarmisten aus dem Hinterhalt
beschossen. Aus diesem Grunde sind bisher verschärfte
Aktionen der Wehrmacht und Polizei nicht durchgeführt
worden.

Die in den Wäldern und sonstigen Schlupf-
winkeln verborgenen Angehörigen der Roten Armae kom-
men vom Hunger getrieben, zum Vorschein und ergeben
sich größtenteils durch Zeigen der weissen Fahne. Die
litauische Bevölkerung ist vorläufig durchweg deutsch-
freundlich eingestellt und hilft den deutschen Solda-
ten, den Polizeiorganen und den im Gebiet bereits tä-
tigen sonstigen Organisationen in jeder Weise. Ihre
Mithilfe erstreckt sich in der Hauptsache auf die Auf-
findung und Jberstellung von litauischen Kommunisten,
versprengten Rotarmisten und Juden. Nach dem Abzug
der Roten Armee hat die Bevölkerung von K o w n o
in einer spontanen Erhebung etwa 2500 Juden erschla-
gen. Eine weitere größere Anzahl von Juden ist durch
den Polizeihilfsdienst (Partisanen) erschossen worden.

Einsatzgruppe A:
Standort R i g a.

1) In K o w n o wurden nunmehr insgesamt 7 800
Juden erledigt, teils durch Pogrom, teils durch Er-
schiessungen von litauischen Kommandos. Sämtliche
Leichen sind beseitigt. Weitere Massenerschiessun-
gen sind nicht mehr möglich, es wurde daher ein
jüdisches Komitee von mir vorgeladen, und ihm er-
klärt, daß wir bisher keinen Anlaß gehabt haben,
in die inneren Auseinandersetzungen zwischen
Litauern und Juden einzugreifen. Voraussetzung für
eine Neuordnung:

Die Errichtung von einem jüdischen Ghetto,
die Kennzeichnung aller Juden durch einen gelben
Davidstern in Größe von 8 x-10 cm Durchmesser auf
der linken Brustseite und die Unterbringung von
eventuell auf unseren Befehl durch die Litauer
freizulassenden Frauen und Kinder durch ein jüdi-

sches Hilfskomitee in dem neuen Ghetto.

Als Ghetto wurde die Stadt V i l i a m-
p o b bestimmt.

Die Umsiedlung muß in 4 Wochen durchgeführt sein. Die Gefängnisse werden nunmehr noch ein-
mal durchgekämmt. Juden, soweit besondere Gründe
vorliegen, verhaftet und erschossen. Es wird sich
dabei um kleinere Exekutionen mit 5 bis 1oo Leuten
handeln. Um ein Zurückströmen von Juden nach
K o w n o zu verhindern, wurde mit dem Höheren ₰-
und Polizeiführer vereinbart, daß Ordnungspolizei
einen Gürtel um Kowno zieht und keinen Juden herein
läßt. Nötigenfalls wird auf die Juden geschossen.
Sämtliche Wehrmachtsstellen wurden von der ge-
troffenen Regelung unterrichtet.

Etwa 2o5 Mann der litauischen Partisanen
wurden von uns als Sonderkommando belassen, unter-
halten und zu eventuellen Exekutionen, auch aus-
wärts, herangezogen.

2) Detachierte Gruppen vom Einsatzkommando 3 sind
z.Zt. in Mariampol und Raseinial tätig. Nach Erle-
digung ihrer Aufgaben treten sie zum Hauptkommando
zu-rück.

3) Die Wehrmacht hat neue Weisung erhalten, die neu-
gebildete litauische Regierung zwar nicht anzuer-
kennen, sich aber ihrer zu bedienen.

4) Metropolit der russischen orthodoxen Kirche
für die baltischen Länder S e r g e i in Riga
ist bereit, einen Aufruf an die Gläubigen Rußlands,
gegen den Kommunismus zu veröffentlichen. Sergei
ist seit 1941 in Riga, war vorher 23 Jahre in
Moskau. Er ist Großrusse. Zivilname: V o s -
k r e s e n s k y. Entwurf des Aufrus wird z.Zt.
abgefaßt.

<u>Einsatzgruppe B:</u>
<u>Standort  M i n s k.</u>

Es liegen keine besonderen Meldungen vor.

Der Chef der Sicherheitspolizei
und des SD

Berlin, den 7. August 1941

- IV A 1 - B.Nr. 1 B/41g.Rs. -

## Geheime Reichsfache!

47 Ausfertigungen
33 Ausfertigung

Ereignismeldung UdSSR. Nr.45.

1) Politische Übersicht.

a) Im Reich:

Es liegen keine Meldungen vor.

b) Besetzte Gebiete:

Untersteiermark und Krain.

Die in der Gegend von St. V e i t bei Laibach
aufgefundenen Flugblätter fordern die Slowenen zum
Boykott aller Veranstaltungen der Besatzungsmächte auf.
Ferner sollen alle Einheimischen, die mit den Besat-
zungsbehörden zusammenarbeiten "wie tolle Hunde gejagt
und erschossen werden". An alle Arbeiter und Angestellte
ergeht die Aufforderung zur Sabotage und zur passiven
Resistenz. Gendarme, Polizisten und ihre Schergen sollen
entwaffnet und umgebracht werden. Jedes Haus muß ver-
nichtet werden, das die Besatzungsmächte fremden Sied-
lern zuweist. Zum Schluß heißt es: "Es lebe der Frei-
heitskampf des slowenischen Volkes. Schulter an Schulter
mit den Völkern der Sowjetunion gegen die faschisti-
schen Okupatoren. Kampf gegen die Verbrecher Mussolini
und Hitler!"

Konservendose für 2 Mann (sehr viel Fische) und dazu
das bekannte harte Brot.

E i n s a t z g r u p p e   D

Standort: O l s c h a n k a  westl. J a m p o l.

Einsatzkommando lo A
Standort: P e t s c h a n k a

In K o k y m a  wurde wegen Aufruhr und Angriffe
auf ehrmacht Razzia gegen Juden durchgeführt. Dabei
wurden 97 Juden erschossen und 1 756 Geiseln festgesetzt. An jedem neuen Ort werden Geiseln festgesetzt
und bei geringsten Anlässen exekutiert. In J a m p o l
9 Juden erschossen.
        Im Bezirke J a m p o l  und E t s c h a n k a
Erntearbeit auf Kolchosen auf 5ooo Morgen organisiert.

Einsatzkommando lo B
Standort: M o g i l e w - P o d o l s k i
Verhindert Judenabstrom in deutsches Interessen-
gebiet, organisiert Ernteeinbringung.

Einsatzkommando 11
Standort: K i s c h i n e w

Hat bei Überholung der wenigen unzerstörten
Dienstgebäude Material und einige Terror- und Sabotage ge-
organisationen erfasst. Führende Agenten erschossen.
Bisher 551 Juden liquidiert, davon 151 wegen Beteili-
gung an Sabotage und 4oo als Vergeltung für Beschiessung
deutscher Sanitätswagen und Geben von Leuchtsignalen
an rote Flieger. Juden im Ghetto abgeschlossen soweit
nicht abgezogen. Einsatz der Kolchosen zur Ernteeinbringung eingeleitet. Volkstumsmässig wird verschüttetes
Deutschtum z.Zt. überprüft. Ermittlungen gegen Terror-
organisationen laufen weiter.

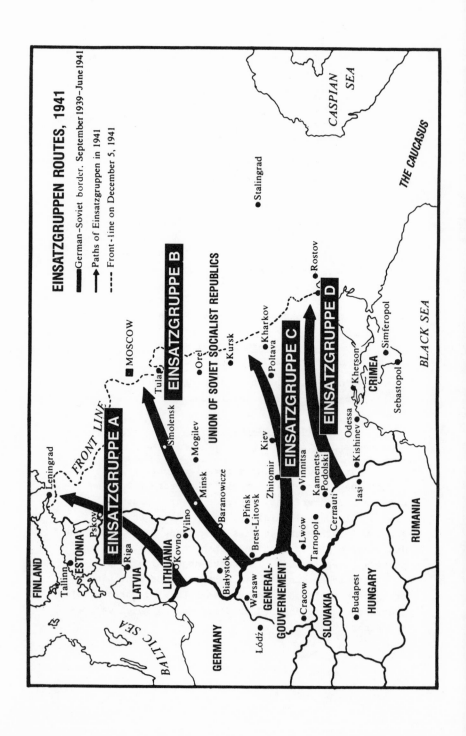

# INTRODUCTION

## Beginnings

The "Final Solution," the complete destruction of European Jewry, was inherent in National Socialist doctrine. In *Mein Kampf* Hitler derisively referred to the Jews as "maggots," "vermin," "parasites." Though this attitude was not unknown in the history of anti-Semitism, what separated the Nazis and made the Final Solution unique was the fact that a progressively harsher persecution was followed by a policy of total extermination — every Jewish man, woman and child was to be killed.

Indeed, the annihilation of the Jewish people was presented to the murderers themselves as a great deed. Addressing SS officers during the war, Heinrich Himmler, Chief of the SS (*Schutzstaffel* — "guard echelon" of the National Socialist Party), remarked, "I should like to talk about the extermination of the Jewish people . . . To have gone through that and to have remained decent just the same . . . is what has made you tough and strong. This is a glorious page in our history . . ."[1]

Rudolf Höss, the commandant of Auschwitz, recalls another address of Himmler's: "Jews are the eternal enemies of the German people and must be exterminated. All Jews within our grasp are to be destroyed without exception . . ."[2]

The logistics of mass murder on a scale never before seen had to be devised. At first the Germans improvised; then the methods were refined. Eventually, a whole apparatus of destruction was in place. Jews were isolated in Ghettos. They were terrorized and starved. They were then forced into the cattle cars that took them to the gas chambers of the death camps or marched into the fields and forests surrounding their towns and cities to face the guns of the *Einsatzgruppen.**

---

1. Speech delivered by Himmler at Posnania, October 4, 1943, cited at the Nuremberg Military Tribunals (NMT — International Military Tribunal for Major War Criminals and the American Military Tribunal), PS. 1919.

2. Rudolf Höss, *Commandant of Auschwitz: The Autobiography of Rudolf Höss* (Cleveland: World, 1959), pp. 83-94.

* In the Soviet Union, Minsk was the only city in which a Jewish ghetto was established. Elsewhere, Jews were murdered outright by the Einsatzgruppen.

The *Einsatzgruppen* were the mobile arms of the German extermination machinery. Composed of elements of the police, security, SS and SD (*Sicherheitsdienst* — the SS security service) forces, the *Einsatzgruppen* were formed initially to arrest and murder active and potential political opponents and to annihilate Jews. Eventually the mass murder of Jews became their primary function.

Though Einsatzgruppen operated in Austria and Czechoslovakia six major *Einsatzgruppen der Sicherheitspolizei (Sipo* — Security Police) with several hundred members each were formed before the Polish campaign of September 1939. Five were attached to the five advancing armies, and one was designated for the Posen area. The units were divided into smaller units (*Einsatzkommandos*) each of which was assigned to an army corps. Their earliest tasks were outlined in an order of the Eighth Corps: "Particularly counterespionage, arrest of the politically unreliable, confiscation of weapons, gathering of evidence important for police intelligence activities, etc."[3]

Shortly after the invasion of Poland, the *Einsatzgruppen* initiated a massive terror campaign against Jews and the Polish intelligentsia and upper classes that claimed tens of thousands of victims.

In a notorious telegram sent to *Einsatzgruppen* commanders in September 1939, Reinhard Heydrich, Chief of the RSHA (*Reichssicherheitshauptamt* — Main Office for the Security of the Reich) for the first time used the word *Endziel* ("final aim") in reference to the "Jewish question in the occupied territories." Toward that end, the concentration of Jews in ghettos and the establishment of *Judenrate* (Jewish Councils) were also discussed.

## The Invasion of the Soviet Union

With the invasion of the Soviet Union in June 1941, the *Einsatzgruppen* were given more extensive tasks.

Preparing for Operation Barbarossa (the invasion of the Soviet Union), Hitler lectured his generals, explaining that the war represented a struggle between two radically opposed ideologies, National Socialism and Bolshevism. The victors would be those who would succeed in totally destroying the opposing ideology and its supporters, and Jews were seen, in Nazi ideology, as "the reservoir of Bolshevism."

---

3. USSR, 509; or Hans Bucheim, in *Anatomy of the SS State*, London, 1968, p. 177.

Nazi ideology consistently presented contradictory images of the Jews. They were at once weak and inferior yet enormously powerful. In his "Orders for Special Areas" in connection with Directive No. 21 (Operation Barbarossa) of March 23, 1941, Hitler declared: ". . . Within the area of military operations, the Reichsführer-SS [Heinrich Himmler, then Chief of the SS and the German Police] will be entrusted, on behalf of the Führer, with special tasks for the preparation of the political administration. These tasks derive from the decisive struggle that will have to be carried out between two opposing systems.

"Within the framework of these tasks, the Reichsführer-SS will act independently and on his own recognizance. Apart from this, the executive power vested in the Supreme Commander of the Army and in the command levels acting under his orders will not be affected. The Reichsführer-SS will insure that the execution of his tasks will not interfere with operations. Details will be worked out directly between the Army's High Command and the Reichsführer-SS . . ."[4]

The "special tasks" refer implicitly to the elimination of the Jews for which the SS under Himmler, and through them the *Einsatzgruppen*, would be the instruments in Soviet territory.

## The Army and the Einsatzgruppen

On March 25, 1941, Hitler's March 23 directive was included in a draft approved by Reinhard Heydrich and the Quartermaster of the Wehrmacht (General Wagner). On March 28, 1941, it was published as a military order signed by the Chief of Staff of the Wehrmacht, General Walter von Brauchitsch. The following were its principal points:

> In order to carry out certain special security-police duties [the mass-murder of Jews] which are outside the army's domain, it will be necessary to employ special SD detachments [*Sonderkommandos*\*] in the zone of operations.
>
> With the agreement of the Chief of Sipo and SD, the employ-

---

4. NOKW-2302, or Documents of the Holocaust, Jerusalem, 1981, p. 375.

\* *Sonderkommandos* were "special units", in this case a special unit of the SS, usually a company; the term is also used in other contexts, as in describing, for example, the designated groups of prisoners that were assigned special slave-labor work in the concentration camps.

ment of the Sipo and SD in the zone of operations will be governed by the following guidelines:

1. *Tasks*

    A. In the army's rear area, prior to the initiation of operations: listing of selected objects (material archives, card indexes of anti-German or anti-Government organizations, associations, groups, etc.) and selected important individuals (leading emigrés, saboteurs, terrorists, etc.). The Army commander is authorized to forbid the utilization of the special detachments in those areas where their employment may affect operations adversely.

    B. To discover and stamp out anti-German and anti-Government movements insofar as these are not part of the enemy's armed forces: provision of general information to the zonal communications commander regarding the political situation.

    Cooperation with field security officers of the Secret Field Police [GFP] will be governed by the 'Principles for cooperation between the State Security Police and the field security units of the Wehrmacht' agreed to by the security branch of the Reich War Ministry on January 1, 1937.

    C. Cooperation between the special detachments and the military authorities in the Army's rear area (see 1A above): The special detachments [*Sonderkommandos*] of the *Sicherheitspolizei* [Sipo] will carry out their duties on their own responsibility. They will be controlled by the armies' movements in the following matters: movement, rations and accommodations.

    This does not affect the authority of the Chief of Sipo and SD in matters of discipline and jurisprudence. They will receive their technical instruction from the Chief of Sipo and SD but, when necessary, their activity will be restricted by orders from Army headquarters (see 1A above).

D. A representative of the Chief of Sipo and SD will be placed in each army area to centralize the direction of these detachments. It will be his duty to inform the appropriate Army commander as soon as possible about the instructions he receives from the Chief of Sipo and SD. The military commander is authorized to give this representative such instructions as may be necessary to avoid interference with military operations. Such instructions will have precedence over all others.

E. The *Sonderkommandos* are authorized, with reference to their tasks to take administrative measures affecting the civilian population on their own responsibility. In this connection, it is their duty to work in closest cooperation with the field security service. Any measures which may effect operations must be agreed to by the commander of the army concerned.[5]

The directive outlined relations and coordination between the army and the *Einsatzgruppen*. The army was technically exempt from participating in mass-murder operations, obliged only to provide logistical support to the death squads. As the *Einsatzgruppen* reports indicate, however, there was extensive cooperation between them. The Wehrmacht's assistance frequently extended far beyond its official limits.

## The Organization of the Einsatzgruppen

At the beginning of May 1941, potential recruits for the *Einsatzgruppen* gathered in the Border-Police School in Pretsch on the River Elbe, northeast of Leipzig. Due to lack of space, some were accommodated in Duben and Bad-Schmiedberg. There, similar units were organized and prepared for the occupation of the Balkans, the Soviet Union and even for Operation Sea-Lion, the invasion of Britain.

There were no specific instructions as to who should be sent to Pretsch, and the RSHA manpower section turned to various depart-

---

5. NOKW-256.

ments of the Sipo and SD in its search for candidates. A large contingent from the Berlin-Charlotenburg Sipo Senior Commanders School, as well as 100 Kripo (*Kriminalpolizei*, or Criminal Police) cadets, were also assigned there.

The commanders of the *Einsatzgruppen* and *Einsatzkommandos* were chosen by Himmler and Heydrich from a list compiled by the RSHA Department One. Of the 75 selected, 42 were members of the SD. In addition to Sipo and SD officers, a support staff of drivers, translators, radio operators and clerks was also assembled. These latter came from all over Germany, though most were members of the SS. Some were conscripted in accordance with the emergency law of 1938. Three of the *Einsatzgruppen* were reinforced by companies from the 9th Police Reserve Battalion.

In Pretsch, companies from the Waffen SS Battalion for Special Duties set up from the First SS Infantry Battalion were attached to *Einsatzkommando* 9 and *Sonderkommando* 4a. (Waffen-SS were drawn from the Wehrmacht.) Later, pursuant to Himmler's directive of July 27, 1941, other units received similar reinforcements.

The division into sub-units and areas of activity was as follows:

| Unit | Sub-unit | Area | Est. Strength |
|------|----------|------|---------------|
| EG-A | SK 1a, 1b; | | |
| | EK 2, 3, 1C | | |
| | (Leningrad) | Baltic countries | 1,000 |
| EG-B | SK 7a, 7b; | | |
| | EK 8, 9; VK | Byelorussia, | |
| | Moscow | Smolensk district | 655 |
| EG-C | SK 4a, 4b; | North and Central | |
| | EK 5, 6 | Ukraine | 750 |
| EG-D | SK 10a, 10b; | South Ukraine, | |
| | EK 11a, 11b, 12 | Crimea, Caucasus | 600 |

(EG = *Einsatzgruppen*; EK = *Einsatzkommando*; SK = *Sonderkommando*; VK = *Vorkkommando*.)

The *Einsatzgruppen* were attached to the commanders of the rear area army groups by June 25, 1941, and had to send forward subunits to join the staff of the Higher SS stationed at the groups' headquarters.

Thus, *Einsatzgruppe A*, headed by SS-Standartenführer (Colonel) Dr. Walter Stahlecker, joined Army Group North in Danzig;

*Einsatzgruppe B*, headed by SS Brigadeführer (General) Arthur Nebe joined Army Group Center in Malo Yaroslavets. *Einsatzgruppe C*, headed at the time by SS Brigadeführer Dr. Otto Rasch, attached to Army Group South at Kiev. *Einsatzgruppe D*, headed by SS-Standartenführer Professor Otto Ohlendorf, joined the headquarters of the Eleventh Army in Piatra-Neamt (Romania) on July 4, 1941. Notably, the *Einsatzgruppen* included many high-ranking officers, intellectuals and lawyers. Otto Ohlendorf, who commanded *Einsatzgruppe D*, had earned degrees from three universities and achieved a doctorate in jurisprudence. One of the commanders of *Einsatzgruppe C*, Ernst Biberstein, was a Protestant pastor, theologian and church official.

## Directives

There were a number of briefings about the aims and activities of the *Einsatzgruppen* in the Nazi-occupied territories of the Soviet Union. The first took place in Pretsch, and it was conducted by Bruno Streckenbach, Chief of Department One of the RSHA. Streckenbach acted as spokesman for Himmler and Heydrich in explaining the Führer's order concerning the murder of the Jews.

The meeting is described in Ohlendorf's testimony at the Einsatzgruppen Trial No. 9 at Nuremberg.[6] It is also mentioned in the affidavit by Dr. Walter Blume, who headed SK 7a: "During June, Heydrich, Chief of the Security Police and the SD, and Streckenbach, head of Office I of the Reich Security Main Office [RSHA], lectured on the duties of the *Einsatzgruppen* and *Einsatzkommandos*. At this time we were already being instructed about the tasks of exterminating the Jews. It was stated that Eastern Jewry was the intellectual reservoir of Bolshevism and, therefore, in the Führer's opinion, must be exterminated. This speech was given before a small, select audience. Although I cannot remember the individuals present, I assume that many of the *Einsatzgruppe* and *Sonderkommando* chiefs were present."[7]

Another briefing was given by Heydrich at a meeting of the leaders of the *Einsatzgruppen* and *Einsatzkommandos* which took place on June 17. There again the Führer's order concerning the murder of the

---

6. NMT (Case 9, Einsatzgruppen), vol. IV, p. 244.
7. NMT, vol. IV, p. 140.

Jews was discussed, as stated by Standartenführer Dr. Walter Blume: "I heard another speech by Heydrich in the Prinz Albrecht Palace in Berlin, in the course of which he again emphasized these points."[8] Ervin Schulz, head of EK-5, testified at the Nuremberg trials that "Some time during the first ten days of June 1941, the chiefs of the *Einsatzgruppen* and leaders of the *Kommandos* were called to the RSHA in the Prinz Albrecht Palace to hear a speech by Heydrich in which he outlined the policy to be adopted, giving us some guidelines concerning the fulfillments of the tasks imposed upon the *Einsatzgruppen*."[9]

At the third meeting, which probably took place shortly before June 22, high-level SS and Police chiefs met in the office of the Chief of Order Police, General Kurt Daluege. As Heydrich was unable to attend, he sent them a memorandum dated July 2, 1941 (dated after the invasion of the Soviet Union), specifying who was to be eliminated:

> *Executions*
> All the following are to be executed:
>
> Officials of the Commintern (together with professional Communist politicians in general);
>
> Top- and medium-level officials and radical lower-level officials of the Party. Central committee and district and sub-district committees;
>
> People's Commissars;
>
> Jews in Party and State employment, and other radical elements (saboteurs, propagandists, snipers, assassins, inciters, etc.) insofar as they are, in any particular case, no longer required to supply information on political or economic matters which are of special importance for the further operations of the Security Police, or for the economic reconstruction of the Occupied Territories . . .[10]

More details are contained in Report No. 111 dated October 12, 1941: "The principle targets of execution by the *Einsatzkommandos* will be: political functionaries, . . . Jews mistakenly released from

---

8. NMT, vol. IV, p. 140.
9. NMT, vol. IV, p. 136.
10. Documents of the Holocaust, p. 375.

POW camps, ... Jewish sadists and avengers, ... Jews in general ..."

According to the testimony of Otto Ohlendorf, head of *Einsatzgruppe D*, dated April 24, 1947, the objective was the "murder of racially and politically undesirable elements." Later on in the *Einsatzgruppen* trial, he said (October 1948): "The goal was to liberate the army's rear areas by killing Jews, Gypsies and Communist activists ..."[11]

Armed with detailed instructions, the *Einsatzgruppen* began their bloody march to the East.

## The Route Taken by the Einsatzgruppen

EG-A: Most of the EG-A reached Guimbinnen, in East Prussia, on June 23, 1941, and from there Stahlecker, at the head of an advance unit, made his way to Tilzit on the Lithuanian border, entering Kaunas on June 25, together with advance units of the Wehrmacht.

SK-1a, which was attached to the 18th Army, organized *Aktionen* (Actions, or police and SS terror operations; used also to describe the deportations from and liquidations of the ghettos) that began on June 27 in the areas of Liepaya and Yelgava, and entered Riga together with EG-A headquarters during the first days of July. EK-1b reached Kaunas on June 28, and Daugavpils on July 8. EK-2 reached Siaulai on June 27, and later continued on to Riga. EK-3 entered Kaunas on July 2, and organized *Aktionen* in Lithuania. On August 9, it relieved EK-9 of EG-B in Vilnius (Vilna).

The headquarters of the EG-A remained in Riga, and for a time supervised operations in Lithuania and Latvia. On July 10, EK-1a began operations in Estonia, while EK-1b operated in the area south of Leningrad — in Pskov, Ostrov and Opotshka. EG-A headquarters wished to enter Leningrad, and for this purpose conducted talks with the fourth Panzer Group, and in particular the SS *Totenkopf* (Death's Head) Division, which was supposed to be the first to enter the city. The headquarters of EG-A moved to Pskov where sections of SK-1a and EK 2 and 3 were then concentrated. When the front ceased to advance at the outskirts of Leningrad, they moved to Krasnogvardeisk (Gatchina).

At the end of September 1941, Stahlecker was appointed commander of the Sipo and SD in the Baltic countries and Byelorussia

---

11. NMT, vol. IV, p. 244.

with headquarters in Riga. SK-1a was divided among the regional offices of the Sipo and SD in Estonia. Large sections of EK-2 were divided between the regional offices in Latvia, and sections of EK-3 in Lithuania. Most of SK-1b was transferred to Minsk, while small mobile units of SK-1a and 1b continued to operate in the Leningrad area. On March 24, 1942, Brigadeführer Heinz Jost replaced Stahlecker after he was wounded and died.

EG-B:  On June 24th, EG-B advanced through Poznan to Warsaw, while SK-7a joined the Ninth Army, marching through East Prussia. On June 30th it reached Vilnius. On July 3, it was relieved by EK-9 and proceeded to Minsk.

SK-7a and *Vorkkommando* (Work Group) *Moscow* were then transferred to the Fourth Panzer Army. On July 4, SK-7b also arrived in Minsk, after passing through Briest, Kobrin, Pruzhany, Slonim and Baranovichi. On July 5, the headquarters of EG-B reached Minsk, where it remained for five weeks. It was then decided that the *Sonderkommandos* would march on with the advancing army units, while the *Einsatzkommandos* would continue to operate in the occupied areas.

EK-8 reached Bialystok on July 1. Moving through Slonim and Baranovichi, it organized mass executions in southern West Byelorussia. It stayed in Minsk from August 6 to September 9, 1941, and then moved to Mogilev, which became its headquarters. From there it operated in southern East Byelorussia by sending sub-units to Bobruisk, Gomel, Roslavl and Klinzy.

EK-9 left Warsaw and reached Vilnius via Treuburg (East Prussia) on July 2. Sub-units were active in Grodno and Bielsk-Podlaski. On July 20, it advanced to the area north of the Minsk-Moscow highway. The main body settled in Vitebsk, and sections were sent to Polotzk, Nevel, Lepel and Surazh. Following the advance on Moscow, the headquarters moved to Vyasma and advance sub-units were sent to Gshatsk and Mozhaisk, close to the Soviet capital. On December 21, 1941, it returned to Vitebsk.

In the meantime, on August 5, 1941, EG-B headquarters moved to Smolensk where *Vorkkommando Moscow* was stationed. An advance unit was attached to the Fourth Panzer Group, which marched towards Moscow. Beginning in October 1941, it joined the advance sub-units of EK-9, while *Vorkkommando Moscow* settled in Medyn and Maloyaroslavetz. After April 19, 1942, it was no longer mentioned in reports.

SK-7a and 7b proceeded with mass murder operations in vast areas to the east and south of Minsk and Smolensk, which included towns like Veliki-Luki, Kalinin, Orsha, Gomel, Tshernigov, Oryol and Kursk. EG-C: The headquarters of EG-C travelled through Upper Silesia to East Galicia, and reached Lvov on July 1. EK-5 and 6 arrived there shortly afterwards and organized the infamous pogrom against the Jews of Lvov. SK-4b acted similarly in Zlotchev and Tarnopol (July 5). SK-4a marched through Crakow, Zamosc and Sokal to Lutsk, where it organized a large-scale murder operation between June 30 and July 2, under the guise of revenge *Aktionen*. On July 6, SK-4a continued on to Rovno, Novograd-Volynskii and Zhitomir, where it was joined on July 19 by the headquarters of EG-C. Divided into sections, it operated in the area to the north, west and southwest of Kiev.

On September 19, 1941, SK-4a entered Kiev and on September 29-30, with the help of the headquarters of EG-C, it organized the infamous murder of 30,000 Jews at Babi-Yar (mentioned in reports 101 and 106). In January 1942, it carried out the murder of the Jews of Kharkov, and marched through Belgorod to Kalach in the direction of Stalingrad. After the German defeat there, it retreated through Bobruisk to Minsk, where it was dispersed.

At the same time, the headquarters of the Higher-SS and Police Leader South, with the help of units from the First SS Brigade and Police Regiment South, murdered 33,600 Jews in Kamenetz-Podolsk and Dnepropetrovsk.

SK-4b marched through Vinnitza, Kirovograd and Krementcug to Poltava, reached Kramatorskaya in December 1941, and Gorlovka in the Donbass region in March 1942. During the advance to the Caucasus in Autumn 1942 it was stationed in Rostov.

EK-5 made its way through Zhitomir to Berditchev and was active in the same area as SK-4a. After the occupation of Kiev, it moved there. Sections of EK-5 were sent to Zhitomir, Vinnitza and Rovno to serve as local Sipo-SD offices. Some sections of EK-5 operated east of the Dnieper River, but in January 1942 the unit was dispersed and its members sent to the Sipo-SD in Kiev.

In August, EK-6 proceeded from Zlochev to Proskurov and Novo-Ukrainka, where the headquarters of EG-C were also located. In September, it was active in Krivoi-Bog, and in October in the Dnieper-Bend in the villages of Dnepropetrovsk, Zaporoshye and Nikopol. In November 1941, it was stationed in Stalino, and by September 1942, in Rostov.

The headquarters of EG-C moved to Kiev on July 25; in September 1942, it was sent to Starobelsk and in February 1943, to Poltava. In view of the immensity of the areas conquered in the East, Schongarth, the Chief of the Sipo and SD in the *Generalgouvernement* (the part of Poland controlled directly by Berlin under the administration of Hans Frank), was ordered to create six units (*Truppen*). They operated in Lvov, Rava-Ruska, Lutak, Kovel, Rovno, Pinsk, Bialystok, Novogrodek, Baranovichi and Grodno.

EG-D: EG-D was attached to the Eleventh Army. It advanced through Bratislava and northern Transylvania and reached Piatra-Neamt, near Bessarabia on July 5, where the *Sonderkommandos* went into action: SK-10a in Beltzi; SK-10b with the Third Romanian Army in Chernauti; and SK-11a in Kishinev.

Though it extended beyond the stated responsibilities of the *Einsatzgruppen*, the Commander of the Eleventh Army used the *Sonderkommandos* for military operations. He asked the *Einsatzkommandos* to wait until he reached the Caucasus, or at least until enough territorial depth had been created in the rear. Ohlendorf, the commander of EG-D, acquiesced, and used the *Einsatzkommandos* to guard the Dniestr border.

The Balta-Pervomaisk line between EG-C and EG-D was only established in the middle of August 1941. The headquarters of EG-D reached Ananyev, proceeding on September 18 to Nikolayev, and from mid-November to Simferopol in the Crimea.

SK-11a reached Nikolayev on August 19. Proceeding to Kherson, it initiated mass-murder operations along the shores of the Black Sea and then waited by the Perekop for the occupation of the Crimea. SK-11a was later especially active in Sevastopol. After August 1941, it was merged with SK-11b into one unit, SK-11. SK-11b had reached the Odessa front, waited for the occupation of the city and entered Odessa on October 16. In mid-December the merged SK-11 moved into the Crimea.

SK-10a and 10b moved along the Black Sea shores to the Crimea where they were active until August 1942. EK-12 was left in the Nikolayev area where it looked after local ethnic Germans. It then also moved to the Crimea.

With the German advance into the Caucasus, SK-10a and 11 and EK-12 moved on. SK-11 was concentrated in the north of the area, in Maikop and Cherkesk, and in October 1942 created *SK-Astrachan* (stationed in Elitsa) to enter the city. EK-12 was active in the south in Piatigorsk, Kislovodsk.

In July 1942, Ohlendorf was replaced by SS-Oberführer Bierkamp. Later, when the retreat began, the EG-D moved back to Ovruch, where it operated as an anti-partisan unit.

During the second half of 1943 the *Einsatzgruppen* began their retreat from the East, leaving behind mass graves containing millions of dead, most of them Jews. Such was the German mentality of the time that special units were created, under the leadership of SS Standartenführer Paul Blobel, to erase all evidence of the murders. Graves were dug up and the bodies burned. Blobel went so far as to develop special combustibles and even experimented with dynamite to destroy the corpses. He ultimately brought his "expertise" to Auschwitz where up to 20,000 victims could be murdered in the gas chambers in a single day, and his experience in the disposing of thousands of bodies at a time could be put to use.

## *The Reports*

As did all other units in the German military bureaucracy, the *Sonderkommandos* and *Einsatzkommandos* reported on their extermination activities to their respective *Einsatzgruppe* headquarters which sent the information to Berlin. There the RSHA compiled concise reports in the name of the Chief of Sipo and the SD. Copies were distributed to high-ranking army, police and SS officers, diplomats, members of the foreign office and even to industrialists as they related to economic factors in the Soviet territories.

The Einsatzgruppen Reports were discovered by the U.S. Army in Gestapo headquarters in Berlin after the war. They were initially impounded by a research analyst attached to the Berlin branch of the Office of the Chief of Council for War Crimes (OCCWC, established under Council Law Number 10 of the Allied occupation authorities). The head of the office, Benjamin Ferencz, who became Chief U.S. Prosecutor at the Einsatzgruppen War Crimes Trials, turned them over to U.S. Army custody. They were sealed and transported to Nuremberg to the office of General Telford Taylor, Chief of Council for War Crimes, for use in preparing for the Einsatzgruppen War Crimes Trial.

During the first days of the Einsatzgruppen Trial the authenticity of the reports was established beyond doubt, after which the German defendants did not challenge their validity.

During the war, the person responsible for the reports as they were received inBerlin was Kurt Lindow, an officer in the RSHA. On July 21, 1947, at the Einsatzgruppen Trial, he identified the reports and gave the following testimony concerning the methods used in their compilation:

> From October 1941 until about the middle of 1942, I first was deputy chief and later chief of subdepartment IV A 1 [of the RSHA]. This subdepartment dealt with Communism, war crimes, and enemy propaganda. Moreover, it handled the reports of the various *Einsatzgruppen* until the command staff was set up in 1942. The *Einsatzgruppen* in the East regularly sent their reports to Berlin by wireless or by letter. The reports noted the various locations of the *Gruppen* and the most important events during the period under survey.
>
> I read most of the reports and passed them on to Dr. Knobloch, Inspector of the Criminal Police, who compiled them at first. The compilation was published daily under the title 'Operational Situation Reports — U.S.S.R.' These reports were stenciled and I corrected them. Afterwards they were mimeographed and distributed. The originals of the reports which were sent to the Reich Security Main Office [RSHA] were mostly signed by the commander of the *Einsatzgruppe* or his deputy.
>
> The reports, 'Operational Situation Reports — U.S.S.R.' [Nos. 114, 115, 118, 128, 138, 141, 142, 144, and 159] as shown to me, are photostats of the original reports drawn up by Dr. Knobloch in subdepartment IV A 1 of which I was chief. I recognize them as such by the red borders, discernible on the photostat, their size, the typefaces, and incomplete borders.
>
> I identify the handwritten initials appearing on the various reports as those of persons employed by the Reich Security Main Office. Considering that six years have elapsed since then, I cannot remember the full names of these persons whose handwritten initials appear on the documents. From the contents of the handwritten notes, I conclude that these were made by Dr. Knobloch. Moreover, I notice that various

parts of the above-mentioned reports are extracted from the original reports of the *Einsatzgruppen* to the Reich Security Main Office.

On the strength of my positions as deputy chief and, later on, chief of subdepartment IV A 1, I consider myself a competent witness, able to confirm that the 'Operational Situation Reports — U.S.S.R.' which were published by the chief of the security police and the security service under file mark IV A 1 were compiled entirely from the original reports of the *Einsatzgruppen* reaching my subdepartment by wireless or by letter.[12]

The *Ereignismeldungen UdSSR* (Morning Reports — U.S.S.R.) were initiated on June 23, 1941, and terminated with No. 195 on April 24, 1942. They were published almost daily. On May 1, 1942, they were replaced by the weekly reports called *Meldungen aus den besetzten Ostgebieten*[13] which appeared until May 21, 1943 (number 55).

The original reports were sent to the National Archives in Washington, D.C. after the Nuremberg War Crimes Trials. In 1960 they were given to the Bundesarchiv (the West German national archives) in Koblenz. Photocopies of all the reports remain in the National Archives in Washington and at Yad Vashem, the Holocaust Museum and Memorial in Jerusalem.

The *Einsatzgruppen* constituted the principle German instrument of annihilation of the Jewish people in the Eastern (Soviet) territories. While other groups fell victim to the *Einsatzgruppen*, only the Jews were doomed as a people in their entirety.

This book contains citations pertaining to the murder of Jews. Sometimes, in order to clarify the frame of reference, general descriptions in whole or in part were included. Excerpts from these reports were previously presented in Nuremberg at the International Military Tribunal and at the American Military Tribunal.

## Trials of the Einsatzgruppen Members

The first trial of *Einsatzgruppen* members was conducted in Nuremberg by the American Military Tribunal. It was Case No. 9 before Tribunal II-A, and was known as "United States of America against

---

12. NMT, vol. IV, pp. 99-100.
13. Report No. 158 is missing.

Otto Ohlendorf and others," or "The *Einsatzgruppen* Case."[14] The judicial panel of three consisted of the presiding Judge Michael A. Musmano, and Judges John J. Speight and Richard D. Dixon. Proceedings began on September 15, 1947 and concluded on April 10, 1948. Of the 24 accused, the case of Otto Rasch (head of EG-C) was dealt with separately, owing to his state of health (he died soon after in prison). Charges against Emil Hausmann were dropped. Mathias Graf was sentenced to the period he had already served in prison.

The sentences of the other defendants were read by the presiding judge, Michael Musmano, as follows:

a) Death by hanging: Ernst Eiberstein, Paul Blobel, Walter Blume, Werner Braune, Walter Haensch, Waldemar Klingelhoefer, Erich Naumann, Otto Ohlendorf, Adolf Ott, Martin Sandberger, Heinz Schubert, Willy Seibert, Eugen Steimle, Eduard Strauch.

b) Imprisonment for life: Heinz Jost, Gustavg Nosske.

c) Twenty years in jail: Waldemar von Radetzky, Erwin Schultz, Franz Six.

d) Ten years in jail: Lothar Fendler, Felix Ruehl.[15]

Of the 21 prisoners sentenced, two *Einsatzgruppen* commanders, ten *Einsatzkommando* leaders and two officers were sentenced to death. One *Einsatzgruppe* commander and one *Einsatzkommando* leader were sentenced to life imprisonment. Two other leaders and one officer were sentenced to twenty years' imprisonment, and two officers to ten years.

Since the Central Prosecution Office of Nazi War Criminals was established in West Germany (Ludwigsburg), proceedings were initiated against more than one hundred members of the *Einsatzgruppen*, among them *Kommando* leaders.

Yitzhak Arad                              William H. Donat
Shmuel Krakowski                          Mark Cohen
Shmuel Spector                  — *Holocaust Publications*
— *Yad Vashem*                            *New York*
  *Jerusalem*

---

14. NMT, vol. IV.
15. NMT, vol. IV, pp. 587-589.

## Operational Situation Report USSR No. 8

*Einsatzgruppe A:*
*EK 1b*
On June 28 Vorkommando[1] has moved into Kaunas. It has started its activity, occupying the former trade union building, the NKVD Building, as well as two other houses. During the night, exchange of heavy fire between Lithuanian insurgents, Jews, and irregulars. Very difficult to secure the prisons, which are totally overcrowded. During the last 3 days Lithuanian partisan groups have already killed several thousand Jews.

---

1. An advance unit.

The Chief of the Security Police       Berlin, July 2, 1941
          and the SD

25 copies
23rd copy

## Operational Situation Report USSR No. 10

*Einsatzgruppe B*[1]

The 17th Army Command has suggested the use first of all of the anti-Jewish and anti-Communist Poles living in the newly-occupied areas for self-cleansing activities.

On July 1, 1941 Chief of Security Police and SD issued the following order to all Einsatzgruppen:

Order No. 2:

Poles residing in the newly-occupied Polish territories may be expected, on the basis of their experiences, to be anti-Communist and also anti-Jewish.

It is obvious that the cleansing activities have to extend first of all to the Bolsheviks and the Jews. As for the Polish intelligentsia and others, decisions can be taken later, unless there is a special reason for taking action in individual cases considered to be dangerous.

It is therefore obvious that such Poles need not be included in the cleansing action, especially as they are of great importance as elements to initiate pogroms and for obtaining information. (This depends, of course, on local conditions.)

This policy is to be applied, of course, to all similar cases. Einsatzgruppe staff have arrived on July 1, at 5 am, in Lvov. Office is in the NKVD central building.

Chief of Einsatzgruppe B reports that Ukrainian insurrection movements were bloodily suppressed by the NKVD on June 25, 1941 in Lvov. About 3,000 were shot by NKVD. Prison burning. Hardly 20% of Ukrainian intelligentsia has remained. Some elements of the

---

1. Renamed on July 11th, *Einsatzgruppe C*.

Bandera-group[2] under the direction of Stechko and Ravlik have organized a militia force and a municipal office. The Einsatzgruppe has created a counterbalance to the Bandera group, a Ukrainian self-policed city administration. Further measures against the Banderaa-group, in particular against Bandera himself, are in preparation. They will be carried out as soon as possible.

EK 4a and EK 4b with Einsatzgruppe staff have also arrived in Lvov.

*Einsatzgruppe C*[3]
*EK 7a*
Location: Vilnius

Confiscation of numerous documents in NKVD Building. National Lithuanian activists have established city committees after the German troops marched in. Leader Zakovasius. For the time being, the committee is recognized by the field commandant. Activists strive for independence as in Slovakia. They appear to be ready to make sacrifices. On July 2, 1941, Commander of Einsatzgruppe C and SS-Brigadeführer Nebe, in coordination with Army Group Center initiated the settlement of this matter. According to a suggestion of the Einsatzgruppen leader, Army Group Center issued the following order on June 30, 1941:

"Civilian prisoners have according to our information, been freed by the Army. They are said to be, at least partially, Soviet political prisoners. Mostly criminal convicts, they are said to have freed themselves from another prison. It is requested that the troops be informed that prisoners are not to be freed. On the contrary, prisoners are to be secured by the Army until they are taken over by the officers of the security police. Care should be taken that prisoners do not free themselves under any circumstances."

EK 7a has initiated arrest actions against Communists and Jews. There are about 8,000 Jews in Vilnius. Most of the leading Communists have escaped.

EK 7b still near Pruzhana, will proceed towards Baranovichi.

EK 9 Location: Vilnivs.

On June 30 Vorkommando ordered to Grodno.

After arrival of IX 9, EK 7a is free for Minsk which, according to reports, is heavily damaged.

---

2. In original written "Pandora."
3. Renamed on July 11th, *Einsatzgruppe B*.

## Operational Situation Report USSR No. 11

*Einsatzgruppe A.*

Location July 2, 1941: Under way from Siauliai to Riga (Communication by radiogram)

*Einsatzkommando 1a*

Location July 3, 1941: Under way from Mitau to Riga (Communication by radiogram)

*Einsatzkommando 1b:* Location Kaunas

*Einsatzkommando 2:* Location July 3, 1941: Siauliai, NKVD Building.

*Siauliai:* 35,000 inhabitants (12-15,000 Jews). About 2,000 Jews are still left. The others have fled. The prison is empty. In order to keep the war plants and the plants vital for the population operational, the Wehrmacht is, for the time being, not in a position to dispose of the Jewish manpower still available and fit for work.

*Einsatzkommando 3*

Location July 3: Kaunas (Communication by radiogram)

*Einsatzgruppe B*

Location July 2, 1941: Lvov (Communication by radiogram)

*Einsatzkommando 4a*

Location: Lvov

*Einsatzkommando 4b:*

Location: Lvov

*Einsatzkommando 5:*

Location: Lvov

According to reliable information, the Russians, before withdrawing, shot 30,000 inhabitants. The corpses piled up and burned at the GPU prisons are dreadfully mutilated. The population is greatly excited: 1,000 Jews have already been forcefully gathered together.

*Einsatzkommando 6* reports on July 2, 1941 that 133 Jews were shot.

*Einsatzgruppe C:*
Location: July 3: Volkovisk.

The group commander reports the result of the conference with Army Group Central Sector about the recognition of the Lithuanian Committee by the field commander. There is unanimity on this. Army Group Central Sector immediately issued a corresponding order.

*Einsatzkommando 7a:*
Location: Vilnius
Officials of the Komsomol and Jewish officials of the Communist Party were liquidated. The Einsatzkommando is trying to push forward to Minsk as fast as possible.

*Einsatzkommando 7b:*
Location on July 2, 1941: Under way to Slutsk.

*Einsatzkommando 8:*
Location July 3, 1941: Volkovisk.
Kommandos in Slonim and Baranovichi.

*Einsatzkommando 9:*
Location: Vilnius
Vorauskommando under way to Lida.

## Operational Situation Report USSR No. 12

. . . . . . . . . . . .

*Einsatzgruppe A:*

Location: July 4, 1941 Riga (communication by radiogram)

Gruppenleiter SS-Brig. Stahlecker entered Riga with the fighting force. Together with EK 1a and parts of EK 2.

Excellent cooperation with 10th Army Headquarters. Smooth integration in advance groups possible. Security measures, in agreement with the Wehrmacht, have been taken against Russians in hiding and armed Communists.

One member of the EK 1a slightly wounded. Entire national leadership of Riga deported or murdered. Pogroms have been started.

Police is being organized, led by the former director of the political police in Riga who was brought from Berlin, and is manned by reliable persons only. It is engaged exclusively in the search for Communists and members of the Red Army. Since, according to 18th Army Headquarters in Libau, civilians were also engaged in the battles against Germans, an EK 2 sub-unit was sent there, in addition to the unit that had been sent previously, with orders to proceed with utmost ruthlessness.

*EK 1b:*

Location July 4, 1941: Kaunas

Only insignificant destruction in Kaunas. Strong sniper activity, particularly in the area of Tauroggen.

Stapo Tilsit has so far carried out 200 shootings.

Lithuanians have less trust in Lithuanian ambassador Skirza in Berlin (under house arrest in Berlin, as already reported) than in General Rastikis. The latter is very popular.

2 groups of partisans[1] in Kaunas:
(a) under leadership of Klimaitis, 600 men, mainly civilian workers
(b) under leadership of the physician Dr. Zigonys, about 200 men.

---

1. In this case "partisans" means Lithuanian nationalists who cooperated with the Germans.

## Operational Situation Report USSR No. 13

. . . . . . . . . . . .

*Einsatzgruppe B:*
Location: Lvov
On July 5, 1941 a non-political and non-party Ukrainian national newspaper appeared for the first time in Lvov.

The first edition contains greetings and introductions by the city commandant General Renz, the Ukrainian-Greek UNIATE Metropolitan Sheptitsky and Mayor Poliansky.

The Metropolitan Graf Sheptitsky, who is highly esteemed by all Ukrainians, will read a Pastoral Letter on July 6, 1941, the contents of which have been agreed upon.

Contents: The Ukrainian people's gratitude for their liberation by the Germans.

*EK 4b*
Location: Tarnopol
Prison full of dead bodies (400-600). All officials have fled.

*Einsatzgruppe C:*
Location July 5, 1941: Slonim.

*EK 7a*
Location: Minsk. The same.

*EK 7b*
As all the officials have fled and archives have been carted off from the former Polish area, it has become necessary to concentrate the entire Einsatzgruppe in Minsk, since it is a bustling center and capital of the White Russian Soviet Republic.

*EK 7b* reports from Baranovichi systematic destruction of archives. Officials and clerks have fled. Church attendance is high. Economic life greatly disrupted due to the Kolkhoz-system; thus, lack of food.

*EK 9*
Location: Grodno

The party building has been requisitioned for the main office in spite of objections from commander Colonel Pickel. Documents and photographs have been secured from the NKVD office. Pogroms are being initiated, heavy destruction, shops looted and demolished; supply situation bad. Church attendance is high.

Bielsk-Podlaski: Supporting troops have taken over all positions. Party officials have fled. Leaders of Jewish intelligentsia (in particular teachers, lawyers, Soviet officials) liquidated. Public feeling towards Germans friendly, especially among peasants. On June 20, 1941 Soviet Russians still deported workers to Northern Russia. Church attendance is high.

EK 9 is relieved on July 5, 1941, in Grodno and moves on to Lida. During July 4 and 5, 1941, Volkovisk and Slonim will be searched by security forces.

## Operational Situation Report USSR No. 14

. . . . . . . . . . . .

*Einsatzgruppe A:*
Tilsit was used as base for three major cleansing actions, as follows:
  in Garsden: 201 persons were shot.
  in Krottingen: 214 persons were shot.
  in Polangen: 111 persons were shot.
In Garsden the Jewish population had supported the Russian border guards repulsing the German attack.
In Krottingen, on the night of the occupation, a [German] officer and two quartermasters were treacherously shot by the population.
In Polangen, on the day of the occupation, another officer was treacherously shot by the population.
In all of these 3 major operations mainly Jews were liquidated. However, there were also Bolshevik officials and snipers among them who had been handed over by the Wehrmacht to the security police.
*EK 1b:*
Location: Kaunas
Reports:
Public feelings among Lithuanians in Kaunas are good and are pro-German. The Lithuanian population does not agree with the self-proclaimed Lithuanian government under Colonel Skirpa. The government is defined as a group of the army who has vested interests, first of all to take advantage of the presently unclear conditions, and to gain material profits. Former Lithuanian parties have already attempted to make contacts. The Roman Catholic Bishop Brizgys, who holds an influential position in Lithuanian church circles, was won over. He maintains a close relationship with General Rastikis. The followers of Woldemaras are starting to be somewhat active. Basically

-10-

they reject General Rastikis, because he is close to Christian-Democratic circles. They strive only for a limited Lithuanian independence, i.e., they want only cultural and economic freedom and are ready to leave foreign politics to the Greater German Reich. General Rastikis will immediately dissolve the temporary Lithuanian government.

Partisans in Kaunas and its surroundings have been disarmed on June 28 by order of the German Feldkommandatur. An auxiliary police force consisting of 5 companies has been created from reliable partisans. Two of these companies were subordinated to the Einsatzkommando. Of these, one company guards the Jewish concentration camp. In the meantime, in Kaunas, Fort VII has been established where executions are carried out. The other company, with the agreement of the Field Commander of the Einsatzkommando, is to be employed for regular police tasks.

In Kaunas reserves of meat and flour will last for 6 more weeks. Fort VII in Kaunas will be organized as a Jewish concentration camp with two sections:

1. male Jews
2. female Jews and children.

Presently about 1,500 Jews are kept in the fort. Guard duty is performed by Lithuanian guard formations. In the central prisons there are:

1860 Jews
214 Lithuanians
134 Russians
1 Latvian
16 Poles.

Another concentration camp for Jews is planned for in Fort IX — Kaunas.

*Einsatzgruppe B*
Location: Lvov
It was established that in Lvov the Russians left behind about 12 agents, their task to sabotage bridges, etc. 2 agents who had cut Wehrmacht cables have been arrested.

*EK 4a:*
Location: Lutsk
Also active with the advanced units in the area of Lutsk. 2,000 shootings, reprisals for the murder of Ukrainians. Archives have been

secured. In Brody, 50-60 steel cabinets with GPU material were secured.

*EK 4b:*

Location: Tarnopol

In Tarnopol 5,000 Ukrainians were taken away, and 2,000 murdered [by the Soviets]. In retaliation, arrest of Jewish intelligentsia has begun, since they are responsible for the murders and have also acted as informers for the NKVD. The number is estimated at 1,000. On July 5, about 70 Jews were assembled by the Ukrainians and finished off with concentrated fire [machine gunned]. 20 more Jews slain in the streets by Ukrainians and soldiers as retaliation for the murder of 3 soldiers who were found in prison, tied, their tongues sliced and eyes gouged out. The German Army demonstrates a gratifyingly good attitude towards Jews. Zlochev was searched for agents and archives.

*Einsatzgruppe C:*

Location so far: Slonim, on the road to Minsk.

Berlin, July 7, 1941

38 copies
(21st copy)

## Operational Situation Report USSR No. 17

. . . . . . . . . . . .

Einsatzgruppe C:
Location: Minsk
First summary report of the activity of Einsatzgruppe C in the Polish and Russian sections of Byelorussia.

1. *Organization and March Route*

On June 23, Einsatzgruppe B met in Poznan in order to continue the march towards Warsaw the following morning. According to the order of RSHA, contact was established with Army Group Center and the commander of the Rear Army Group Area 102 in Warsaw.

As was agreed, Sonderkommando 7a started the march on June 26 attached to 9th Army HQ and Sonderkommando 7b on June 27 to 4th Army HQ. Sonderkommando 7a marched via East Prussia in order to enter Vilnius with the troops. After being relieved by the Einsatzkommando 9, it proceeded on road 4, and turned south towards Minsk by order of Einsatzgruppe C in order to secure archives in Minsk, the capital, and arrived on July 4.

Sonderkommando 7b marched via Brest, Kobrin, Pruzhany, Rushana, Slonim, Baranovichi, Stolpce, via Route 2 towards Minsk and arrived there with the Vorkommando on July 4.

*Einsatzkommando 9:*

Proceeded towards Vilnius on June 29 according to instructions issued by the commander of the Rear Army Group Area.

Einsatzkommando 8 proceeded, according to orders of the commander of the Rear Army Group Area, to Bialystok on July 1, and marched on with the two commands towards Slonim, Novogrudok and Baranovichi. The staff continued towards Bialystok on July 3 with the advancing units of the Rear Army Group Area.

In conjunction with the commander of the Security Police for the General Gouvernement, six supporting units were set up for Byelorussia, who relieved the Sonderkommandos and Einsatzkommandos on July 3 and advanced from Warsaw to the assigned areas.

Based on these tactics, all towns in the Polish and Russian sections of Byelorussia are occupied as far as the fighting zone. A supporting unit is posted in Brest, one supporting unit in Pinsk and another in Slutsk with the aim of marching into Gomel after occupying the area. One supporting unit is posted in Bialystok with the task of also taking care of Bielsk. One supporting unit is in Vilnius, with the task of also taking care of Grodno and Lida. One supporting unit will be moved forward to Minsk in order to assume the work in Minsk after Einsatzgruppe C will march on to Moscow.

*Einsatzkommando 8*

is stationed, until further notice, in Bialystok. Einsatzkommando 9 is stationed in Vilnius so that it can be moved via Minsk towards Moscow at a later time. The staff of Einsatzgruppe C[1] has been posted in Minsk since July 6 with its headquarters in the Soviet building of the USSR.[2]

Because of the encirclement and due to the highway system, a rear and a front line cannot be delineated. Thus the Sonderkommandos 4a and 7b, as well as their staff, are constantly in the fighting zone and have been exposed on the highways to Russian sniping. At this time, Minsk is still in the fighting zone. Army Group B HQ is located 150 km in the rear in Baranovichi. After consultations in Minsk, Sonderkommando 7a was transferred from the 9th Army HQ, which is to march to the north of Moscow, to the newly formed 4th Armored Army HQ. Sonderkommando 7a is joined by a Vorauskommando with translators and persons familiar with Moscow, under the direction of SS-Standartenführer Dr. Six. The former army HQ 4 is now Army HQ 2, and Sonderkommando 7 has been put at its disposal.

In the course of further advances, the towns of Gomel, Mogilev, Vitebsk, Orsha, and Smolensk are to be bypassed.

2. *Police Work*

According to instructions by RSHA, liquidations of government and party officials, in all named cities of Byelorussia, were carried

---

1. Also called 3.
2. Obviously, it is meant to be the building of the Council of BSSR.

out. Concerning the Jews, according to orders, the same policy was adopted. The exact number of the liquidated has not as yet been established. On June 22, almost all the officials of the Communist party had fled, probably following higher instructions, and had taken with them all well-prepared documents. It is likely that some of the officials will try to return. Some will be identified with the help of the network of informants. The city of Minsk was an exception, although the officials had fled from there; surprisingly, the documentation remained intact in the sole government building — the house of the BSSR Soviet that had not been destroyed. On the other side, in destroyed Minsk, the NKVD and the internal party materials were destroyed by fire caused by the bombardment. Evaluating reports on Minsk follows.

. . . . . . . . . . . .

*Special report on the political situation and on activity in the area of Vilnius*
    *Police Matters*
The Lithuanian police branches in Vilnius, subordinated to the Einsatzkommando, were given the task of drawing up current lists of names of Jews in Vilnius; first the Intelligentsia, political activists, and wealthy Jews. Subsequently, searches and arrests were made and 54 Jews were liquidated on July 4, and 93 were liquidated on July 5. Sizeable property belonging to Jews were secured. With the help of Lithuanian police officials, a search was started for Communists and NKVD agents, most of whom, however, are said to have fled.

A search was also started for hidden weapons of the Polish secret military organizations, of which the Lithuanian police has as yet not made an accurate estimate. The establishment of a Jewish quarter is being prepared. Upon suggestion of the EK, the Jewish quarter will be declared to be out of bounds to military personnel by order of the Field Command HQ.

## Operational Situation Report USSR No. 19

. . . . . . . . . . . .

For organizational reasons the designations of the Einsatzgruppen is changed, effective immediately, as follows:

Einsatzgruppe Dr. Stahlecker — Einsatzgruppe A
Einsatzgruppe Nebe — Einsatzgruppe B, up to now C
Einsatzgruppe Dr. Rasch — Einsatzgruppe C, up to now B
Einsatzgruppe Ohlendorf — Einsatzgruppe D.

For technical reasons the designations of the Einsatzkommandos remain unchanged.

In the border region of Lithuania, the Stapo Tilsit carried out further large-scale operations. Thus, on July 2, 133 persons were shot in Tauroggen; on July 3, 322 persons (among them 5 women) in Georgenburg; in Augustowo 316 persons (among them 10 women); and in Mariampol 68 persons.

In addition, the following executions were carried out:

1. GPP. Schirwindt
   in *Wladislawo* (Newstadt) and vicinity 192 persons
2. GPP. Laugszargen
   in *Tauroggen* and vicinity 122 persons
3. GPK. Memel or GPP. Bajohren
   in *Krottingen* and vicinity 63 persons
4. GPP. Schmalleningken 1 person

Thus, till now *a total of 1743 persons* have been shot.

The higher SS and Police Commander, the commander of the Army's Rear Area North, SS-Gruppenführer and Generalleutnant (Lieutant General) of the Police Preutzmann reports:

The commander of the Army Area North offered to take over security in the area from the border of the Reich to the line Grodna-

Kaunas-Jubarkas-Tauroggen-Rietavas-Darbona-Baltic Sea to the temporary Corps Headquarters 1, together with his forces. The commander of the Army Rear Area has proposed a corresponding motion to the Quartermaster General. The area to be covered has become too large, as a consequence of the fact that the eastern boundary of the Army's Rear Area has been moved forward. Thus, I have ordered the commander of the ORPO in Königsberg/Prussia, in accordance with the authorization given by the Reichsführer-SS and Chief of the German Police and Chief of the ORPO, to take over the area of Lake Wystit-Mariampol-Kaunas-Jurbarkas-Tauroggen-Tietaveas-Darbenai-Baltic Sea with his own forces. An agreement with the commander of the Army Rear Area North and the temporary corps headquarters has been reached. In cooperation with the commander of the Army Rear Area North and the commander of the ORPO Königsberg/Prussia, the forces needed have been determined. The area will probably be taken over on July 12 or 13, 1941.

Otherwise the situation in the area of Kaunas is quiet. Only in isolated cases members of the Red Army who had been separated from their units were lying in ambush and shooting at units. This is the reason why up to now the Wehrmacht and the Police did not carry out more severe measures.

The members of the Red Army who were hidden in the woods and in other hiding places, driven by hunger, surface and surrender, in most cases by showing the white flag. The attitude of the Lithuanian population is friendly towards the Germans so far. They help the German soldiers, the police officials, and the other organizations already functioning in this area as much as possible. Their cooperation consists chiefly in looking for and turning over Lithuanian Communists, dispersed Red Army soldiers, and Jews. After the retreat of the Red Army, the population of Kaunas killed about 2,500 Jews during a spontaneous uprising. In addition, a rather large number of Jews was shot by the Auxiliary Police Service.

*Einsatzgruppe A:*
Location: Riga
1. In Kaunas, up to now a total of 7,800 Jews have been liquidated, partly through pogroms and partly through shooting by Lithuanian Kommandos. All of the corpses have been removed. Further mass shootings are no longer possible. Therefore, I summoned a Jewish committee and explained that up to now we had no reason to interfere

with the internal arrangements between the Lithuanians and the Jews. Foundations for a "New Order":

The establishment of a Jewish ghetto; identifying all the Jews with a yellow Star of David, 8 by 10 cm. in size, to be worn on the left breast; and the separate housing of women and children, for possible release on our orders by the Lithuanians and by a Jewish Relief Committee in the new ghetto. The town of Viliampol was designated as the location of the ghetto.

The resettlement must be carried out within 4 weeks. Prisons now are being searched once more. Some Jews, for special reasons, are being arrested and shot. This will involve a minor number of executions, only 50 to 100 persons. To prevent Jews from returning to Kaunas, an agreement was made with the Higher SS and Police Leader that the ORPO draw a cordon around Kaunas not allowing any Jews to enter the town. If necessary, Jews will be fired upon. All Wehrmacht agencies were informed about the directives.

About 250 men of the Lithuanian [anti-Soviet] partisans were left and are being sustained by us as a Sonderkommando and are being employed for future executions outside the town.

2. Units of Einsatzkommando 3 are presently working at Mariampol and Raseinial. After finishing their tasks, they will rejoin the Hauptkommando.

3. The Wehrmacht has received a new directive ordering it not to recognize the newly formed Lithuanian Government, but to make use of it.

4. In Riga, Metropolitan Sergei of the Russian Orthodox Church for the Baltic countries is prepared to make a proclamation against Communism to the believers in Russia. Sergei has been in Riga since 1941 and was in Moscow for 23 years before that. He is a Great-Russian. Civilian name: Voskresensky. Draft of the proclamation is now being prepared.

*Einsatzgruppe B:*
Location Minsk.
No special reports received.
*Einsatzgruppe C:*
Location: Rovno.

Einsatzkommando 4a is still in Rovno where executions of 240 Bolsheviks, predominantly Jewish, officials, agents, etc. took place. Vorkommando of 4a, set to march via Chudnov to Zhitomir as soon as that area is secure to some extent. Another section of 4a, in accordance with a wish expressed by Army Headquarters, takes over the area south of Rovno, in an area 20 kilometers wide, to the East, as a security measure. One section of the Special Task Commando from Lublin has arrived.

*Einsatzkommando 4b*
has finished its activity in Tarnopol. 127 executions. Parallel to that, liquidation of 600 Jews in the course of the persecutions of Jews as inspired by the Einsatzkommando.
In Zborov, 600 Jews liquidated by the Waffen-SS as a retaliation measure for Soviet atrocities.

*Einsatzkommando 6:*
On July 8, 1941 at Zlochev, 16 Communist officials and informers, among them 3 Jewesses, executed.
Group staff will proceed to Zhitomir.

*Einsatzgruppe D:*
Location: Piatra.

*Einstzkommando 10a:*
Location: Paleski, north of Jassy.
Vorkommando had already reached Belci; however, was forced to leave again because Soviet forces counter-attacked and re-occupied the place. Vorkommando was under fire. No casualties. Bolshevization not conducted extensively.
Paleski considerably devastated. Rumanians content themselves with looting everything. Pogroms could not be accomplished so far.

*Einsatzkommando 10b:*
Location: Chernowitz.
Einsatzkommando was fired upon in the center of the town. No casualties. Vorkommando made an attempt to reach Khotin. Contrary to statements by the Rumanian Army, the place was still occupied by Soviet forces. Vorkommando fell back under fire causing no casualties. Good cooperation with Rumanian Gendarmerie. Rumanians have taken over the civil administration at Chernovtsy. Action against Jews until the arrival of the Einsatzkommando spotty. Rumanian soldiers looted all the houses. Above all, Ukrainians were ill-treated. The city is destroyed. The ghetto, including most of the Jews, is completely destroyed by Red artillery. Einsatzkommando stopped harassing of Ukrainians, and contacted the National Ukrainian Organization (OUN).

*Einsatzkommando 11*
Location: Barlad.
Good cooperation with the Rumanian Army.

Berlin, July 12, 1941

12 copies
(11th copy)

## Operational Situation Report USSR No. 20

. . . . . . . . . . . .

*Einsatzgruppe B;*
Location: Minsk
The industrialized areas are only slightly damaged. The town is without light and water. Political and government officials have fled. The population is very depressed. Many people have lost their shelter and the food situation is worsening. To protect the communication lines and prevent acts of sabotage, the Field Commander ordered the arrest of all male inhabitants between the ages of 18-45. The civil prisoners are being screened at this time. The attitude of the population toward the Germans is one of wait-and-see. The Byelorussians show a friendlier attitude towards the Germans. However, the entire population hopes that the occupation will enable them to live a normal life in the near future.

According to the last report of Einsatzgruppe B, wooden houses in the western part of Minsk were set afire. Apparently the houses were set on fire by Jews because the Jews were supposed to evacuate their homes for returning Byelorussian refugees. At present the population is in a mood to launch a pogrom. Their fury caused certain anti-Jewish actions. A number of Jews were liquidated for this act.

*Einsatzgruppe C:*
Location: Rovno
1. *Actions*
On July 5, 1941, 15 Jews were executed as reprisal for the bestial murder of the Ukrainian nationalist leader Dr. *Kirnychny* in Rudki. The Ukrainian population on their part set the synagogue and Jewish houses on fire. 150 Ukrainians were found murdered in Stryj. In the course of a search, it was possible to arrest 12 Communists who were

responsible for the murder of the Ukrainians. It concerns 11 Jews and 1 Ukrainian who were shot with the participation of the entire population of Stryj.

## Operational Situation Report USSR No. 21

. . . . . . . . . . . .

*Einsatzgruppe B:*
Location: Minsk
A civilian prison camp was built in Minsk by the first troops passing through. Almost all the male inhabitants of the town were placed into it. The Einsatzgruppe was asked to screen the camp together with the Secret Field Police. Only persons were set free who were able to clear themselves beyond reproach and who were neither politically nor criminally implicated. The remainder, left behind in the camp, will be subjected to a careful investigation. Each case will be decided upon in accordance with the results of the investigation. 1050 Jews were subsequently liquidated. Others are executed daily. With regard to the non-Jews left in the camp, liquidation of the criminals, the officials, the Asiatics, etc. was started. A Jewish committee was also formed, a ghetto was set up, and the identification of Jews on outer garments started. The Bolsheviks set free the inmates of the Minsk prison except the political ones. These were shot by the Bolsheviks before their retreat. A search has been started for the criminal prisoners who have been set free.

In Vilnius by July 8th the local Einsatzkommando liquidated 321 Jews. The Lithuanian Ordnungsdienst which was placed under the Einsatzkommando after the Lithuanian political police had been dissolved was instructed to take part in the liquidation of the Jews. 150 Lithuanian officials were assigned to this task. They arrested the Jews and put them into concentration camps where they were subjected the same day to Special Treatment. This work has now begun, and thus about 500 Jews, saboteurs amongst them, are liquidated daily. About 460,000 rubles in cash, as well as many valuables belonging to Jews who were subject to Special Treatment, were confiscated as property belonging to enemies of the Reich. The former Trade Union building in Vilnius was secured for the German Labor Front (DAF) at their request, as well as the money in trade union bank accounts, totaling 1.5 million rubles. The arrest of several repeatedly convicted armed robbers indicated that in the future we shall have to reckon with such bandits. The Einsatzkommando was informed by Lithuanians that the Poles residing in Vilnius at the time of Bolshevik rule had formed armed cadres with a total strength of 12,000 men who had amassed considerable ammunition supplies. A search for these hordes of ammunition has been started.

Einsatzkommando 2 in Vilnius has confiscated vast documentary materials in the local Jewish museum which was a branch of the central Moscow Institute for Jewish Culture.

Apart from 215 Jewish and Bolshevik officials, 15 more NKVD agents were shot in Bialystok. The NKVD office had been completely burnt down. Only in the cellar vaults was it possible to secure various lists. The executions continue all the time at the same rate. The Polish section of the population has shown that it supports the executions by the Security Police by informing on Jewish, Russian, and also Polish Bolsheviks. The security of the city and of the surrounding districts is not, at present, sufficiently assured, owing to a lack of Byelorussian police forces. When the Soviets entered Bialystok in 1939, they sent all police and judicial officials to Siberia, and set up a new administration. This set-up was, however, completely dissolved by the Russians before the Wehrmacht occupation. All official files and documents were destroyed. An auxiliary police force was formed, subordinate to the Einsatz unit in Bialystok, by recruiting the White Russian forces and former Polish criminal-police officials.

Only 96 Jews were executed in Grodno and Lida during the first days. I gave orders to intensify these activities. The headquarters of the Grodno Communist party was seized and the materials found in it were confiscated. A card index with photographs was found in the NKVD building. Other photographs were also found which provided information on the killing activity of the GPU. Notes of a Russian officer were also found, showing individual preparations for war by the Soviets.

The activity of all the Kommandos has progressed satisfactorily. The liquidations, in particular, are in full swing and usually take place daily. The carrying out of the necessary liquidations is assured in every instance under any circumstances.

It emerges more and more clearly that the main responsibility lies with the rear section of the army area for the seizure of resistance groups, partisans, Red functionaries, and Jews. This is due to the gradual surfacing of fugitives who had escaped into the forests and swamps. It is, therefore, not practical to pull the Einsatzkommandos out of the area of the security sectors.

Berlin, July 14, 1941

30 copies
(22nd copy)

## Operational Situation Report USSR No. 22

. . . . . . . . . . . .

*Einsatzkommando 1b:*
Location: Chernovtsy, Vorkommando at Khotin. The following was ascertained at Chernowitz:

1. The Rumanians declare North Bukovina to be Rumanian territory.

2. A great number of Jews of the poorer class are in Rumanian prisons. Nearly no intelligentsia.

3. The Rumanians are inclined to exterminate the upper echelon of Ukrainian leadership in order to settle the Ukrainian problem in the North Bukovina once and for all, taking advantage of the present situation. 22 Ukrainians are under Rumanian arrest in Chernowitz. 1b has been given the following orders in this respect:

a. To influence the Rumanian authorities to take severe measures concerning the Jewish question. They must raid Jewish meetings and uncover conspiracies in order to stimulate Rumanian activities against the Jewish intelligentsia and to enable us to take a hand ourselves.

b. To hold or to turn over to us important Ukrainians; similarly, Ukrainian Communists will be put at the disposal of the Rumanians.

10b finished its tasks at Khotin. Intelligentsia from the Soviet party and public life, Jewish agitators, teachers, lawyers, and rabbis were apprehended with the help of Ukrainian informants in the course of several raids. Jewish physicians were not arrested in order to administer to the medical needs of the population.

The Chief of the Security Police               Berlin, July 15, 1941
and the SD

32 copies
(21st copy)

## Operational Situation Report USSR No. 23

. . . . . . . . . . . .

*Einsatzgruppe C:*

Former Polish officers and Jews play an important part in the Honved Army. The translators are almost without exception either Jews or scoundrels. Names of individual Polish officers have been established. All the leading military Hungarian circles sympathize with the Poles, most of them also with the Jews. Poles were preferred in Zaleshchiki and Stanislovov. The Hungarian Feldgendarmerie is apparently favoring the setting up of Polish units.

In the area of Zaleshchiki, the Poles cooperate with Soviet Russian gangs who are still hiding in the forests. Hungarian circles deny knowing of Polish activities in connection with Bolsheviks. All the intelligence officers are either Jews or under Jewish influence. I personally had dealings with 6 officers in the area who were undoubtedly Jews. A Polish officer, Dabrowski, holds a leading position.

. . . . . . . . . . . .

Isolated actions against Jews were carried out by the militia (Ukrainian). As a consequence, the Hungarian Army intervened immediately. In Stanislovov one could see leading officers together with many Jews in the restaurant "Kiev."

The Chief of the Security Police          Berlin, July 16, 1941
and the SD

33 copies
(23rd copy)


*Operational Situation Report USSR No. 24*

. . . . . . . . . . . .

*Einsatzgruppe A:*
Location: Riga
*EK 1b*
Location: Daugavpils
Daugavpils was occupied by the German troops on July 6. The greater part of the town was burned down during the following 2-3 days. Only a relatively small part of the town was damaged through direct fighting. The fires on the days that followed were caused by arson. Before leaving the town, the Russians released a proclamation in which they ordered the town to be burned. The Jews are said to have participated in the burnings. 5 Jews were caught red-handed during the first 3 days and were immediately shot.

Of the vital services, the electrical works are totally gutted by fire. Only the reservoirs and water towers of the waterworks are destroyed; thus, a limited supply of water is available for the population. The water system is intact.

The population, with the exception of a very few, had fled from the town. At present, there are approximately 8,000 persons in town again. A steady flow of returning inhabitants can be observed.

The attitude of the Latvians is absolutely positive. They are solely interested in creating conditions in Daugavpils that will enable the population to renew the most vital services for normal life.

So far, no political involvement has been observed. Activity and interest of the leading Latvians are absolutely guided by the conditions caused by the destruction of the town.

The Latvians, including the leading activists, have been, so far, absolutely passive in their anti-Semitic attitudes, not daring to take action against Jews. Until now, Dünaburg had about 45,000 inhabitants, 50% of whom were Jews. They ruled the town absolutely. As the Russians left, the Jews spread the rumor that the Russians would return soon. Thus, unlike the Lithuanians who have an active attitude, the Latvians are hesitatingly organizing and forming a front against the Jews. The Latvian population has been further weakened as the Russians, during the last fourteen days before the war's outbreak, deported about 500 Latvian families belonging to the intelligentsia to Central Russia.

Since July 3, the Latvians have a town administration and an auxiliary police force. Both organizations are headed by the former Latvian captain, Petersons.

The auxiliary police force consists of former police constables, members of the former Latvian Army, and members of the former ATZSARGI organization (Organization for Self Defense). The latter was founded during the Ulmanis dictatorship in 1934. Its individual members did not swear allegiance to him; so it is reported.

Owing to the initative of the EK (Einsatzkommando), the auxiliary police force at present consists of 240 men and has been strictly organized. New men are currently being enlisted. They help the EK as auxiliary police and are on duty in the 6 police districts established so far. Some members have been assigned to criminal police and security police work.

By July 7 the Latvians arrested 1125 Jews, 32 political prisoners, 85 Russian workers, and 2 women criminals, the greater part during the last days. This is due to the EK backing the Latvians. Actions against the Jews are going on in an ever-increasing number. Conforming to a suggestion of the EK, the Jews are being evacuated by the auxiliary police force from all houses still standing. The apartments are being allotted to non-Jewish inhabitants. The Jewish families are being driven out of town by the Latvians; most of the men have been arrested.

The food supply is inadequate as nearly all stocks were destroyed by fire.

The arrested Jewish men are shot without ceremony and interred in previously prepared graves. Until now the EK 1b has shot 1150 Jews in Daugavpils.

The advance units of EK 1a Sandberger are located in Pskov, Fellin, Pernau, and before Dorpat, EK 1b Ehrlinger is in Zilupe (Rosenhof), and Ostrov.

In Riga, Einsatzkommando 2 sifted through the entire documentary materials, searched all offices, arrested the leading Communists as far as they could be found. These actions initiated against Jews were headed by SS-Sturmbannführer Barth and were carried out in an exemplary manner. At present, 600 Communists and 2,000 Jews are under arrest. 400 Jews were killed during pogroms in Riga, since the arrival of EK 2; 300 by the Latvian auxiliary police and partly by our units. The prisons will be emptied completely during the next few days. Outside of Riga, within Latvia an additional 1,600 Jews were liquidated by EK 2.

The political conditions are still not clear. Various Latvian groups have finally come together. With German officials they try to commence their work, but so far, with no success. Clarification of these conditions would be highly desirable, as well as an indication of the expected directions of political developments. Because of the urgency in settling the economic questions, contact has been made with the higher SS and police leaders and the German Army. Agreement has been achieved.

*Einsatzgruppe B:*
Location: Minsk
*EK 8:*
Location: Baranovichi.
An advance Kommando unit moves slowly towards Slutsk which is already occupied by EK 7b. EK 8 has the task of carrying out rather dangerous actions against officials, kommissars, etc., who are hiding in the forests.

*Einsatzkommando 9:*
Location: Vilnius.
Has orders to send an advance unit to Vileyka. Because of a short surprise fire fight against the Vilnius Security Police Headquarters a special liquidation was carried out in excess of daily liquidation quotas.

*Sonderkommando Moscow*
The situation at the front permitting, the Sonderkommando will proceed cauttiously to Smolensk on 16 July.

*Einsatzgruppe C:*
Location: Zviahel (Novograd-Volynski)

I. *General Situation on Arrival.*
Before leaving, the Bolsheviks, together with the Jews, murdered

several Ukrainians; as an excuse, they used the attempted Ukrainian uprising of June 25, 1941, which tried to free their prisoners.

According to reliable information, about 20,000 Ukrainians have disappeared from Lvov, 80% of them belonging to the intelligentsia. The prisons in Lvov were crammed with the bodies of murdered Ukrainians. According to a moderate estimate, in Lvov alone 3-4,000 persons were either killed or deported.

In Dobromil, 82 dead bodies were found, 4 of them Jews. The latter were former Bolsheviki informers who had been killed because of their complicity in this act. Near Dobromil an obsolete salt mine pit was discovered. It was completely filled with dead bodies. In the immediate neighborhood, there is a 6 × 15m mass grave. The number of those murdered in the Dobromil area is estimated to be approximately several hundred.

In Sambor on June 26, 1941, about 400 Ukrainians were shot by the Bolsheviks. An additional 120 persons were murdered on June 27, 1941. The remaining 80 prisoners succeeded in overpowering the Soviet guards, and fled. Concerning their numbers it should be noted that Sambor has a total of 26,000 inhabitants, among them 12,000 Poles, 10,000 Jews, and 4,000 Ukrainians.

As early as 1939, a larger number of Ukrainians was shot, and 1,500 Ukrainians as well as 500 Poles were deported to the east.

Russians and Jews committed these murders in very cruel ways. Bestial mutilations were daily occurrences. Breasts of women and genitals of men were cut off. Jews have also nailed children to the wall and then murdered them. Killing was carried out by shots in the back of the neck. Hand grenades were frequently used for these murders.

In Dobromil, women and men were killed with blows by a hammer used to stun cattle before slaughter.

In many cases, the prisoners must have been tortured cruelly: bones were broken, etc. In Sambor, the prisoners were gagged and thus prevented from screaming during torture and murder. The Jews, some of whom also held official positions, in addition to their economic supremacy, and who served in the entire Bolshevik police, were always partners in these atrocities.

Finally, it was established that seven [German] pilots who had been captured were murdered. Three of them were found in a Russian military hospital where they had been murdered in bed by shots in the abdomen.

This atrocity apparently stems from a Russian instruction to "exterminate" all German pilots and parachutists.

II. *Behavior of the Ukrainian Population.*

In the first hours after the Bolshevik withdrawal, the Ukrainian population displayed commendable activity against the Jews.

For example, the Dobromil synagogue was set on fire and 50 Jews were killed by the enraged crowd at Sambor.

Maltreating them, the Lvov inhabitants rounded up about 1,000 Jews and took them to the GPU prison which has been occupied by the Wehrmacht.

III. *Measures of the Einsatzgruppe.*

Approximately 7,000 Jews were rounded up and shot by the Security Police in retaliation for the inhuman atrocities.

73 men were discovered to be functionaries and spies of the NKVD and were likewise shot.

40 men were liquidated on the basis of well-founded denunciations made by inhabitants. Mainly Jews between 20 and 40 years of age were rounded up, artisans and specialists being set aside as far as possible. Apart from these executions in Lvov, reprisal measures were carried out at other places also: 132 Jews, for instance, were shot in Dobromil.

Since 32 Ukrainians had been murdered in Yavorov, 15 Jews were liquidated in retaliation.

*EK 4a*

Moved from Cracow via Zamosc to Sokal and from there into the Lutsk district.

Among the civilian prisoners found in Sokal, 17 were discovered to be Communist functionaries, agents and snipers, and were executed on June 28, 1941.

With the help of the Ukrainian militia, another 117 active Communists and agents of the NKVD were found on June 29 and executed the same day.

With the assistance of reliable Ukrainians, residents of Sokal, 183 Jewish Communists were also caught. They were liquidated on June 30.

Furthermore, Horokhov details the discovery of 7 Communist functionaries on June 30 who were shot on the spot.

An advance unit dispatched to Lutsk on June 27 found the larger part of the town in flames. According to information from the town commander, only Jews can be held responsible for the arson. Prior to their withdrawal, the Bolsheviks shot 2,800 out of 4,000 Ukrainians imprisoned in the Lutsk prison. According to the statement of 19 Ukrainians who survived the slaughter with more or less serious injuries, the Jews again played a decisive part in the arrests and shooting. In the town itself everything was still in wild confusion. All shops were looted by the population. After the arrival of the Einsatzkommando all available men were sent to assist the town commander. They succeeded at least in safeguarding the extensive food supplies.

Afterwards, the official buildings were systematically searched. Other investigations were started to find the Jews and Communists responsible for the arson and the looting.

300 Jews and 20 looters were arrested and shot on June 30.

On July 2 the corpses of 10 German Wehrmacht soldiers were found. In retaliation, 1160 Jews were shot by the Ukrainians with the help of one platoon of the police and one platoon of the infantry.

Finally, 50 Polish agents and informers were discovered who were liquidated also.

The methodical searches carried out everywhere by the Einsatzkommando before the arrival of the intelligence units and the Secret Military Police were also successful. Thus, it was possible to find on June 28 lists of agents and other important documents in three party buildings as well as in the bank after the safes had been forced open.

On July 1, 1941, the offices of the Russian District Military Headquarters were searched and all files secured which, among other matters, contained secret instructions relating to mobilization.

Moreover, important material, including, among other things, records relating to Russian agents in various countries, was discovered in the buildings of the Lutsk Soviet authorities as well as in different Communist centers after the safes had been forced open.

Einsatzkommando 4b is at work at present in the Tarnopol area. It is planned to have the Kommando proceed to Proskurov.

Of the 54 Poles and Jews who had been working as agents for the NKVD, 8 persons, two of them Jewish women, were arrested and executed, the remainder apparently having taken to their heels.

At Tarnopol 10 [German] soldiers were also found among the murdered in the prison, 1 of them a lieutenant of the air force, 6 pilots, and 3 soldiers of the mountain troops. Of the Jews assigned to disinter the corpses, about 180 were slain, some in the prison courtyard, some in the streets. Moreover, Jewish residences were destroyed by members of the Waffen-SS with hand grenades, and then set on fire. According to the statements of Ukrainians, the number of German members of the Wehrmacht murdered by the Russians is estimated to be much greater. Reliable Ukrainian circles ventured to say that numerous Ukrainians serving with the Russian army would like to desert immediately. But, like the Russians, time and again, they had been impressed by the fact that they would be shot on the spot by the Germans if they were taken prisoners of war; thus, they had refrained from deserting from sheer fright. Furthermore, the Russians are said to have ordered the complete destruction of all crops in case of a retreat to former Russian territory. They also asked the farmers to retreat with the troops for, otherwise, they would likewise be shot by the Germans.

This being the situation, Ukrainian circles suggest a large-scale leaflet propaganda campaign directed at Ukrainian soldiers and peasants. Apparently, such a propaganda campaign has not as yet begun. At any rate, nothing of this kind has become known at Tarnopol.

A Kommando of the Group Staff participated in an action in Zlochev on July 7, 1941, which had only been superficially purged earlier by Einsatzkommando 4b when it passed through the town. In the NKVD office essential secret documents were seized which were already sealed and ready to be sent off.

The investigations at Zlochev proved that the Russians, prior to their withdrawal, arrested and murdered indiscriminately a total of 700 Ukrainians, but, nevertheless, included the entire [local] Ukrainian intelligentsia. By order of the Wehrmacht, the militia retaliated by arresting and shooting several hundred Jews. The number of the Jews liquidated may run to about 300-500.

Repeatedly it could be observed that *Politruks* [party members] who had escaped raided villages at nighttime for food.

The influence of the Bandera group is very strong in Zlochev. A revolutionary Ukrainian administration has been established there which welcomes the Germans as their allies with posters and leaflets.

At Rocsiczau[1] three saboteurs were arrested who had cut a Wehrmacht telephone line leading to the forward German lines; they had then passed information on to the Russian troops. As a result, German soldiers have been made prisoners of war by the Russians.

These Communist saboteurs were likewise shot.

---

1. Probably Rozhishche in Volhynia.

## Operational Situation Report USSR No. 25

. . . . . . . . . . . .

*Einsatzgruppe D*
Location: Piatra-Neamt.
*EK 10:*
Location: Belzy.

We must be aware that a Rumanian major from Jassy delegated by the Rumanians will arrive. For the time being, administrative business is carried out by a suitable personality who has connections with the EK and was delegated by the local Kommandatur. Before the arrival of the local Kommandatur, the commander initiated some preparatory measures for the reopening of the supply factories. These measures are being continued by the local Kommandatur.

During the past days and nights, considerable excesses were carried out repeatedly against Jews by Rumanian soldiers. The number of Jews killed cannot be established, but might, however, reach several hundred. On the evening of July 10, Rumanian military authorities rounded up some 400 Jews of all ages, including men and women, in order to shoot them in retaliation for attacks on Rumanian military personnel. Fault was found, however, in the lengthy technical planning. Following the wish of the commander of the 170th Division, the Rumanian commanding general restricted himself in the last moment to the shooting of 15 male Jews.

Rumanian police gather up the Jews who are capable of working, and keep them under arrest. These Jews are also used for clearing and cleaning jobs [removing rubble, etc.].

Before yesterday in accordance with the wish of the commander of the 170th Division, about 70 hostages were arrested. This number is to be increased to 200, in order to protect the army against repeated insidious attacks that have occurred. A few hostages were shot as retribution for the attack on a German army car in a suburb of Belzy. All the leading state and party officials have fled. Interrogation of various Ukrainians in the P.O.W. collection centers has demonstrated that they all had joined the war without the slightest enthusiasm and that they awaited the Germans as their liberators. They had been told by the Russian soldiers that the Germans would shoot them in case they were captured, but as they knew how their fathers had been treated as German P.O.W.s in World War I, they realized that these were only lies of the Red Rulers. Other sources also confirm that many Ukrainians kept away from actively resisting the German advance.

## Operational Situation Report USSR No. 26

. . . . . . . . . . . .

*Police unit — Tilsit*
reports that so far 3302 persons were liquidated in the course of the cleansing operation on the other side of the former Soviet-Lithuanian border.

*Einsatzgruppe A:*
Location: Pleskau [Pskov]
EK 1B reports:
As the German troops marched in, most of the Jews fled to Russia and into the surrounding forests. Most of the cases of arson in the town are committed by Jews. As the German troops marched in, they found some 60 totally mutilated Latvians, whereupon 80 Jews were liquidated. Police prefect Matsch has taken the liquidation upon himself. The former Latvian judge, Alexander, was entrusted with the management of the local criminal police. He is under the control of the Security Police. He was instructed to choose capable people among the former active Latvian police officials and to give them criminal-police tasks.

*Einsatzgruppe B:*
Location: Minsk
*Einsatzgruppe C:*
Location: Zviahel (Novograd Volynskiy)

## Operational Situation Report USSR No. 27

. . . . . . . . . . . .

*Einsatzgruppe B:*
Location: Minsk

A meeting of the commander of the Rear Army Area 102 with the higher SS and Police Leader has resulted in complete agreement concerning our further activities.

The rear security divisions attach great importance to cooperation with the security police.

Liquidation continues daily. If they are not caught red-handed [in some dereliction], persons are liquidated according to lists. It has been repeatedly observed that Jews escape into the forests now and try to hide there. The employed White Russians have shown little activity so far. It has been explained already to Dr. Tschora what is expected from their support, particularly concerning the cooperation in the apprehension of Communists, officials, commissars, intellectuals, Jews, etc.

*EK 8:*
Location: Baranovichi

With the Vorkommando to Slutsk and Lachoviche. Special action [Sonderaktion] was carried out against 60 Communists.

*Einsatzgruppe C:*
Location: Zhitomir

Zhitomir had a population of 90,000, of which about 30% were Jews, 15% Poles, the rest Ukrainians, and about 4,000 Volksdeutsche. Now there are approximately 40,000.

Zhitomir is heavily damaged by arson committed by the Russians. The population greets the Germans as they march in.

*Einsatzgruppe D:*
Location: Piatra-Neamt

## Operational Situation Report USSR No. 28

. . . . . . . . . . . .

*Einsatzgruppe A:*
Location: Pleskau [Pskov]
Einsatzgruppe A has transmitted secret instructions (a copy of which is enclosed) concerning the deportation of anti-Soviet elements from Lithuania, Latvia and Estonia.

. . . . . . . . . . . .

I. Following consultations with Army Group South, the agreement stands that all the Einsatzkommandos as well as the Group staff stay close to the fighting troops whenever possible. This guarantees that the advance Kommandos as well as the main Kommandos will march into Kiev as soon as possible after its capture, which is expected shortly.

. . . . . . . . . . . .

II. According to the report of an eyewitness from Tarnopol, an officer of the German Air Force was led through the city by the Russian police, followed by a large crowd of Jews, and was insulted and ill treated. The population is in general convinced that it is mostly the Jews who should be held responsible for the atrocities that are committed everywhere.

. . . . . . . . . . . .

IV. So far, a total of 240 executions have been carried out in Rovno: mostly Jewish Bolshevik agents and informers of the NKVD. The advanced Kommando Lublin for special tasks arrived here yesterday and together with the militia will now proceed to undertake the further purging of the town and its environs.

As it was learned that the Russians before they left have either deported the Ukrainian intelligentsia, or executed them, that is, murdered them, it is assumed that in the last days before the retreat of the Russians, about 100 influential Ukrainians were murdered. So far the bodies have not been found — a search has been initiated.

About 100-150 Ukrainians were murdered by the Russians in Kremenets. Some of these Ukrainians are said to have been thrown into cauldrons of boiling water. This has been deduced from the fact that the bodies were found without skin when they were exhumed. In retaliation, the Ukrainians killed 130 Jews with sticks.

In Dubno, where the activities have essentially come to an end, a total of 100 executions were carried out. Among them was a Ukrainian who since 1940 has worked without interruption for the NKVD. He confessed he was responsible for the murder or deportation of Ukrainians into Central Russia; in addition, two Communist officials and confidants of the NKVD who instigated sniper-warfare; one Communist who had revealed every activity of the Ukrainian nationalists to the Russians and had initiated the evacuation or deportation of many local families. Finally, there were also two Russians who were found in possession of shoulder-straps, leather-wear and army underwear of German soldiers. Before leaving Dubno, the Russians, as they had done in Lvov, committed extensive mass-murder.

Altogether 127 executions were carried out in Tarnopol. Before their flight, as in Lvov and Dubno, the Russians went on a rampage there. Disinterments revealed 10 bodies of German soldiers. Almost all of them had their hands tied behind their backs with wire. The bodies revealed traces of extremely cruel mutilations such as gouged eyes, severed tongues and limbs.

The number of Ukrainians who were murdered by the Russians, among them women and children, is set finally at 600. Jews and Poles were spared by the Russians. The Ukrainians estimate the total number of victims since the occupation of the Ukraine by the Russians at about 2,000. The planned deportation of the Ukrainians already started in 1939. There is hardly a family in Tarnopol from which one or several members have not disappeared. In the town, containing about 40,000 inhabitants, among them 12,000 Ukrainians, 18,000 Jews, and 10,000 Poles, there are fewer than 10,000 Ukrainians left. The entire Ukrainian intelligentsia is destroyed. Since the beginning of the war, 160 members of the Ukrainian intelligentsia were either murdered or deported. Inhabitants of the town had observed a column of about 1,000 civilians driven out of town by police and army early in the morning of July 1, 1941.

As in Lvov, torture chambers were discovered in the cellars of the Court of Justice. Apparently, hot and cold showers were also used here (as in Lemberg) for torture, as several bodies were found, totally naked, their skin burst and torn in many places. A grate was found in another room, made of wire and set above the ground about 1m in height, traces of ashes were found underneath. A Ukrainian engineer, who was also to be murdered but saved his life by smearing the blood of a dead victim over his face, reports that one could also hear screams of pain from women and girls.

The troops passing by who saw these horrors, in particular the bodies of the murdered German soldiers, killed approximately 600 Jews and burned down their houses.

## Operational Situation Report USSR No. 30

. . . . . . . . . . . .

*Einsatztgruppe C:*

Location: Zhitomir, reports:

187 Soviet Russians and Jews turned over by the army, some as civilian prisoners, were shot in Zhitomir.

One car of Einsatzgruppe 4a was shot at from a house in Zhitomir. The young culprit, aged 12, was arrested. Inquiries are not yet completed. Retaliation measures initiated.

Since Communists and Jews are said to hide in the area of Zhitomir, systematic search activity has started in cooperation with the army... Despite the independence propaganda of the Bandera group, the mood of the Ukrainians, particularly in the provincial towns, continues to be good. They are only worried about the advance of the Hungarian troops into Ukrainian territory.

Polish officers are serving with the Hungarians and are hostile toward the Ukrainian militia. They prefer German occupation to Ukrainian rule. Rumor propaganda from the resistance movements is being notices.

## Operational Situation Report USSR No. 31

. . . . . . . . . . . .

*Einsatzgruppe B:*
Location: Borisov
5. *Einsatzkommando 9*
Location: Vileyka
*Mood and Situation in the Occupied Territories*
Up to now, Jewry has shown restraint. The harsh measures against the Jews and, in particular, the executions, have increased the anti-German attitude considerably. They are also attempting to become aggressive. Reports that Jewish circles spread horror propaganda and other incitements against the Germans among the population become more and more frequent. They try to intimidate and threaten the White Russians who remain undecided whether to carry out pogroms.

The Jews have organized a signal service and, as soon as a SiPo kommando appears, escape into the surrounding forests and swamps. At least 1½ million Jews live in the Byelorussian area; their sociological structure differs from that of the former Polish and Soviet regions. While the Jew did not have any official function and did not enjoy any special protection as a Jew in what was formerly Poland, in the Soviet Union, he regarded himself, without any question, as a member of the ruling strata. The Polish Jew always had to be aware of anti-Jewish demonstrations from the population, and where he was not in the majority, he considered it better to appear reserved and timid. The Soviet Jews, on the other hand, were strengthened in their self-confidence to a great degree during the quarter century of Jewish-Bolshevik rule. They appeared to be not only self-assured but even arrogant in many cases when the German troups entered. The liquidations of Jews carried out by the Einsatzgruppe brought about a rapid external change. Nevertheless, the Jew remains dangerous and hostile in this area. Because of his education and tradition, he is ideally suited and also willing in most cases to inflict significant damage.

A solution of the Jewish question during the war seems impossible in this area because of the tremendous number of Jews. It could only be achieved through deportations. However, to work out a flexible basis for the immediate future, the Einsatzgruppe B has, wherever it arrived, enforced the following measures:

Appointed a chairman of the Judenrat [Jewish Council]; in every town he was charged with setting up a Judenrat consisting of 3-10 persons. The Judenrat bears the collective responsibility for the behavior of the Jewish population. Besides, the Judenrat has to start immediately with the registration of Jews living in the area. In addition, the Judenrat must organize work groups consisting of all male Jews aged 15-55, to carry out cleaning and other work for German [civilian] offices and the Army. Also a few female work groups are to be set up from the same age-group.

The German soldiers are not always able to distinguish between the Jewish and the local non-Jewish residents, resulting in some unpleasant situations. Thus, it was ordered that all male and female Jews over the age of 10 are to wear, as of now, the yellow Jewish patch on the breast and the back.

The Judenrat is subordinated to the temporary town-commissar. The position of town-commissar has been given to reliable Byelorussians who were suggested and chosen by the Einsatzkommandos.

Because of their great numbers, the housing of the Jews in the ghetto itself presents a particularly difficult task. The fulfillment of this task is already in progress. Suitable town-districts have been chosen, in collaboration with the military and civilian headquarters.

Economic life has come to a standstill for the time being because of destruction and looting. Some factories in Minsk and Borisov have renewed their work. Kolkhoz workshops have been destroyed by looting and requisitions. This has influenced the supply situation. Presently, money has almost no value and bread is issued in lieu of payment.

Continued tension persists between Lithuanians and Poles in the Vilna district, but no open clashes occur, due to the German Army's presence. Many rumors are circulating concerning imminent Polish action. Four additional Lithuanian-organized groups were uncovered which have, so far, not been active, according to our information. The control of the sermons in Vilnius has resulted in a generally positive political attitude.

A Jewish-Polish secret organization exists in Vilnius and its environs. It has set itself the task of reestablishing by force Polish sovereignty. The organization which is said to be very large in number is divided into sections in the town and country of the Vilnius district. They are said to have machine guns, rifles, pistols and hand grenades. The organization is also said to possess a secret transmitter. An agent was planted in the organization. We expect to uncover it within 2-3 days.

There exists complete agreement with the commander of the Rear Army Area concerning the treatment of partisans and soldiers in civilian clothes. Large actions are initiated with participation of the security police. Proceedings are carried out with utter ruthlessness.

The number of liquidations reported on July 14, 1941 is 4,243 and by July 19 has increased by an additional 3,386.

As of now, there is an order to dissolve the Communist party and Communist organizations. Confiscations of valuables, reports, and files, etc., are assured. The Einsatzgruppe is constantly kept informed as to all confiscations and other activities that occur by the local Kommandatur, etc.

The Chief of the Security Police      Berlin, July 24, 1941
and the SD

41 copies
(41st copy)

*Operational Situation Report USSR No. 32*

. . . . . . . . . . . .

*Einsatzgruppe B:*
Location: Orscha
Reports:
1. Police activity
In addition to reports from Brest-Litovsk, Minsk, Bialystok, Baranovichi, and Slonim, we have received reports on activity of EKs from: Novogrudok, Brazianka, Lizejka, Vsielub, Niekhnierviche, Koreliche, Stankiewiche, Zdzenciol, Lida and Lakhoviche. We have succeeded in arresting 67 NKVD agents and officials; among these were three Red Commissars from these small localities; they have been liquidated. Cooperation between the EK 8, based in Baranovichi, and the appropriate Army units is particularly success-ful. Together with the local military and civilian headquarters the for-mation of Jewish Councils, registration and concentration of Jews were brought about, as well as a renewed registration of all civilians. With the help of the GFP, the Abwehr units,[1] and the Field Gendar-merie, actions were carried out continuously against Bolshevik ag-ents, political commissars, NKVD members, etc. Another 301 per-sons were thus liquidated in Baranovichi. This accounts for Jewish ac-tivists, officials and looters. Approximately 25,000 rubles in cash were confiscated.

The Teilkommando which was dispatched to Slonim has carried out with the police major action [Grossaktion] against Jews and other Communist elements. During this action about 2,000 persons were arrested because of Communist activity and looting. Of these, on the

---
1. Inteiiigence.

same day 1,075 persons were liquidated. The Kommando alone liquidated another 84 persons in Slonim.

In addition, during the Lakhovich liquidation-action, 323 Russian infantry rifles, machine guns, and automatic pistols were confiscated and handed over to the Ortskommandatur [municipal occupation headquarters]. The police, supported by the local Einsatztruppe, have liquidated 4,435 persons, among them 400 Russians and Byelorussians. Quite a number of NKVD buildings were searched for political material. Several card indexes, lists, etc. were found.

In Minsk the entire Jewish intelligentsia has been liquidated (teachers, professors, lawyers, etc., except medical personnel). A Jewish Ordnungspolizei [Ghetto police unit] has been established. It is to maintain order in the new Jewish quarter. The Jewish police is at the disposal of the Jewish Council. It has to help carry out the orders issued by the German authorities and the municipality of Minsk. A Jewish health service, which is subordinated to the city health department, has been set up in order to prevent epidemics in the Jewish quarter.

At present the population of Bialystok cooperates actively in the elimination of the Bolshevik system. They report regularly on partisan groups in the surrounding area of Bialystok; thus, together with the army, action against them can be taken. As requested by the 162nd Infantry Division, the security police carried out an action against former Communist officials who now live in a small locality near Bialystok. 17 Communist officials were liquidated. In Bialystok proper, another 59 NKVD informants were liquidated.

## Operational Situation Report USSR No. 33

. . . . . . . . . . . .

*The Jewish Question in the Byelorussian Territories*
More than half of world Jewry lives on a relatively narrow strip of
east-central Europe along the Riga-Bucharest line, the so-called Jewish segment of Europe. Here, one can find the human reservoir of
western Jewry which cannot renew itself on its own, depending on
a steady transfusion from the east. It is simply impossible to trace the
family lines of any leading personality of world Jewry without going
back to the ghetto of some town in east-central Europe.

The Jews came to these regions following the migrational routes
taken by people on the way from the south to the south-east. A small
part also came from Germany. They stopped there as a result of tsarist
Russia's laws closing areas further east to Jews until World War I. The
zone that was open to the Jews in tsarist Russia included the districts[1]
of Kaunas, Grodno, Vilnius, Volhynia, Podolia, Minsk, Vitebsk,
Mogilev, Kiev (without the city of Kiev), Chernigov, Poltava,
Jekaterinoslav, Tauria (without the cities Nikolayev, Sevastopol and
the tsarist summer residence in Yalta), Bessarabia and the 10 districts
of the Russian part of Poland. The Jews that were already settled in
Kurland and Livonia were given permission to stay there.

Despite this the Jews frequently broke through into the forbidden
zone which was not difficult because of the corruption of the Russian
police. There were also some legal opportunities since academicians
and businessmen of the first and second guilds were also permitted
to live officially outside the Jewish zone. Of course, all these exceptions only concerned relatively small numbers.

---

1. Gubernia (Russian for 'province').

-47-

The 1917 February revolution lifted the Jewish settlement ban. The central part of Russia was also opened up by law to the Jews. Particularly under Bolshevik rule (which began half a year later) they rushed in ever increasing numbers to the Russian east, especially to the big cities. This development was of too short a duration to cause a noticeable de-Judaization[2] of the east-central European region until now. Only the very large natural population surplus of Eastern Jewry was diminished.

The Byelorussian area of settlements also belongs to the area of maximal Jewish-density. According to the 1926 Soviet census, at that time there were more than 400,000 Jews in the Byelorussian Soviet Socialist Republic (BSSR). In the western regions, formerly part of Poland and inhabited mainly by Byelorussians, the districts[3] of Bialystok, Novogrudok, Polesie and Vilnius had a Jewish population of more than 500,000 according to the last Polish census of 1931. Only a fraction of the Jews living here are included in this number since only those who admitted being Jews were registered as such in this census. The Polish census, for instance, reveals that in most of the Polish census regions, the number of those who admit to belonging to the Mosaic faith is higher than the number of persons who admit that they are Jews. Converted Jews and children of mixed marriages[4] are of course not registered as Jews. Conditions are similar in the Soviet Union. There, religion was not included in the census; however, in the same region, in many cases, more people declared Yiddish as their mother tongue than were registered as Jews. The estimate of 1½ million Jews in the Byelorussian territories is rather too small than too high.

These Jews lived formerly scattered all over the country with special preference for small towns, some of which are even today almost totally Jewish as their population consists of up to 80% or 90% Jews. Around the turn of the century, particularly after World War I, a tendency to move to the big cities set in, with a preference for living in the larger towns such as Grodno, Bialystok, Brest, Baranovichi, Pinsk, Mosyr, Gomel, Bobruisk, Mogilev and particularly in Minsk, where there were 100-120,000 Jews in a population of 238,000.

The sociological structure of the Jews in the west is not the same

2. In original — "Entjudung"
3. Wejewodztwo (Polish for 'province')
4. Judenmischlinge

-48-

as in the east. In both regions one thing is similar. While a small portion of the Jews can be counted as belonging to the upper strata, it is extraordinarily high in relation to that of the host nation. Most of the Jews live in great poverty and exist from small workshops, home artisanship and, most of all, from small trade and small commission jobs. On the other hand, there are only a few workers and even fewer peasants among the poor Jews.

In the former Polish areas, as well as in the former Soviet part of Byelorussia, almost all the key positions in spiritual and cultural life are occupied by the Jews. Universities, schools, newspapers and theaters were under Jewish influence. Jews formed an overwhelming majority among physicians and lawyers. The Jewish political influence in the former Polish areas, however, was felt mainly through their very strong economic position. Direct influence on politics in former Poland was exerted mainly by camouflaged descendants of Jews. They are in very great numbers among the Polish intelligentsia, with very many descendants of mixed marriages. Polish and Jewish estimates calculate the number around 2 million.

The use of power by the Jews to influence politics played a smaller role in the Soviet Union, though they quickly learned to take over the leading and economically most profitable posts in the nationalized economy. Their main ambition, however, was to occupy the decisive posts in the government itself and in the Communist party, especially in the real power centers, the Central Committee of the KP (B) SU. How fast and with how much success they managed to do so is proven by the fact that in Lenin's time, the Jews, though constituting 1.77% of the entire population, were represented in the Communist party with 5.2%, in the party's Central Committee with 25.7% and in the Politburo with 36.8%. At the end of the Lenin period their participation in the Politburo was up to 42.9%. In the area of high Jewish density, as in Byelorussia, this participation was accordingly higher.

These statements do not reflect the actual conditions accurately. There were and are strong anti-Semitic tendencies inherent in the Russian people, even if they are latent at present. Although the death penalty for anti-Semitism existed in the Soviet Union, the Jews deemed it prudent to camouflage themselves as much as possible. The most frequent means for this was a change of name which is very easy to effect in the Soviet Union, where a notification at the appropriate office is sufficient. In former years such a change was announced in a government publication so that the number can be estimated with some precision. These publications have stopped lately, but it is certain that the changes of names h ave rather increased than decreased as the Jews have gone far in their camouflage. After the political crises in 1936 and 1937, they gave up in many cases obvious posts, concentrating instead on those posts that are less obvious and representative in public life, but having politically more power where the influence of state and party meet. Here the Politburo occupies the first place.

. . . . . . . . . . . .

Recapitulating, one can state that:

At least 1½ million Jews live in the Byelorussian (region).[5] Their social structure is not uniform as in the former Polish and Soviet parts. Immediate measures were taken for the solution of the Jewish question by installing Jewish councils, identifying all Jews over 10 years of age with special badges, setting up labor gangs of all Jews aged 15-55. The establishment of ghettos is already in progress and already partly accomplished.

---

5. The term in the German is "Lebensraum," living space.

## Operational Situation Report USSR No. 34

. . . . . . . . . . . .

*Einsatzgruppe B:*
Location: Orsha
Reports:
Einsatzkommando 9 is in Vileyka and Molodedechno, though a Rear Kommando is still in Vilnius. Einsatzkommando 8 is in Minsk, with detachments in Borisov and Slutsk. Detachment Bonifer has taken over the task of the security police in Baranoviche since July 24, 1941.

*Sonder Kommando 7* reports from Vitebsk:
Before the occupation there was a commissar for public health at Vitebsk; subordinated to him were the managers of the health insurance offices, mostly Jews. The newly appointed physician, Dr. Muraschki, states that prior to this there were 200 physicians; at present only 40 among them are Jews. There are four hospitals, four clinics, and a medical college. Clinics formerly did not take in sick persons. The Army took over 3 hospitals. The municipality now has its hospital with 40 beds, a medical college with 500 beds, and clinics. The chief of the clinics, Dr. Kupreyev, is an optometrist. Allegedly epidemics have not occurrred recently. The most frequent diseases are tuberculosis and typhus. For tuberculosis, one hospital with 40 beds available is presently occupied by 12 patients.

The sewer system is still operating and remains relatively intact. Waterworks are partly in operation again. Water supply locations are installed within the city; water, however, must be boiled. So far, about 3000 Jews are registered by the appointed Jewish Council. Badges for Jews introduced. At present they are being employed with clearing rubble. For deterrence 27 Jews who had not come to work were publicly shot in the streets.

The Chief of the Security Police
and the SD

Berlin, July 28, 1941

43 copies
(32nd copy)

## Operational Situation Report USSR No. 36

. . . . . . . . . . . .

*Einsatzgruppe B:*
Location: Minsk
I. *Police Activity:*

a. In the course of an extensive search action, 38 more persons were arrested in cooperation with the GFP. A larger number of weapons, radios and files has been secured. Further action led to the liquidation of 193 Jews. Two armed robbers caught red-handed were also liquidated. A Jewish-Polish secret organization was discovered and was infiltrated by secret agents. They will be uncovered only after more details are available. An organization plan of the NKVD and NKGB was set up in Vilnius with the assistance of secret agents. For the time being, one cannot know for certain if this plan is complete in all its details.

b. Until further notice, about 200 persons are being liquidated daily in Minsk. This concerns Bolshevik officials, criminals, Asiatics, etc. They are being sorted out from among civilian-camp prisoners. Among those already liquidated were also the former politically oriented staff commissar, Gregory Bylich, born 1890 in Lesog, and his wife. Both had been very active in the deportation of Byelorussians to Siberia. Actions were further carried out in Rakov, about 40 km from Minsk, and in the forest region north of the Minsk-Borissov-Krupka line. 58 Jews, Communist officials, and agents, prison inmates as well as soldiers in plain clothes suspected of having contact with partisan groups, were liquidated. In addition, 12 Jewesses who were proven to be agents for the KP during the Polish campaign were shot.

c. Concerning their KP memberships: Our experience up to now shows that a majority of members at heart rejected the Bolshevik

Weltanschauung [world outlook]. The Soviet leading class had exerted strong pressure on the population to join the KP. Those who refused were in many cases sent to Siberia, thrown into prison or shot. The percentage of the population that was forced to join the party varied, however, within the diverse groups of peoples. In general, the Jews belong to the party out of inner conviction. The same goes for the Russians who lived in Byelorussian areas. Also the Poles were forced into memberships. However, coercion to join the KP was often the case with the Byelorussians. The Kommandos have been ordered to consider these facts carefully in the course of the liquidations.

II. *Civilian Life Activity:*

a. The activity of the Roman Catholic Church, which has in the Byelorussian area mainly Polish leadership, is very noticeable and clearly attempts, with the Byelorussian clergy, to do missionary work.

b. Preference of Byelorussian personnel for "leading and organizational" positions in the former Polish areas as well as gradual removal and relief of the Poles partly causes reactions in their mood.

c. Ruthless requisitions have had a negative influence on the general public mood as well as the prevailing conditions in Minsk and its rural environs. A price list has been drawn up, and the question of wages was handled in Minsk. Free trade will be opened up soon. The Reichskreditkasse has granted the city of Minsk a substantial loan for its reconstruction expenses. For the time being financial resources are drawn from forced loans from the Jewish population. The appointed head of the Minsk district has appointed an administrator of the kolkhozes [collective farms]. The following immediate projects have been ordered:

A survey of cattle and cultivated fields has to be drawn up; furthermore, all the distributions in the kolkhoz-factories were cancelled. The immediate publication of a newspaper in the Byelorussian language is planned. The first 5,000 copies are to be printed. The content: general information, German Army reports and news from the front. For the time being, political issues are not to be touched. Radio station Baranovichi lacks material to transmit; there are not enough records either.

d. It is evident that the population rejects the Bolshevik rule in the area around Orscha, Krupka, and Shklov, 200 km east of Minsk; however, this is so mainly for economic and social reasons. The population is still greatly intimidated. Economic life is completely paralyzed, food very scarce. The population rummages in demolished places for things which they could use. Einsatzkommando 7b has set up appointed town administrations in Krupka, Shklov and other places. Four-fifths of Shklov are destroyed, mainly by arson. Citizens are afraid to assume an office in the town hall for fear that the leaders of the Komsomol might take revenge. We succeeded nevertheless in forming a city council consisting of 8 Russians who carried out the following:

1. Clearing of houses inhabited by Jews and placing the Jews in ghettos (cases of leprosy and scabies were observed among the Jews).

2. Distribution of flour to the population from army reserves.

3. Work in city kolkhoz was begun.

e. The antagonism between Poland and Lithuania continues in the district of Vilnius. Poles feel disadvantaged in the distribution of goods. Lithuanians believe that they have the right to arrest Poles and to confiscate their belongings. There is, however, a general agreement with the measures taken by the Germans, particularly with the proceedings against the Jews. It was established that the above-mentioned Lithuanian organization has dissolved spontaneously with the advance of the German forces. The active forces went over to the activist [collaborating] groups. Activity of Schaulists has increased in the university. Tension between Fascist and Catholic groups can be noticed there. Fascist groups are in the minority.

The Chief of the Security Police
and the SD

Berlin, July 29, 1941

45 copies
(45th copy)

## Operational Situation Report USSR No. 37

. . . . . . . . . . . .

*Einsatzgruppe C:*
Location: Zhitomir
Reports:
There were about 30,000 Jews living in Zhitomir, that is somewhat more than 30% of the entire population. The greatest part of them fled before the occupation of the German Army. According to conservative estimates, there are now about 5,000 Jews (9% of the entire population) in Zhitomir. Many Jews, particularly the intelligentsia, were active as informers for the NKVD. They were given preferential treatment by the Soviet authorities. They were mainly employed as administration officials, managers of warehouses, kolkhozes and sovkhozes [state farms]. (80% of the Soviet officials in the area of Zhitomir were Jews.) They had hardly any difficulties from the Soviet authorities in practicing their religion. Unlike the Orthodox churches, the synagogues were at the disposal of the Jews for their religious ritual. The Jews have not given up hope that the Bolsheviks will return in the near future. Because of the Jewish behavior during the time of the Bolshevik government, the population, with only few exceptions, is consciously anti-Semitic.

The Ukrainian population, at least the older generation, is at heart generally religious. Churches which were not used for public purposes were destroyed by the Soviets. There were, however, itinerant priests who went from village to village gathering the believers around them. A tremendous need for religious activity prevails. As could be established so far, [Soviet] anti-religious propaganda has been in general ineffective in the areas that are now occupied by German troops.

The 6th Army HQ presently prepares a special order because of the uncontrolled requisitioning of houses, cattle, and machinery by German troops. There is also a plan to try and release Ukrainian prisoners of war after a short inquiry, so that they can return to their homes, if they are now under German Army occupation. Thus, it is hoped that through these means it will be possible to proceed with the harvest without damage.

Since the Kommandos have marched into the Old-Russian area, it has become evident that work is much more difficult and frequently ineffective. This might be so because the Russians have spared the Western Ukraine. Now the Russians destroy everything systematically, as they retreat.

This assumption is confirmed by the circular letters which were found in Zhitomir. According to these, a summons was issued by the Soviet central organization of trade, economy and handicraft, to destroy the entire property of the state, i.e. buildings and supplies. In addition, they ordered the political commissars, Russians and also Jews, to retreat together with the Russians. This also explains the fact that the search for political commissars, etc., is not too successful at this time.

In Zhitomir itself, Gruppenstab and the advance Kommando of EK 4a have to date shot approximately 400 Jews, Communists, and informants for the NKVD. Thus, Einsatzkokmmando 4a has carried out 2531 executions.

In Zhitomir, a large prison camp has been set up which also contains civilian prisoners. It is highly probable that there are, particularly among these civilian prisoners, former political commissars who, apparently on instructions, left their units in time to procure civilian clothes for themselves.

Thus, three political commissars in civilian clothes who eventually admitted their identity were apprehended.

In each case attempts to obtain the truth about their assignments and activities failed. It is clear from their manner of infiltration and by their conduct that they were acting according to definite instructions.

As reported already, a Jew aged twelve, who had fired at a vehicle of Einsatzkommando 4a, was arrested. All attempts to seize any adult instigators behind him proved in vain. As retribution another action will be carried out against the Jews.

While almost everywhere the Soviets have destroyed or removed all the material, Einsatzkommando 5 has succeeded in securing important material, chiefly pertaining to the NKVD, at Kremenets. The material has been passed on.

*Einsatzgruppe D:*
Location: Piatra
*Einsatzkommando 10a:*
Location: Iswary

. . . . . . . . . . . .

*Report from the district Belzy*
Belzy is a district town (Kreisstadt) of 55,000 inhabitants of whom approximately 2//3 are Jews. The whole district comprises about 600,000 people. It is subdivided into 14 rayons (counties) with 350 villages.

*Police Work*
1. The town of Belzy is extensively destroyed. Present population, therefore, not ascertainable.

2. Searches in state and party buildings without result. Communist functionaries of Belzy have fled.

3. Rumanian police operates in political police area under the Kommando's directions.

4. Partisan warfare.

During the night of July 11-12 a German military vehicle was fired at in Belzy. Consequently 10 hostages were executed and a public announcement was made by the Rumanian police. During the evening of July 15 military vehicles were again fired at and 20 more hostages were dealt with by a summary court. During the night of July 15-16 German pioneers were murdered by decapitation. Countermeasures are not fixed at present.

5. Jews
Rumanian police in and around Belzy act harshly against Jews. The precise number of shootings cannot be ascertained. On the evening of July 15, the Kommando appropriately punished the Jewish Council of Elders in Belzy and other Jews totalling 45 for failing to comply with security police directives and as retribution for attacks on German military personnel.

The Chief of the Security Police          Berlin, July 30, 1941
and the SD

45 copies
                                                (45th copy)


## *Operational Situation Report USSR No. 38*

. . . . . . . . . . .

1. *Political Survey:*
b. *Occupied territories*

### Russian-Poland

The Commander of the security police and the SD in Cracow reports from the occupied border territories:

I. *Activity report:*

At the time of the report, another 416 persons, most of them Jews, were shot because of Communist activity, such as Communist commissars in the Red Army, murderers of Ukrainians who had nationalistic views or as agents of the NKVD. More than 1,000 persons were arrested because of similar offences or for lootings, gang-raids, etc.

The offices of the party committees, NKVD and border guard were constantly searched. Prior to their retreat, the Russians were able to destroy or take with them in some cases all of their documents. Some of the files and maps were seized and are still being evaluated. A gun repairshop of the NKVD with 1,000 guns, 2 H.M.G.s, and 70 boxes with ammunition, was discovered in Lvov and removed. The searches for NKVD agents are becoming more and more difficult as they are constantly changing their quarters.

15 persons were arrested in Lvov because of activity as part of the Polish terrorist group ZWZ.

With the arrest of NKVD agent Sekunda in Lvov, assistant to the well-known captain Orlov, the names of persons who had been sent as spies into the General Gouvernement after special training were revealed.

II. *Situation report:*
(former Russian-Poland)

Jews:

Behavior continues to be offensive and provocative. In the rear areas, some of the Jews who had fled are returning. Illicit trading is stopped, markets in smaller towns are full of Jews hoarding. A "Jewish Community" has been established in Lvov by an official order. Their task: taxation, registration of Jewish population, and organization of social self-help.

2. *Reports of the Einsatzgruppen and kommandos:*
*Einsatzgruppe C*
Location: Zhitomir
Reports:

Arson is still frequent. In agreement with General Reinhardt and with German Army support a major action was carried out which ended with the arrest of 200 Communists and Jews. After having established the personal data and examining the cases, 180 Communists and Jews were shot. The interrogations have again shown that, like in other towns, the important personalities are no longer there. It is, however, possible that for the time being, Jews in particular remain in hiding in the surrounding areas of the town. They will be caught when the villages are systematically searched in the near future.

A 12-year-old Jew was brought forward who admitted to having set fire to a whole street. He admitted during the investigation that his parents and a third person had incited him.

According to a report of EK 4a constant sabotage activity is going on in Zwiahel (Novograd-Volynskiy). The German Army now drives all the civilians together and, as retaliatory measures, carries out executions. In cooperation with the German Army and the Ukrainians, 34 political commissars, agents, etc. were plucked from civil-prisoner camps. In the meantime, they have been finished off. Two of them pretended to have important information about an arms cache in the forest. However, it became obvious on the way there that the two Russians intended to deliver the Kommando into the hands of the Russians and that they did not mean to locate the cache at all. Thereupon the two were shot on the spot. A short while later, we could observe about 100 Russians fleeing hurriedly into the forest. On the march back, a large arms cache was actually discovered.

In Proskurov the entire documentation is either destroyed or removed. All the officials have disappeared. 22 political prisoners were found dead, they were obviously starved in a cellar. Many Ukrainians and Poles have been deported.

Considering the situation, the relationship of Volksdeutsche [ethnic Germans] towards the Ukrainians was good. There exists, however, a pronounced lack of confidence on the part of the Volksdeutsche towards the Ukrainians. This rests on the fact that they are and will be a minority in the future.

Executions:

Proskurov — 146; Vinnitsa — 146; Berdichev — 148; Shepetovka — 17; Zhitomir — 41; Khorostov — 30.

In this last place, 110 Jews were slain by the population.

## Operational Situation Report USSR No. 40

. . . . . . . . . . . .

*Einsatzgruppe A:*
Location: Novoselya

. . . . . . . . . . . .

B. *Concerning the People*

It was very easy to convince the Lithuanian circles of the need for self-purging actions to achieve a complete elimination of the Jews from public life. Spontaneous pogroms occurred in all the towns.

National consciousness in Latvia has remained strongly intact and was nourished by the obscure political situation. If no one will interfer organizations like the Perkonkrust[1] with its definitely national political aim will find no obstacle in its way to awaken strong national pride in the Latvian population. Although in Latvia one part of the intelligentsia has completely disappeared, the pronounced Nordic outward appearance of the population in Riga as well as in the small towns is striking. The population of Latgale which differs greatly in its way of life from the population of the rest of the country reveals a very bad racial picture. The high rate of criminality and alcoholism can be due to the admixture of Russian-Polish-Latvian descent.

Self-cleansing operations are very late in starting in Latvia. Although Jews are completely eliminated from public life, they can still be seen in the streets of Latvia's towns. The impertinence of the Jews has contributed towards increased self-cleansing activities. Thus in all Latvian towns pogroms, destruction of synagogues, and liquidations of Jews and Communists occurred. The 1,550 Jews who had still

---

1. Thunder Cross: A national pro-Nazi party.

remained in Jelgava (Mittau) and its surroundings were removed without any exception by the population. Self-cleansing activities in Latvia still continue at this time.

The population of occupied Estonia is in general very sympathetic. Their pronounced Nordic type, their quiet, rather clumsy but open manner in which most of the population meet the Germans, the cleanliness of their homes and courtyards, adds considerably to this impression. Since there are relatively few Jews in Estonia, the solution of the Jewish question will not pose any problem. In Latvia and Estonia, one can note a strong aversion to the Russians who live in their countries, also to old emigrants, and the Greek-Orthodox church. Frequent articles have appeared in the Latvian press bringing to mind the suppression of the Latvians during the time of Tsarist Russia.

. . . . . . . . . . .

### D. Details

In the self-cleansing actions in Lithuania, Latvia and Estonia over 20,000 Communists and Jews were liquidated by the self-defense organizations (Selbstschutz-organisationen). These organizations are now being dissolved as part of the reorganization of the official order and security matters in these regions. These forces will be taken over in smaller numbers by the local auxiliary order-police.

. . . . . . . . . . .

*Einsatzgruppe C*
Location: Zhitomir
*Attitude of the population towards Bolshevism.*

As in the areas that have been dealt with so far, the population in the Berdichev area can be divided into 3 groups according to its attitudes toward Bolshevism. The Bolshevik party played a decisive role in the life of the population; the main officials in the party were the Jews. With a few exceptions, the Jews were also the sole beneficiaries of the system. Leading positions were held almost without exception by the Jews. They were the absolute rulers and had extensive economic privileges.

Only a few non-Jewish members of the Communist party were employed who were not treated as equals by the Jews.

The population in general rejected the Bolshevik ideology privately without, however, being able to muster the strength to change the regime. Jews, insofar as they did not belong to the party, were removed from the masses through the help of their Jewish brothers, who were in high positions.

. . . . . . . . . . .

*Einsatzgruppe D*
1. *Arrests and Liquidations.*
In cooperation with the Rumanian police in Chernovtsy 682 of the approximately 1,200 arrested Jews were killed.

So far 16 of the arrested 50 Communist officials have been liquidated. Those remaining are still needed for interrogations, since it may be expected that as a result of the interrogations material from the Soviet offices will be found.

The area of Czernovtsy and Khotin has been searched thoroughly and as a result 150 Jews and Communists have been liquidated. In Mogilev-Podolsk no operation is necessary since the Russians have evacuated the entire population and have destroyed and devastated the town completely.

2. *Economic Life.*
At present, almost all the shops in Czernovtsy are closed — either because they were destroyed during the looting or because the managers of the nationalized enterprises do not dare to show themselves, as their position proves that they were reliable Communists. In addition to this, most of them are Jews whom the Rumanian authorities have prohibited from doing business. Reorganization of trade and commerce on a cooperative basis is planned.

In the future Jews are to be excluded from trade. The practical ex ecution of this plan seems more than questionable since the Rumanian authorities are very corrupt and the Rumanians are very incompetent in the economic field as well. The fields are in relatively good condition; there is quite a large number of cattle. Soviet-Russian destruction is limited also in agriculture in North Bucovina. In the meantime, the question of property has been solved. All nationalized property in the Russian area, except property belonging to Jews, will automatically return to the owner. Only former Jewish property remains the possession of the state, and is to be divided between deserving soldiers, officers and officials after the war. The question what is to become of the very considerable transfer of real estate possessions in North Bucovina remains to be solved. The Soviets did not compensate for this and no compensation should be given if the possession can be nationalized. The possessions of the deportees or of their representatives have to be taken over by the German "Treuhand Gesellschaft" in accordance with new Rumanian law. The German claims must be registered immediately to avoid other dispositions by the Rumanians.

## Operational Situation Report USSR No. 42

. . . . . . . . . . . .

*Einsatzgruppe C:*
Location: Zhitomir

In the Zhitomir area, a Russian civilian was brought to the EK. He turned out to be a parachutist who had jumped together with a group of 16 men, all of them in civilian clothes, from a height of 2,000 m on July 30 at 03:30 o'clock. He was instructed to hide in the forests during daytime and to blow up bridges, attack military formations and destroy fuel transports at night. He communicated after landing by means of hand-clapping and pass words. This group arranges signals by means of pieces of material in the shape of Russian letters: KH-kharosho-good, in case of success; P-plokho-bad, in case of failure. On July 27 two parachutists were dropped near Warsaw with a similar task. Groups of 5-6 men jumped into East Galicia, Volhynia and Byelorussia. Armed Jews and Communists were also dropped in the rear of German lines with the task of organizing [Resistance] groups.

The arrested man belongs to the 212th Parachute Brigade. They number 1350 men and are organized into 3 battalions and 9 companies. When examining suspicious civilians, attention should be paid to parachute equipment. It consists of: a carbine and 150 rounds; a pistol and 30 rounds; hand grenades, as well as on occasion a few kilos of explosives with detonator and string. Explosives are the size of a piece of soap, and called "tol" by the Russians. Their food supply consists of meat preserves, chocolate, tobacco, and 100 rubles in cash. Not only Russians, but Jews, Poles, Ukrainians and Asiatics are dropped as parachutists.

The 212th Parachute Brigade alone has dropped 250 men in July.

Further drops occur constantly, according to our information. The German Army has been informed. Other E-groups have been alerted.

## Operational Situation Report USSR No. 43

. . . . . . . . . . . .

*Activity Report of the Security Police in the former Polish Russian
Territories.*

3,947 persons were liquidated between July 21-31, 1941. Individual Einsatzkommandos participated as follows:

Lvov: 1,726; Brest: 1,280; Bialystok: 941; more than 7,000 persons were arrested.

In Lutsk, barns sheltering an artillery platoon were set on fire simultaneously in different places and burnt down. A German soldier was seriously wounded by a shot in his chest on an airfield near Lutsk. Communist agitators, particularly Jews, tried to disrupt work in various places. In order to achieve this aim, they spread the rumor that the German troops in the east were retreating and that the Red Army would shoot anybody who has as much as moved a hand on behalf of the German cause.

Looting still occurs frequently. In this connection, the Jews are the worst. Single stragglers from the Red Army and criminals who picked up weapons discarded by the Russians and committed gang-attacks, were shot. In all of the area's sections an order has been issued that the Jews are to wear a white arm-band with the star of Zion. Jewish Councils, Jewish work groups and, in some places, separate housing districts have been set up or started. In some places measures had to be taken against the Ukrainian militia and its leaders as looting and ill treatment occurred regularly. They murdered Polish families in Tarnopol and Rovno. In many places, the local and field commandants disarmed and dissolved the militia and arrested their leaders. Part of the militia behave in such a way that even the Ukrainian peasants call them "Bolshevik hordes."

The Ukrainians in Drohobych are issued identity cards and passes with the signature "Ukrainian National Council." Ukrainians showed themselves to be unreliable as translators for the German Army; they violated secrecy rules.

The attitude of the Poles varies. There are reports from the northern regions that they receive the Germans gratefully as their liberators and are generally loyal. However, the secret organizations in East Galicia energetically resume their activities. Polish leaflets expressing animosity towards the Germans are distributed; meetings, some of them in homes of priests, and tuning to English radio transmissions in Polish are frequent. The former combatants' associations are the chief protagonists of this resistance. Leading persons of the resistance movement in Kremenets have fled to the General Gouvernement. Dissemination of rumors is general. It was possible to seize NKVD agents who are suspected of being spies by the Security Police offices of the General Gouvernement. They will be handed over to the proper commanders. A central workshop of international dimensions for forging passports was disclosed in Lvov, in the flat of the fugitive Jew Essigmann.

No reports from Einsatzgruppe A.

*Einsatzgruppe B:*

Location: Smolensk

1. *General Mood and Situation*

The mood in the former Lithuanian region is greatly influenced by the nationality struggle between Lithuanians and Poles. Since these national groups are still not sure what the political future will be, they observe with considerable suspicion all the German orders. For example, Lithuanians interpreted a poster put up by the German Command stating that Lithuanians, Byelorussians and Poles have the equal right to use their mother tongue as a measure aimed at stopping accusations of Lithuanization. They are also afraid that their struggle for independence, which they have not abandoned, will not be respected sufficiently. Only a part of the Lithuanian intelligentsia seems to realize that the three million Lithuanians can exist only with the support of the great power, Germany. The Lithuanians are said to demonstrate pronounced self-assurance. It expresses itself first of all in their relationship to the other nationality groups and this, naturally, has also influenced the behavior of the Poles. However, neither the Poles nor the Lithuanians have shown any open antagonism towards the Germans. According to previous reports, the Polish part of the population is very friendly towards the Germans. This can be explained by the fact that they suffered more than anyone else under the Soviet regime.

A negative turn in the mood of the population of the former Byelorussian Soviet Republic has been noted, caused, first of all, by looting and requisitions by the German troops in city and countryside. Nevertheless, the attitude of the population in general, at least in the areas of Vitebsk, Orsha, Mogilev, can be described as friendly towards the Germans. The Bolshevik rule is rejected everywhere but mainly for economic and social reasons. The population hopes that the German regime will improve their personal living conditions. Right now, the population living to the east of Minsk is still greatly intimidated. The food situation is catastrophic since the Soviets have destroyed all reserves. There is practically no Byelorussian national consciousness left in that area. A pronounced anti-Semitism is also missing, as already observed in Minsk and the former Polish regions.

In general the population harbors a feeling of hatred and rage towards the Jews and approves of the German measures (establishing ghettos, labor units, security police, procedure, etc.) but it is not able by itself to take the initiative in regard to the treatment of the Jews. Altogether it can be said that generally the population lacks political initiative. The reason for this fact is probably, to a certain degree, their treatment by the Soviets. This is disclosed among other things in self-administration.

2. *Relations between National Groups*

The behavior of the Jewish population is influenced by the development of the security measures that have become more extensive lately. The anti-German mood can not be hidden. Expressions and actions show that the Jew gradually disregards all precautions. The fear of "actions" has caused a constantly increased chase for "certificates." Thus, during an action against 157 Jews in Baranovichi, 140 produced certificates that testified to their indispensability to the German offices. Since these certificates are now without value, the Jews have organized a system of signals. As soon as a SiPo Kommando appears, they escape into the surrounding forests and swamps. There are increasing reports concerning horror and incitement propaganda by Jewish circles among the population. Prostitution is to be regarded as a special Jewish problem. According to a report it is flourishing again in Baranovichi without any supervision.

. . . . . . . . . . . .

6. *Operational Activity.*

On the one hand the operational activity in the Byelorussian area is geared to the principle of hitting the Jewish-Bolshevik upper class as efficiently as possible. On the other, however, it should interfere as little as possible with the Russian economy needed for the German war effort. One has also to be careful not to disturb the process of inner disassociation of the Byelorussian population from the Bolshevik system as a result of executive measures.

As was to be expected, almost the entire higher Bolshevik leadership has escaped, thereby evading arrest by the advancing German Army and our Vorkommando. The same goes for the persons who are listed on the search list issued by the Reich Security Main Office. The same difficulties are encountered with the confiscation of politically important materials. They were either destroyed in great quantities by party officials and agents, often by setting fire to the buildings, or were taken along to the hinterland. The material that was nevertheless seized by the Einsatzkommandos is, at first, collected in Minsk and Vilnius and, as far as it is relevant, handed over to the Reich Security Main Office or to the Army. The Einsatz and Sonderkommandos have also been instructed to call upon the population in public announcements to turn over any political writings and propaganda material.

Under these conditions, in the course of time, it will be possible to seize more prominent Bolshevik officials with the help of a well organized system of informers, as they have found refuge in villages and towns of other regions. The Einsatzkommandos are ordered to report regularly to Einsatzgruppe H.Q. all information concerning escaped officials. Search lists are then drawn up and transmitted to the Einsatzkommandos and supporting troops. Searches and collections frequently suffer, however, because of missing report lists. Another obstacle in searches for people is the prevailing feeling that the areas presently occupied by the Germans may be reconquered by the Soviets. The population is, however, called upon to cooperate in the search for officials, agents, criminals, etc. and by proper instructions their fear concerning return of the Soviets can be laid to rest. The denunciations that have reached us prove already that the Byelorussians are slowly starting to cooperate in the search for functionaries. It was, however, almost impossible to stage pogroms against the Jews because of the passivity and the political disinterest of the Byelorussians.

As for membership in the Communist party: Experience gathered so far has taught that the majority of the members inwardly reject Bolshevik ideology. The Soviet leadership exerted intense pressure on the population to join the party. Persons who refused to join the party and its organizations were frequently sent to Siberia, thrown into prison, or shot dead. The percentage of persons forced into joining the party varied, however, within the nationality groups. Jews, as a rule, joined the party from inner conviction. The same goes for the Russians living in Byelorussia.

. . . . . . . . . . . .

The emphasis of the operational activity was, therefore, directed, first of all, against the Jewish intelligentsia. Byelorussians were rendered harmless only when it was established that they had been, without any doubt, convinced Bolshevik functionaries or agents. Among the functionaries seized so far were also Russians, Poles, many Asiatics (Kirghizes, Tartars, Tibetans, etc.) who had been transplanted by the Bolshevik ruling classes to Byelorussia in order to demoralize the region, or who had been henchmen, helpers and assistants.

Wherever it was necessary and possible, ghettos were set up in collaboration with the local and field commanders. Jewish Councils were installed, marking off the Jews with special badges was accomplished, labor units were formed, etc. In order to keep order in the newly established living quarters, a Jewish Order Police was set up. In order to prevent contagious diseases from spreading, it was necessary to create Jewish health services in the Jewish living quarters.

Since the man-power at the disposal of the Einsatzgruppe is hardly sufficient, considering the huge territory, Order Police stations are to be created that will be subordinated to the Einsatzkommandos. The Lithuanian political police that was formed in Vilnius was dissolved. The officials in question work under the command of the Einsatzkommando which is stationed there.

Executive police measures were taken in Baranovichi, Bialystok, Braciarka, Borisov, Brest, Grodno, Kopis, Krointnichi, Kropka, Lachoviche, Lida, Lizajki, Niechniviche, Novogrudok, Oshmyana, Pinsk, Podrechie, Shklov, Slonim, Slutsk, Stankeviche, Stolpce, Vileyka, Vilnius, Volkovisk, Vsielub, Zarovche, Zdzienciol, Zelva and other small places. In all those places Bolshevik party officials, NKVD agents, active Jewish intelligentsia, criminals, looters, saboteurs, partisans, etc., were arrested and, after screening, were rendered harmless. Besides, a number of searches were made in party and state buildings for political material. The assets of elements hostile to the Reich were confiscated for the Reich Treasury.

Upon demand of the 162nd Infantry Division, a security police action was undertaken against former Communist party officials living in a small locality in the neighborhood of Bialystok. 17 party officials were seized and liquidated in the course of this action.

The unit of Einsatzkommando 8 which is stationed in Baranovichi is particularly successful in its cooperation with the relevant units of the German Army. Together with the field and local commandants, they organized Jewish Councils, registration, and separate living quarters for Jews, as well as a new citizen registration. The current actions against Bolshevik agents, political commissars, NKVD members, etc. were continued with the participation of the GFP, the defense force, and the field gendarmerie. All the party offices as well as a great many Jewish private houses were searched.

Successful searches for Communist officials were carried out in Borisov. Among them were found the chairman of the city council in Borisov, criminals, asocial elements and Asiatics with contagious diseases. In Brest it was possible also to render harmless party officials, NKVD-agents and partisans. The German Army and the 307th Police Battalion were helped in cleansing actions directed against groups of partisans. Quite a number of NKVD buildings were searched for political material. Several card indexes, lists, etc. were seized. In Grodno, the NKVD building was searched. A card index with photographs as well as a Bolshevik library in German was secured. A great number of Jews who had worked during the Soviet regime for the NKVD and had instigated the population to resist against the German troops, were rendered harmless.

. . . . . . . . . . . .

In Lida, besides successful search activities, lists of party officials and Bolshevik propaganda material were seized. The German Army was extensively supported in Minsk in searches of civilian prisoner camps which had been set up by them. The sorting-out was carried out from the economic point of view, with the aim of securing urgently needed manpower and rendering harmless political and criminally dangerous persons. The regiment commissar, Gregory Bylich, born

1890 in Lesog, who was largely responsible for the deportation of Byelorussians to Siberia, was among those who were seized. All the party and government buildings were searched for political material. Among other things it was also possible to find a list of all leading party members in Byelorussia. At the request of the 87th Division, a commando numbering 60 men was put at their disposal against Russian cavalry. Two Russian officers were also removed from a private house. A group of partisans, who had already cut cables repeatedly, was caught near the radio transmitter along the road to Moscow, and liquidated.

Further successful partisan actions were carried out near Hajna. On this occasion hand grenades, machine-guns, and pistols were captured. The local support unit noticed irregular Russian soldiers on the night of July 8/9 1941, near Novogrudok. It moved into the big forests east of that location where there are still Russian units led by officers and Red commissars. An army commando that passed through Novogrudok as well as the Feldkommandatur was immediately given the necessary information from the support unit. The security police activity took place in Kropka, Lizajki, Niechnievichi, Oshmyana, Pinsk, Podrechie, Shkiow, Volkovisk, Vsielub, Zaroviche, Zdzienciol and Zelva. The cooperation with the German Army in Vilnius was especially successful. The NKVD building was searched and enormous amounts of political material were found. The Trade Union house and a sum of 1.5 million rubles were secured for the DAF.

. . . . . . . . . . . .

*Einsatzgruppe D*
Location: Piatra
*Einsatzkommando 10a*
Location: Balta
Since July 22, 1941, Einsatzkommando 10a is situated in Yampol with the purpose of advancing to Balta. As the majority of the inhabitants of Yampol have fled and the offices did not contain any material, the EK has produced an overview of various regions based on interrogations and its own observations.

1. *Situation of National Groups:*
The district town with the 29 villages belonging to this area is inhabited by a vast majority of Ukrainians and also by a few families of

Russian and Polish nationality. The center of Yampol is inhabited by Jews.

There are no national upper-class Ukrainians in that district. Although there is no leadership, the Ukrainian nationality has been preserved. The Ukrainians live in accordance with their national customs, speak only Ukrainian with their children and members of their family. They have no particular customs that would help preserve Ukrainian tradition. But for a few exceptions, the Ukrainians have preserved their racial pride during the last 2 decades. They hate the Jews from the depth of their soul. According to Ukrainian information, they had been entirely disadvantaged in public life. Even in legal matters, their punishable offenses were dealt with much more strictly than were those of Russians or Jews.

The deeper reason for the Ukrainians' hatred of the Jews comes from the fact that the Jews were settled in tsarist times by a special order of the Tsar who wanted to weaken their strong [Ukrainian] national feelings by equalizing the population groups in Russia.

At the time of the revolution, particularly in the year 1919, the Ukrainians took revenge on the Jews instigating veritable pogroms which killed thousands. The deep, insurmountable conflict between the Ukrainians and Jews found its expression in this action.

A spark of this hatred survives also within the present Ukrainian older generation. But they will not expend the energy, given their present mood, to proceed towards the total destruction of the remaining Jews. The Soviet rule has made them feel insecure.

. . . . . . . . . . . .

### 6. *Suppression of Ukrainians in Northern Bucovina*

Considering the disgusting conditions in Rumania, it is quite obvious that the gendarmes have the opportunity to finish off their personal enemies, to rob the village inhabitants and to take bribes from all sides.

An example is the village Doroschivci. There Botianu, a sergeant major of the Rumanian gendarmerie, was bribed by the local Communists and Jews to murder Zvizda, the country's leader of the OUN, thus demonstrating where all this might lead.

In general, there are complaints that the gendarmerie is bribed by the Jews who incite them against the Ukrainians because of their anti-Jewish attitude. This was reported at the same time from several communities and confirmed by personal observations. Under these conditions there is a definite danger of clashes breaking out between Ukrainians and Rumanians. In some communities the Ukrainian peasants fled into the forests because of Rumanian pressure; and, at that time, they have attacked the Rumanian gendarms. In other villages, the Ukrainian leaders declare that they can no longer prevent their people from anti-Rumanian reprisals.

Under these circumstances it seems advisable to enable the active Ukrainian nationalists, who wish to participate in the fight against the Bolsheviks, to go to Galicia. In this way the danger of armed clashes will be avoided.

The Chief of the Security Police    Berlin, August 6, 1941
and the SD

47 copies
(47th copy)

*Operational Situation Report USSR No. 44*

. . . . . . . . . . . .

*Situation in former Russian Poland*
*Jews*
Despite current liquidations, their behavior is impertinent and insolent. The Jewish population is the source of rumors hostile to Germans. Serious transgressions committed by the Hungarians are reported by the population from the East Galician areas which are occupied by the Hungarians. The population has fled from many places
to the German-occupied areas, as they are afraid of the violence of
the Hungarian troops. The Jewish population supports the Hungarians extensively. Leading Ukrainians have repeatedly turned for help
to the Germans with the request that the Hungarians should be forbidden to act in this manner. The population is greatly worried about
the presence of Jews and Poles who fled from Poland to Hungary
starting in September 1939. The population is systematically worried
by rumors spread by these elements against the Germans. Local
Poles are urged to organize themselves in resistance movements.

The Chief of the Security Police          Berlin, August 7, 1941
and the SD

<u>47 copies</u>
(33rd copy)

*Operational Situation Report USSR No. 45*

. . . . . . . . . . . .

*Einsatzgruppe D*
Location: Olschanka, west of Yampol
*Einsatzkommando 10A*
Location: Petshanka
Because of riots and attacks against the German Army, raids were carried out against Jews in Kodyma. In the course of these raids 97 Jews were shot and 1756 hostages were taken. Hostages are taken in each new place, and they are executed on the slightest pretext. 9 Jews were shot in Yampol.
*Einsatzkommando 10B*
Location: Mogilev Podolski
Prevention of the mass departure of Jews into territory where German interest predominates. Harvesting is organized.
*Einsatzkommando 11A*
Location: Kishinev
In the course of renovating the few official buildings which were not destroyed [EK 11] has seized material and discovered several terror and sabotage organizations. Leading agents were shot. Up to this point 551 Jews have been liquidated, of these 151 for participating in sabotage acts, 400 in reprisal for shooting at German medical trucks and for lighting signal flares for Red aviators. Jews are confined to the ghetto if they have not fled.
*Einsatzkommando 11B*
Location: Thigina
Jews in Thigina concentrated. 155 Jews liquidated as a reprisal for signaling to the Red Army.

*Operational Situation Report USSR No. 47*

. . . . . . . . . . . .

The commander of the Security Police and the SD in the General
Gouvernement reports:
I. *Security Police Activities in the Former Polish-Russian Area.*
The Einsatzkommando in Brest-Litovsk liquidated 510 persons,
and in Bialystok 296 persons. 1500 persons were arrested. Groups of
bandits continue their attacks in full strength. Agents [partisans] near
Lutsk tried to disrupt the harvest by active Communist propaganda.
About 200 parachutists were dropped between Rovno and Lutsk, and
most of them were caught. They all made the same statement, namely, that they were ordered to sabotage and, in particular, to disrupt
the German supply forces, destroy the harvest, etc.

Jews continue to display hostile behavior: they sabotage German
orders, especially where they are strong in numbers. As was previously done, Ukrainian commanders of the [Auxiliary SS] Militia have
persons shot who displease them. They demand more ammunition
and uniforms in order to protect themselves against alleged Communist attacks. They increasingly make false statements.

*Einsatzgruppe C.*

Headquarters: Zhitomir.

1. *Manner of Action of Einsatzkommandos*

In agreement with the commander of Einsatzgruppe D, a small
squad of 15 executive officials with an additional 15 members of the
Waffen-SS has been sent to Chernovtsy. The main task of the squad,
after the withdrawal of Kommando 10a of the Einsatzgruppe D, is to
take care of the interest of the absolutely unprotected and helpless
Ukrainians.

Owing to the slow progress of the military operations the task of the Einsatzkommandos has been rendered rather difficult insofar as Security Police matters are concerned. The whole of the present operationl area of the group was systematically evacuated by the Soviets and their party followers long before the German forces had arrived. The Kommandos are, therefore, for the time being, advancing, so to speak, into empty areas. For instance, in Vinnitsa, it was found that the NKVD had left 11 days before the occupation by the Germans and had systematically either taken with them all essential records or destroyed them. A thorough search of the houses of the functionaries or of the Jews has yielded hardly any material. Under these circumstances the present operations of the Einsatzkommandos must necessarily follow a different course. As a primary measure the Kommandos are searching the small villages away from the main roads. Here the population is continually complaining that at night, bands of marauding troops loot and rob them under threats of violence. As far as they can, the Kommandos, whose members are limited, successfully carry out the systematic clearing of the woods in the vicinity of the villages.

In Vinnitsa a search of the town for leading Jews was unsatisfactory. For this reason, the leader of Einsatzkommando 4b resorted to new methods. He called the town's most prominent rabbi ordering him to gather within 24 hours all of the Jewish intelligentsia. He then told the rabbi that they would be required for work. When this first group was judged insufficient, the assembled intellectuals were sent back with the order to collect the remaining intellectuals and to appear with them on the following day. This method was repeated for a third time. In this manner nearly the entire intelligentsia was trapped and liquidated.

Furthermore, at the present time all civilian persons are systematically searched on the highways. This proved again and again that many former prisoners of war were incorrectly discharged on the basis of their uncorroborated claims that they were Ukrainians. A large percentage of suspected elements among these people have been found. Apart from the language, the best test for the investigation is a painstaking interrogation concerning the immediate surroundings of their alleged home. All Asiatics found on the highways are also liquidated. The news evidently had spread that the Einsatzkommandos would, immediately following the advance of the German troops, systematically search the occupied areas. Therefore, for the time being, the Kommandos changed their methods, postponing actions on a larger scale. They first concentrated their efforts to look for reliable agents coming chiefly from Ukrainians and ethnic Germans. Then, after a lapse of time they carried out systematic actions. It soon became apparent, in the meantime, that some of the inhabitants with bad political records had returned; they could now be apprehended. At times, a search of the prisoner camps was carried out systematically. These searches disclosed that sometimes camp commanders gave special preference to ethnic-German prisoners for administrative assignments.

Last but not least, systematic reprisals were carried out against marauders and Jews. Particularly, in Jewish houses the searches, time and again, produced stolen goods. In Berdichev, in 45 Jewish houses, stolen goods were secured which were distributed among the suffering Ukrainian population. Furthermore, in Berdichev they found spacious underground passages which the Jews used not only for their meetings but also for storing their loot. Under the pretext of trying to locate their husbands in the prisoner camps, hundreds of women of the surrounding villages were frequently seen loitering about the town. They then took advantage of every opportunity to steal everything that was not nailed down from unoccupied houses. When the luggage they carried was searched, stolen goods (especially textiles, leather goods, foodstuff and tobacco) were brought to light.

Carefully planned attempts made at an earlier date to incite pogroms against Jews have unfortunately not shown the results hoped for. They were successful in Tarnopol and in Chortkov, where 600 and 110 Jews respectively were disposed of. The reason for this failure may be the fact that the Ukrainian population is still too fearful in view of the strong position the Jews held formerly. They are also still afraid of a possible return of the Soviets.

. . . . . . . . . . . .

3. *Executions:*

In Zhitomir about 400 Jews, mostly saboteurs and political functionaries, were liquidated during the last few days. In Trojanor, where a unit of engineers stationed there had already shot some Communists, another 22 Jews were liquidated. In Korostyschev 40 Jews were liquidated for sabotage, spying, and looting as it had become known that returning Jews terrorized the population and had kept close contact with the armed guerrillas in the vicinity.

At the same time a raiding party was sent out to look for parachutists who had been reported to have landed wearing civilian clothes. First caught was a soldier of the Red Army wearing civilian clothes, roaming in the woods. He could not identify himself and made very contradictory statements about himself and the reasons why he was there. He was shot on the spot, being strongly suspected of espionage.

In cooperation with the Ukrainian Militia they next caught a civilian who was identified as a Soviet parachutist. Information of this was passed on immediately to the respective competent German Army authorities. In Chernyakhov 110 Jews and Bolshevists were liquidated, also 2 Jews, Communists who tried to ambush a few small units.

In Berdichev a squad of Einsatzkommando 4a operated before the arrival of Einsatzkommando 5. 148 Jews were executed for looting and for Communist activities. Einsatzkommando 5 shot an additional 74 Jews by this date.

In Zaslav 2 political functionaries and saboteurs were shot. In Miropol 24 Jews who had refused to work and had given support to the guerrillas were shot.

In Polonne 20 persons were found to be Communist functionaries and were liquidated. Among them was a Ukrainian who was a Bolshevik informer. In addition in his position as leader of the kolkhoz he terrorized the inhabitants and fled, taking with him 150 horses after distributing the rest of the livestock among the Jews.

In Proskurov 146 Communists were liquidated.

In Vinnitsa where 30 murdered bodies were found under a layer of top soil, 146 Jews were liquidated, among them a member of the NKVD. He had been furnished with a false German passport and with German money and had been instructed by his headquarters to stay on in the occupied area and to keep on operating there.

In Makarov a raiding party seized 14 Jews, all of whom had been active as snipers and informers for the NKVD or had been responsible for deportations.

An ethnic German, called Grünwald, who had been head of a kolkhoz in the vicinity of Zhitomir since 1935, was also arrested. He was accused by the local population, a German colony, of closely cooperating with the NKVD for the systematic deportation of ethnic Germans. He was also charged with having terrorized the German population in every imaginable way. Because he was an ethnic German who most emphatically denied all accusations, all the evidence against him was re-examined very carefully. However, it was proved that all the accusations were true. Thus, he was liquidated.

Furthermore, a 60-year-old Jew was arrested today who admitted that he had been a Bolshevik since 1905 and had served as a People's Judge since 1918. When interrogated he admitted up to a total of about 1000 murders. He and his executioner will be publicly hanged tomorrow in the market square of Zhitomir in the presence of the entire population.

The Police Regiment operating in the areas of Shepetovka and Rovno has concluded its actions. The Higher SS and Police Leader sent the following radiogram to the Army Group South: "Purging of the Shepetovka-Rovno area finished. 370 Russians and 1,643 Jews shot as instigators and accomplices."

## Operational Situation Report USSR No. 48

. . . . . . . . . . . .

*Einsatzgruppe A*
Location: Novoselye
Security Police work develops according to plan. Both in Kaunas
and Riga efficient offices have been set up which may be considered
to be permanent. At the same time, accommodations for the men of
the operational units and married quarters for later use (sufficient for
the time being), were provided. The mopping up of the rear zone,
partly with the assistance of Lithuanian and Latvian auxiliary units,
continues according to plan. In all 29,000 persons were liquidated in
this district. As the combat troops had gained only little terrain during the past fortnight, the forces of the security police in the combat
zone proper, with the armored group of the 16th and 18th Armies,
were busy mopping up what little terrain had been gained, and fighting the partisans.

. . . . . . . . . . . .

During his stay in Riga, the SS Reichsführer mentioned that he in-
tends to set up police formations consisting of Lithuanians, Latvians,
Estonians, Ukrainians, etc., employing them outside of their own
home areas. This is possible right away if this is done here in the old
Soviet areas. After this task is completed, they will be used as police
units, also outside their own home areas. Since the Army Group urgently demands a quick solution because of the difficult situation with
the partisans and the difficulties involving the dual front, the
Einsatzgruppe urgently asks for general instructions how to deal with
this question.

The Chief of the Security Police      Berlin, August 12, 1941
and the SD                      48 copies
(36th copy)

## Operational Situation Report USSR No. 50

. . . . . . . . . . . .

Census of population in some towns provides the following result:
Lvov: 370,000 inhabitants, of these 160,000 Jews, 140,000 Poles,
70,000 Ukrainians.

Pinsk: 30,000 inhabitants, of these 28,000 Jews.

Grodno: 48,000 inhabitants, of these 18,500 Jews, 21,500 Poles,
5,000 Byelorussians (the rest, Russians and others). Simultaneously
with the registration of the population, food ration cards are being
introduced. The posts of mayor and vice-mayor are occupied by Byelorussians. These measures are aimed at preventing further penetra-
tion of Polish elements into the municipal administration. The Polish
population is in a bad state. In Grodno, the administrational apparatus is almost entirely in Polish hands. Good cooperation with German
offices. 72 Order Police are exclusively Polish. In Lutsk, a German
mayor and a German so-called "Gebietsleiter" (district leader) have
been installed. The Gebietsleiter is to prepare taking over the civil
administration.

*Ukrainians*

In Volhynia, the Bandera group is particularly active. Ukrainians
engaged by the German Army use their positions for national and party purposes. They install members as mayors and exert strong influence on the entire Ukrainian Militia. Some observations on Brest-
Litovsk where the Ukrainians, despite their small number, are very
active, generally expecting that an independent state will be created
after the occupation of Kiev. In the district of Galicia, preparations
are made for setting up an Ukrainian aid committee according to the
pattern of the aid committees in the General Gouvernement. The
Bandera group is undecided as to the attitude to be taken.

*Einsatzgruppe B*
Location: Smolensk

Various combats took place between Einsatzkommandos and partisan groups. Thus, a partisan group that had repeatedly cut cables was caught and liquidated in the neighborhood of the Minsk transmitter along the highway to Moscow. The concerned persons had frequently extorted food in the surrounding villages at night. SS-Sturmmann Krause, of the Hq of the Higher SS and Police Leader was shot and dragged away by partisans of kolkhoz Vishevka, 18 km northwest of Minsk. Action was initiated by an advance kommando of the Higher SS and Police Leader and by a sub-unit of the Einsatzgruppe. So far no success.

Executions were carried out in Minsk, Baranovichi, Slonim, Lakhoviche, Stolptse, Zaroviche, Vileyka, Oshmyana, Kopie, Alexandria, and Shklov. In Minsk search of the camp for civilian prisoners and the liquidation of politically dangerous persons or criminals continue steadily.

In Baranovichi interrogations were carried out of a large number of persons who were fanatical supporters of the Soviets or were recognized as agents of the NKVD. In the course of these examinations, 31 persons were liquidated. The Sondertrupp (special unit) Slonim executed them and in the surrounding area 52 additional persons who were recognized as active followers of Bolshevism and some of whom were also looters, among them 16 Byelorussians. In Lakhoviche, 22 Bolshevik officials were arrested and liquidated in the course of a cleansing action. It was established that some of those executed had committed political murders after the Soviet Russians entered the area in the fall of 1939. 76 more persons were liquidated in Stolptse. They were mainly activist Jewish intelligentsia. About 1½ million rubles which were kept in a safe of a branch of the Russian National Bank were secured. The entire male Jewish population of Vileyka has been liquidated by the Kommando that had passed through. Therefore, a search there resulted in the arrest of only 5 persons who were executed. All of the important buildings, like a Komsomol house, a [Communist] party house, the police archives, offices of the city police, the law-court, the NKVD building, etc., were searched for political material.

Among other things, the following lists and materials were found in Vileyka: leaders and political officials of Vilnius; agitators who were active in preparing the elections; instructions for the Communist party; lists of informants; members of the Young Communists and of Bolshevik officials. In the course of further search actions, 527 Jews were liquidated in Oshmyana. In Vitebsk, the population participated in liquidating the Bolshevik system by reporting their members. 332 Jews were shot, among them 5 Bolshevik officials. 27 Jews were shot in public because they had refused to go to work. At first, 84 Jews had to be executed in Shklov, among them 22 arsonists, 25 looters, 22 terrorists, 11 officials and snipers, as well as 4 persons who had spread harmful rumors. 7 officials were liquidated in Kopie.

## Operational Situation Report USSR No. 52

. . . . . . . . . . . .

*Situation Report (Galicia District)*
*Administration:*
Total but temporary disorganization because the military administration has been relieved and the civil administration is not yet established. Conflicting and double occupancy of various positions appointed by the military government and the governor of the [G.G.].[1]
Self-administration very difficult because of the lack of suitable persons. Most of the mayors who were installed by the Ukrainians must
be relieved as they are not suitable. In Lvov and in the rural towns
it is planned to set up Ukrainian-Polish autonomous bodies according
to the pattern of Polish autonomy in the General Gouvernement. The
Ukrainian mayor in Lvov will be replaced by a German one. A
Ukrainian police force numbering 3,000 men is being assembled.
They are selected from a Militia now numbering 31,000 men. Pre-
condition: Previous service in the Polish or Austrian army; leadership: headed by Germans; further leadership: Ukrainians, as officers
and non-commissioned officers, former members of the Austrian
army and lower ranks who have served in the Polish army.
*Einsatzgruppe C*
Location: Zhitomir
*Report Concerning Ukrainian Development*

. . . . . . . . . . . .

2. *What are the national political aims of the Ukrainians?*
The Rumanian army encounters even now many serious difficul-

---

1. General Gouvernement.

ties with the Ukrainians in the East Ukrainian areas occupied by them. German offices had to intervene. It is certain that the Rumanian administration will turn the area into one of constant unrest. This possible development causes real dismay in military circles and they regard:

1. The area between the Dniester and Dnieper as an essential military goal of German politics.

2. It is feared that the threatening guerrilla war of Bolshevik partisans (many parachutists in civilian clothes have landed lately) will find extraordinarily fertile soil in the Rumanian administered zone.

3. It has been established that the Rumanians in Chernovtzy were forced to work together with the Jews. As the Ukrainians are more intelligent and gifted than the Rumanians, the solution of the Jewish question is definitely in worse hands with the latter. Since the Jewish percentage is very high, it constituted a problem requiring careful examination from the economic point of view as well. In addition, the solution of this problem can be approached only within a German-Ukrainian framework. Until the final solution of the Jewish question for the entire continent is achieved, the superfluous Jewish masses can be excellently employed and used for cultivating the vast Pripet swamps, the northern Dnieper swamps as well as those of the Volga.

The Chief of the Security Police    Berlin, August 15, 1941
and the SD

48 copies
(36th copy)

## Operational Situation Report USSR No. 53

. . . . . . . . . . . .

*Einsatzgruppe A*
Location: Riga
A. *General Matters*
The sub-units of the EK 1a entered Pernau and Dorpat on the first day of occupation and were under enemy fire, and are now finally free of contact with enemy forces. The EK 1b that was assigned to the 16th Army advances with its frontline units.

The preparations of the EG-A units which are supposed to enter Petersburg is taking place in Novoselye, 1 km to the northeast of Pskov. The main units of EK 2 and 3 continue their pacification work in Riga and Kaunas.

Every day in the North Estonian and old-Soviet-Russian areas there is an increasing number of partisan groups consisting of 5-30 men. There are constant reports of railway lines and bridges that have been blown up; of smaller columns and single vehicles that were attacked by day and night. Reports arrive from villages about partisan groups that terrorize and extort food from the inhabitants and threaten them. Sub-units of the Einsatzkommandos had to be employed again and again against such groups in order to secure the continuation of the pacification work. This happened particularly in the area of Novoselye and in the area around the location of the 4th Armored Group's H.Q in Strugi. In the last few days, two security divisions of the Army Group North and a batallion of the Police Regiment North were dispatched to pacify the endangered areas.

B. *Political Situation*
Clarification of the general political situation in the entire occupied area has not yet been achieved. The uncertainty of the popula-

tion leads to rumors, although everywhere there are voices advocating an attitude of patience, waiting until the end of the fighting.

Since July 25th the Reichskommissar for Ostland, Gauleiter Lohse, and the Military Commander, Lieutenant-General Bremer, are operating in Kaunas. District commissars have been assigned to Lithuania and to the areas west of the Dvina, and they have gradually started their work. It appears that nowhere are there concrete plans and guiding principles. The commissars started their work in various ways. While the town commissar in Kaunas proceeded promptly in [initiating] the first actions, in a manner similar to those in Polish areas, district commissars approached the competent Einsatzkommandos with the request to execute Communists and Jews. Elsewhere, among them Kaunas, talks were arranged between the responsible commanders of the Security Police and the district commissars which will, hopefully, result in successful cooperation.

The Reichskommissar for Ostland in Kaunas has prepared a draft of a decree concerning guidelines for the treatment of Jews in the area of the Reichskommissariat Ostland and has handed it to the Higher SS and Police Commander.

The draft is similar to those issued in Holland, the Polish areas, etc. We foresee its distribution among the Higher SS and Police Commandos. However, it doesn't mention the cooperation with or the competence of the Security Police.

The Chief of the Security Police      Berlin, August 16, 1941
and the SD

<u>48 copies</u>
(36th copy)

*Operational Situation Report USSR No. 54*

. . . . . . . . . . . .

*Einsatzgruppe A*
Location: Riga
*EK 3*
Kaunas
*Organization of the Catholic Church in Lithuania*
The attitude of the Church regarding the Jewish question is, in
general, clear. In addition, Bishop Brisgys has forbidden all clergymen to help Jews in any form whatsoever. He rejected several Jewish
delegations who approached him personally and asked for his intervention with the German authorities. In the future he will not meet
with any Jews at all. Conversion of Jews to the Catholic faith did not
take place so far. The Church would also object to this type of conversion. It is convinced that the Jews would not come [to be convert-
ed] out of conviction but because of the possible advantages connected with it.
*Executive Activity*
Special actions (Sonderaktionen) were carried out as follows:
July 22, 1941: Pagirai: 1 Jew liquidated
July 23, 1941: Kedainiai: 125 persons (83 Communist Jews, 12
Communist Jewesses, 14 Russian and 15 Lithuanian Communist of-
ficials, 1 Politruk liquidated)
July 25, 1941: Mariampol: 103 Jews (90 men, 13 women) liquidated
July 28, 1941: Panevezys: 288 persons (234 Jews, 15 Jewesses, 19
Russian and 20 Lithuanian Communist officials)
July 29, 1941: Raseiniai: 257 persons (254 Jews, 3 Lithuanian Com-
munist officials) liquidated

July 30, 1941: Agriogola: 30 persons (27 Jews and 11 Lithuanian Communist officials) liquidated

July 30, 1941: Wendziegola surroundings: 15 persons (Jews and 2 murderers)

July 31, 1941: Utena: 256 persons (235 Jews, 16 Jewesses, 2 Lithuanian Communist officials, 1 double robber and murderer)

August 1, 1941: Ukmerge: 300 persons (254 Jews, 42 Jewesses, 2 Lithuanian Communist officials, 1 former mayor of Janova who had set fire to the town, 1 Political Commissar)

August 2, 1941: Kaunas: 209 persons (171 Jews, 74 Jewesses, 4 Lithuanian Communist officials, among them one Jewish couple)

Between July 22 and August 3 the Kommando has liquidated 1592 persons.

The auxiliary police service companies were taken over by the regular police. They were given green armbands marked "Schutzmannschaften."

Again, vast political material was captured in Kaunas. Besides, political material was secured in offices and flats.

The ghettoization of the Jews in Kaunas, numbering about 25,000, is in full swing. Altogether, about 10,000 Jews have been resettled. The registration office (of the Lithuanian Sipo) has completed, under German supervision, a card index containing data on all Jews in Kaunas. The Jewish committee will also report soon on the financial situation and the professional use of the individual Jews.

## Operational Situation Report USSR No. 56

. . . . . . . . . . . .

*Activity Report on Former Russian-Polish Areas*

In the period August 5-11, [19]41, 2,808 persons were liquidated as follows:

by the EK in Lvov: 619; in Brest-Litovsk: 1296 and in Bialystok: 373. 5,000 persons were arrested. There is a considerably increased circulation of pamphlets in German, Polish and Ukrainian languages. Poles and Ukrainians are incited to resist Germany. German troops are incited to desert. There are reports of landings of parachutists, particularly from the area around Lutsk and Rovno, but also from Galicia. Isolated fights and destruction of scattered smaller Russian units that had sought refuge in the woods. Police and Army are too weak in many places to conduct systematic searches in the forests. The quiet is still disturbed by attacks from the [Resistance] groups. Communists and Jews continue in their activities. The insubordination of the Jews increases. For some time now one instigation has led Ukrainian Communist laborers to stop work on the Kovel-Lutsk road. The brewery in Lida was burned down by a Pole. Because of the lack of German propaganda, the propagation of rumors is unusually strong.

Robbery, ill treatment, and murders do not stop within the Ukrainian militia's area as Ukrainian mayors and militia commanders were held responsible for hostile utterances against Germany, for ignoring German orders, and for tearing up German regulations. Poles are equated with Jews and partly have to wear [identification] arm bands as well. In several places, units were formed by the Ukrainian militia, like "Ukrainian Security Service," "Ukrainian Gestapo" and others. Local and field commanders are disarming the militia at this time.

The OUN in Lvov sells war-loan stamps and releases pamphlets demanding Bandera's return. From Lvov, posters are released declaring that a "free and independent Ukraine" must be created according to the motto "Ukraine for the Ukrainians, under the leadership of the OUN." Orders of the German Army are frequently ignored and looted goods are regarded as private possessions. In Lutsk retired Colonel Diatschenko has tried to centralize the militia under his command. At a later stage this command should be located in Kiev. The execution of this plan was prevented by the followers of Bandera.

## Operational Situation Report USSR No. 58

. . . . . . . . . . . .

*Executive activity in the former Polish-Russian area August 12-15, 1941*

4,988 persons were liquidated, more than 6,000 were arrested during the period of report.

Instigation and incitements by the Jews continue to increase. In Pinsk, Jews shot a guard of the city-militia. A member of the militia was shot dead from an ambush near Pinsk. As a reprisal, 4,500 Jews were liquidated.

A list of 43 agents and couriers who had mainly worked for the Russian secret service in the district of Lublin was found at the NKVD frontier guard office in Luboml. Several arrests have already been made. Disturbances and attacks by bands [partisans] continue to increase. An Ukrainian band, numbering 20-30, continues committing excesses near Pinsk. They spread terror using the motto: "Out with the German administration; we want a free Ukraine without Germans, Poles and Russians."

Massive distribution of pamphlets by Russian pilots continues. In this manner, Poles in particular are urged to commit acts of sabotage.

The resistance movement in Tarnopol has put up posters.

Nine persons were arrested in Lvov in a new passport forging operation.

*Einsatzgruppe A*

Location: Novoselye

An exchange of fire took place on August 15, [19]41, between partisans and 2 sub-units of the Waffen SS platoon attached to the Einsatzgruppe A near Boskina near the H.Q. of the Einsatzgruppe A. 13 partisans were killed, one has probably escaped. In the course of the fight, SS-man Polster was shot in his head while SS-man Isbanner was wounded by a shot in his pelvis and later passed away in the military hospital. In addition, SS-men Hinov and Haas were wounded by shots in their thighs and brought to Pskov.

. . . . . . . . . . . .

*Einsatzgruppe C*
Location: Novo-Ukrainka

## I.

Search measures are carried out by the Einsatzkommandos. By now, almost all the villages and larger localities in the more distant surroundings of Berdichev and Zhitomir have been systematically searched.

In Rajkie, the commissar of the NKVD who was at the same time leader of the Red Militia, was found and executed.

It was possible to liquidate the Communist director of the local school, Katjucko, in Nova-Chartorya and also another member of the Communist party. Katjucko, until a short time ago an influential official, had arranged meetings and given inflammatory speeches against the Germans. He has repeatedly threatened to shoot a few resident ethnic Germans whom he and the other Communists were supposed to guard. He coined the following phrase at his last meeting: "Hitler comes with his pig's-nose into our peaceful garden."

Nine Jews who were suspected of being Communists were found and executed in prisoner-of-war camp Berdichev.

In Janushpol, a town with about 25% Jews, Jewish women particularly have displayed an impertinent and provocative behavior in reaction to recently imposed restrictions. They tore off their own clothes and those of their children. In retaliation, the Kommando that arrived after quiet had been established shot 15 male Jews. Further retaliatory measures are to follow.

In Veherayshe, 22 officials, looters, and saboteurs were shot on the basis of information received from the militia.

In Chervonne, from where all the main officials had fled, it was still possible to finish off five officials.

A number of active Communists still remained in Holodki after the Red troops left. Of these, it was possible to liquidate six veteran party members, mayors, kolkhos managers and co-workers of the NKVD.

There it was also possible to arrest the political commissar of a Russian regiment; however, his interrogation has as yet not been completed.

With the help of a platoon of the Waffen-SS, 29 Communists, five agents of the NKVD were arrested in Brusilov and liquidated on the spot.

Following an urgent call for help from the local commander of Radomyshl, a sub-unit and part of a Waffen-SS platoon moved in and immediately found unbearable conditions. The newly established mayor was unmasked as an informer for the NKVD and CP member since 1925. It was proven that until recently he had contact with Communist bands. His deputy was a Bolshevik as well. Furthermore, a citizen was discovered who caused the deportation of ethnic Germans and Ukrainian families. Finally, also Jews were arrested who openly opposed the German Military, refusing to work for the OT,[1] etc. In the course of these actions, nine out of 113 persons arrested were shot.

In the area north of Zhitomir, 12 villages were searched and 15 officials were liquidated there.

In the course of a search action, 31 Jews were executed in the village of Chernyakhov; they had been active Communists and some of them also had been political commissars.

On the occasion of an action in Rudnya and Troyanov, 26 Jewish Communists and saboteurs were arrested and shot.

. . . . . . . . . . . .

As was already briefly mentioned in Operational Situation Report No. 47 of August 9, 1941, in Chernyakhov it was possible to arrest the former chairman of the Troika[2] for that area, and his accomplice. Immediately after the entry of the German Army into Chernyakhov everything was quiet. Thus, the local Jews were forced to restrain themselves. One day later, after the troops had moved on, Einsatzkommando 4a found that the Jews in the meantime, having maintained contact with the scattered Russian bands, terrorized the entire place as elsewhere. A kommando that was sent out following these observations arrested all male Jews who could be found in town. Simultaneously, it extended its search activities for terrorists

1. Organization Todt: military labor units, primarily for construction work.
2. Court presided over by three NKVD judges.

who were still in hiding. In addition to the main culprit, Judge Kieper, 15 GPU members, and 11 other informers were found. After prolonged hearings, it was possible to convict Kieper and his accomplices for the mass murders which they were accused of committing. The main witness, also a Jew, was convicted of having committed 78 murders. Then Kieper finally confessed. He described the atrocities which he had committed with typical Jewish cynicism. Already at the age of 18, he worked as a Zionist agitator in 1905 and formed illegal bands against the then prevailing order. He instigated strikes, robbery, attacks on state organizations, and prepared for the disintegration and fall of the tsarist regime. In the district of Chernyakhov alone he has committed 25 murders during the years 1905-1917; 500 more during 1917-1919; and in 1919-1925 another 800 murders of Ukrainians and ethnic Germans. He gave vent to his hatred for everything that was not Jewish by new methods of murder. He particularly preferred shooting, stabbing, slaying, poisoning and drowning. Whenever he could not get hold of his victims, he brutally mistreated members of their families. Thus a crippled girl was found (who is grown up now), whose right foot was actually smashed with a club while she was nursing at her mother's breast; he did this in his fury because he had not been able to find the child's father, a tsarist officer. In 1933, the year of the great famine, Kieper was again particularly outstanding. He personally lured to a swamp some half-starved Ukrainians and ethnic Germans who had come to him for help. Then he pushed the weakened people into the swamp in order to "help them," as he literally admitted during the trial. Although he himself had been repeatedly convicted to prison terms for embezzlement and other frauds, he managed again and again to arrange influential positions for himself. At least 1,350 murders are on his record which he committed as a terrorist in tsarist Russia, as a GPU agent, and as a member of a Troika.

The Einsatzgruppe has by now finished off a total of more than 8,000 Communists and Jews. The share of the Einsatzkommando 4a in this was 4,335.

## II.

The relationship with the German Army is as cordial as it was previously. In particular, Army circles show a steadily growing interest in and understanding of tasks and matters concerning the work of the

Security Police. This could be observed particularly during the executions. On the other hand, the Army itself endeavors to further the tasks relating to the Security Police. Thus, all the offices of the Einsatzgruppe are continually receiving reports from the Army concerning arrested Communist officials and Jews. It even happens at times that the Security Police is the last resort of the Army. Thus, for example, on August 5, [19]41, the local military commander of Radomyshl called for the help of the Einsatzkommando 4a requesting support, since he was unable to cope with the prevailing conditions.

The Chief of the Security Police   Berlin, August 21, 1941
and the SD

<u>48 copies</u>
(36th copy)

## Operational Situation Report USSR No. 59

. . . . . . . .. . . . . .

*Einsatzgruppe A*
Location: Novoselye

### Fight against partisans

As per agreement with the 16th Army, a sub-unit of the Sonderkommando 1b was transferred to Yaski, 20 km southeast of Porchov, to carry out security police tasks with the advance regiment. The investigations revealed that small partisan units were active in the vicinity of Yaski. One managed to locate a fully operational Soviet Russian telephone exchange in the post office in the village Porevich. The postmaster, 2 technical workers, and two female telephone operators were found and arrested. The investigations revealed that a group of partisans, numbering 15 men, had settled in Porevich. They had established connection with the telephone exchange by branching off a separate line outside the village. Via this telephone, the partisans conversed with Soviet Russian military positions in Staraya Russa. Since the investigations revealed that the postmaster had placed the telephone line at the disposal of the partisans and that both telegraph workers as well as the telephone operators assisted with establishing the connection, they were shot.

*Einsatzgruppe C*
Location: Novo-Ukrainka

### Executive measures

Korosten, north of Zhitomir, which was occupied long ago, has been searched by a unit of a platoon of the Einsatzkommando 6 according to Security Police instructions, immediately after the occupation.

As elsewhere, it was found that the influential Jews and officials had fled and that all the files were destroyed. Only 53 Jews and two officials could be liquidated.

After the German troops entered Staro-Konstantinov (the present seat of the Higher-SS, the Police Chief, and of the Military Commander of the Rear Area), Jews were employed for cleaning the barracks. Since the Jews did not report for work lately, the military authorities had to round up the Jewish labor force early in the day. The Jews were impertinent and even refused to work. Out of about 1,000 Jews that were recruited for field work, only 70 appeared on the following day. Moreover, it was established that harvesters were sabotaged. Finally, the Jewish Council of Elders[1] spread the rumor that the Russians were advancing again; whereupon the Jews publicly threatened and abused the Ukrainians. Finally it was established that Jews were conducting a flourishing trade with stolen cattle and goods.

In reprisal, the 1 SS-Brigade carried out an action against the Jews in the course of which 300 male and 139 female Jews were shot.

Similar facts relating to the behavior of the Jews could also be established in Radomyshl, where a part of a platoon of an Einsatzkommando had regularly been active. During a search action, once again many Jews were discovered who had been influential partners in the deportation of Ukrainians and ethnic German families to Siberia. Here, as in Staro-Konstantinov, Jews also refused to perform jobs assigned to them by the local military commander. Furthermore, a Ukrainian was detected who had intended to blow up the big bridge leading to Radomyshl. Another Ukrainian who was a co-worker of the NKVD denounced six families and was instrumental in their deportation to Siberia. In the course of this and later actions, a total of 276 Jews, Communist officials, saboteurs, Komsomol members and Communist agitators were finished off.

---

1. In the original, "Ältestenrat," another term for "Judenrat."

## Operational Situation Report USSR No. 60

. . . . . . . . . . . .

*Einsatzgruppe A*
Location: Novoselye
*Report by the 4th Armored Group on Activities and Experiences in Combatting Partisans*

As agreed, units of EK 2 and 3 were placed in the region of the 4th Amored Group for extensive purging and pacification activities, mainly in the area bordered by the lines connecting Pod-Gora, Novoselye, Shtrugi and Krassnyje, Ozjerewo, Shcheyednov.

As a result of this assignment, it was possible to arrest the remaining Communist officials, other active Communists and Jews. In the first stage of the action, interrogation of the civilian population and of the 86 Red Army soldiers (some of whom had discarded their weapons and roamed the forests and villages), revealed the existence of quite a number of partisan groups in the area about to be searched. These interrogations led to the conclusion that other partisan groups also passed through this area. At the same time, it became known that almost daily partisan groups attacked motor vehicles traveling alone, demolished bridges on the Pskov-Luga highway, blew up and attacked the Pskov-Shtrugi-Krassnyje railway line.

. . . . . . . . . . . .

*Einsatzgruppe C*
Location: Novo-Ukrainka

## I. Location

A sub-unit of Einsatzkommando 4b has arrived in Kirovograd. The rest of the Kommando will follow by August 14, [19]41. In the meantime, the advance unit of the Einsatzgruppe was recalled as the attack on Kiev is planned in the near future. The advance unit that was also sent by Einsatzkommando 4a to Vasilkov remains there for the time being in order to search the area. It has become known that precisely in that area, Russian spies with definite reconnaissance orders are constantly being dispatched from Kiev through the lines into German rear positions.

According to the facts that could be ascertained by the AOK, thus far, about 25 spies have been assigned to this area. According to the information at hand, there is a large intelligence center in Kiev, which apparently just started with the methodical assignment of its agents. At the request of the 6th Army H.Q., a sub-unit will participate in the search actions against these agents.

*Executive Operations*

It has already been pointed out in previous reports that the Jews no longer show any restraint. This observation has been confirmed again by the latest actions.

Thus, for instance, at Korosten the Jews flashed light signals to the Russians even after the town was occupied by German troops. One Jew set his house on fire after it had been seized as a billet for the German Army. Another Jew dared tell a German soldier that a box which had been found and was actually filled with black powder was harmless and not inflammable. Another soldier with a lighted cigarette who joined them was burned and seriously injured.

In the area around Brusilov-Kornin Jewish-Bolshevik gangs have been formed terrorizing the Ukrainian population. Although these gangs are not numerically large, they are terrifying the Ukrainian population. These gangs ruthlessly take action at night against villages which had already been cleared of Jews and Communists. They set houses on fire by throwing hand-grenades and stealing cattle and vehicles. Now they go so far as to kidnap Ukrainians. In the vicinity of Khmielnik the terror caused by Jews had reached new heights.

After the former local military commander had been relieved and before a new one was appointed, the Jewish population at once turned this occasion to their advantage. They terrorized the Ukrainians and spread the rumor that the Russians would come back to take bloody revenge. According to the reports of an inhabitant, Jews and Communists killed 25 Ukrainians in a neighboring village. The Jews tried to block the approach to Khmielnik by stretching a rope across the road, thus trapping motor vehicles. The commanding officer of a construction company and a fully loaded personnel-carrier evaded the trap at the very last minute.

Extensive actions have been launched to fight these Jewish outrages and banditry. The localities concerned are surrounded and first of all cleared of prominent Jews and Jewish Communists. Above all, in each case, the ghetto is systematically purged. In collaboration with the local authorities and with the militia, lists are compiled containing the names of the well-known and still present Communists; then they are sought out. In Khmielnik as many as 100 Jews and Communists were listed.

In view of these unprecedented Jewish actions it is intended to round up the Jews in certain villages, to liquidate them, and to raze the villages to the ground.

In Turchinka, to the north of Zhitomir, about 400-500 peasants, coming from 12 villages, were caught while looting a railroad depot. First of all, firearms had to be used in order to restore peace and order. Then, together with 26 peasants, one Ukrainian was held responsible for the restitution of the looted goods. In case they refused to return the stolen items, they were threatened with the severest punishment.

Furthermore, the peasants were ordered to start bringing in the harvest immediately under newly assigned kolkhoz leaders. Up to now 110 peasants have returned the looted goods.

In Chernyakhov 13 more Jews were executed, among them a former kolkhoz leader who had also been a GPU agent and caused the deportation of several indigenous families.

In several villages to the northwest of Berdichev eight leading Bolsheviks were apprehended and liquidated. They were convicted of having terrorized their villages for years, either as leaders of a kolkhoz or as NKVD agents. Above all, these Bolsheviks are responsible for the deportation of numerous Ukrainians. It is a proven fact that after the arrival of the German forces, some of the Bolsheviks acted as snipers against German troops. Moreover, they all participated in the destruction of supplies and agricultural machines and the scattering of the livestock. At first, all of them fled, but they have returned now, and, as already mentioned, it became possible to liquidate them.

In the village of Polychynca the population was freed from a radical Communist who was responsible for the crimes of violence. In 1931, he had set the village church on fire entirely on his own initiative.

The villages Koziatyn and Vcherayshe were cleared a second time in order to apprehend the Communists who had returned. In the course of this operation a total of 22 party officials and Jews were liquidated.

One platoon of Einsatzkommando 5 was again in action in Zviahel where 230 civilian prisoners who had been transferred there were screened.

161 persons were executed. They were Jews, Communists, looters and saboteurs.

The Chief of the Security Police    Berlin, August 23, 1941
and the SD
48 copies
(36th copy)

## Operational Situation Report USSR No. 61

. . . . . . . . . . . .

*Einsatzgruppe D*
Location: Ananyev
EK 12:

### Harvesting action

The kolkhozniki [collective farm workers] started to bring in the harvest on their own initiative. The population, almost without exception, showed itself extremely willing to work. Only in Babchinzy was there some resistance to an orderly harvesting caused by the instigation of Jewish inhabitants and some Jews who came to this area a few months ago. By spying on the population, these Jews had already created the basis for numerous deportations to Siberia. As a countermeasure, 94 Jews were executed.

The population was visibly relieved by these measures and hardly knows how to show its gratitude. This measure, as well as protecting the population from looting Rumanian soldiers, which was necessary in many cases, led to the fact that the population put absolute confidence in the Germans. This is reflected by the number of people reporting for work. In Yaruga, for example, 940 people out of a total of 1,200 inhabitants are occupied with bringing in the harvest.

. . . . . . . . . . . .

### Conduct of the Rumanians

In different places on the second bunkerline west of Yampol, looting Rumanian soldiers were intercepted. Plans are being considered for the use of this material by the German troops in Yampol.

Rumanian troops in quest of plunder had moved in with Jews in Borovka and looted from there. The Rumanians were apprehended and handed over to Rumanian officers.

Looting Rumanian soldiers were also apprehended near Sokol and Yelenovka and delivered into the hands of Rumanian officers. It was also possible to apprehend a Rumanian band [of soldiers] that had moved into a sugar factory.

The Chief of the Security Police
and the SD

Berlin, August 25, 1941

<u>48 copies</u>
(36th copy)

*Operational Situation Report USSR No. 63*

. . . . . . . . . . . .

*Einsatzgruppe C*
Location: Novo-Ukrainka
On August 16, 1941, Einsatzkommando 6 of Sipo and the SD were located near Novo-Ukrainka. While purging the area, the Einsatzkommando group encountered a suspicious looking civilian who escaped and was pursued. In the course of that pursuit, members of the EK-6-SS Stubf.[1] von Koskull, SS-O-Scharf.[2] Werner Schulz, SS-Scharführer Schwarz became involved in a shooting incident with nine hidden Soviet officers. SS-O-Scharf. Schulz fell in that fight.

Five of the Soviet officers were shot. Lieutenant-General Sokolov, the commander of the XVI Soviet armored corps, was among the Soviet officers. S. was severely wounded in the course of the exchange of fire and taken prisoner after the other officers had been overpowered.

*Einsatzgruppe D*
Location: Ananyev

. . . . . . . . . . . .

The solution of the *Jewish question*, one of the most important problems, has already been tackled, though only in a hesitant manner. Before the war, there were some 60 to 80,000 Jews in Kishinev. A great many of them left when the Russians withdrew. When the

---

1. Sturmbannführer.
2. Oberscharführer.

town was occupied there were approximately 4,000 Jews as some of them had returned.

On the initiative of the Einsatzkommando the Rumanian town-commander established a Jewish ghetto in the old part of the town which, at present, comprises about 9,000 Jews.

The Jews are divided in labor groups and put at the disposal of the various German and Rumanian offices for rubbish clearance and other work.

## Operational Situation Report USSR No. 64

. . . . . . . . . . . .

*Einsatzgruppe D*
Location: Ananyev

### Situation in Kodyma

*A. Economy*
Business and trade in Kodyma and Kotovsk are almost exclusively under Jewish management. All the stores and shops and storehouses have been destroyed as a result of the war; the rest was looted by the population.

*B. Cultural Situation in Kodyma Region*
*1. Nationalities Situation:*
In the district of Kodyma as well as in the West Ukrainian areas that have been so far in touch with the Kommando, the Ukrainian character is decidedly prevalent. Concerning the nationalities situation, it is the same as in the regions of Yampol and Pechenka.

40% of the population, numbering 6,000, are Jews. The remaining 60% consist of Ukrainians and a small Polish group that has no influence whatsoever.

*2. Education and Communist Influence*
There are three Soviet schools in the region of Kodyma, namely, one comprising ten classes, one eight, and one seven. The schools of ten and seven classes were used mainly by Jews. That school was transformed from a Jewish to a Russian school ten years ago. Soviet personnel policy concerning the school system provided for a staff of teachers who were in charge of the three schools. With one excep-

tion, directors and managers of the schools were either Jews or Communist activists.

### C. Jewish matters

40% of the 5,000 inhabitants of Kodyma were Jews. In addition to the local Jews, there is a large number of refugees from Bessarabia. Most of the local Jews who were close to Bolshevism, that is members of the Communist party, have fled with the Soviet army.

Immediately after the Soviets arrived in Kodyma, the Jewish organizations were dissolved. Thus, their activities took place within the framework of the Communist party organizations. In 1935, the synagogues in Kodyma were transformed into schools. Prayer houses were not subsidized officially; therefore, the cult was practiced in private homes. These meetings were held secretly as the authorities collected high taxes for this. Also, Jewish Soviet employees and workers would have endangered their position. Therefore they frequented the prayer houses secretly.

The Jews in K. did not lead a traditional Jewish way of life. They were active in all of the decision-making positions and had influence in Communist organizations, clubs, and economy. Of the six Jewish physicians, one dentist, two lawyers, one pharmacist, only one female physician has remained in K. The rest of them have fled.

Jewish intelligentsia in Kodyma took great interest in the activities of the Communist party and held, as already mentioned, leading positions in the CP. The poorer part of the population were tradesmen. All of them were sympathetic to Bolshevism. Only a few Jewish families are members of the collectives.

. . . . . . . . . . . .

## Situation in the region of Khotin-Mogilev

### 1. Jewish Question

At present there are about 4,000 Jews in the town of Mogilev who are part of the population. Approximately 7,000 Jews live in the immediate proximity of Mogilev. They were deported from Rumania into this area before its administration was taken over [by the Rumanians]. One transport of Jews, consisting of about 6,000 persons, was escorted to the other side of the Dniester, in spite of considerable protest by the Rumanian officer in command of the bridge. The number of Jews increases daily on account of their return to the town.

It is intended to concentrate the Jewish population into one quarter of the town. The Jews who were deported into this area by the Rumanians are being confined in three camps. Jews fit for work were detailed to clear away rubble in the town as well as to bring in the harvest.

. . . . . . . . . . . .

### Relations with the Rumanian Army

Though the town was not damaged by the effects of the war, it was plundered almost entirely by the Rumanian troops as they passed through. Shootings and rapes are daily occurrences. All the complaints to the Rumanian commanders have not had any success worth mentioning. Therefore, together with the Ukrainian auxiliary police, a permanent street control has been introduced. In many cases, serious conflicts arose as looted goods were taken away again from the Rumanian troops.

## Operational Situation Report USSR No. 66

. . . . . . . . . . . .

*Einsatzgruppe for Special Duties*
Location: Lvov

### Reports: Activity Report in the former Polish-Russian areas

2,117 persons were liquidated as follows: by Einsatzkommando Lvov 1,154; Brest-Litovsk 769; and Bialystok 194. Almost 3,000 persons were arrested. The Communists continue their illegal work in full strength. The spread of rumors and the dropping of leaflets by Russian airplanes are continuing. On August 15, 1941 a large ammunition depot, formerly Russian, exploded not far from Lvov apparently as a result of sabotage. Communists want to delay additional sabotage acts until after the harvest has been brought in. In Klusk near Kovel, 45 full barns burned down on the night of August 15-16, 1941. It is very easy to supply the numerous bands with weapons as military installations are unguarded.

The Jews continue to be extremely hostile and commit acts of sabotage whenever one does not react most energetically.

Members of the 10th Hungarian Hunter Battalion have expelled more than 1,000 Hungarian Jews over the Dniester to Galicia. Einsatzunit Tarnopol promptly sent them back. Members of the same Hungarian unit tore down Ukrainian flags, threw stones into the windows of Ukrainian priests, and entertained themselves with the Polish clergy. The dissolution of the Ukrainian militia is going on everywhere to the satisfaction of the greater part of the population. Activity of the Bandera supporters increases. An inscription on the cooperative store building in Klusk near Kovel demanded removal of the "foreign government" and the return of Stefan Bandera. The popular proclamation of the Ukrainian state was to be read in public in Luboml.

Functionaries coming from the General Gouvernement especially solicit the young people to join the Polish resistance movement.

The Chief of the Security Police     Berlin, August 29, 1941
and the SD

<u>48 copies</u>
(36th copy)

*Operational Situation Report USSR No. 67*

. . . . . . . . . . .

*Einsatzgruppe for Special Duty*
Lvov

### Activity in the former Polish-Russian areas

During the period of this report, 2,739 persons were liquidated, and approximately 2,800 persons were arrested.

The illegal work of the Communists continues. It is expressed in horror propaganda, distribution of pamphlets, and acts of sabotage. In the area of Einsatzkommando Lutsk, army guards were repeatedly shot at by such elements. Adequate retaliation measures were carried out. Communist propaganda by pamphlet continues and is enhanced by propaganda material that is dropped from Russian aircraft (particularly in Volhynia).

The Polish resistance movement is again evident (Rovno, Lutsk). In Kostopol, district Lutsk, illegal organizations, "Bund der Schützen" and "Kampflegion des Todes,"[1] were uncovered. The officials and members whose names were ascertained were liquidated.

The behavior of the Jews is hostile and partly impertinent. They are the main source of anti-German propaganda.

*Einsatzgruppe A*
Location: Pesje

. . . . . . . . . . .

---

1. The Union of Sharpshooters and The Fighting Legion of Death.

*Einsatzgruppe B*
Location: Smolensk

. . . . . . . . . . . .

## Fight against partisan groups

The current actions against partisan groups are continuing successfully. Members of the Gruppe H.Q. had to liquidate 26 Jews in Monastyrshchina, about 70 km south of Smolensk, who were cooperating with the partisans, terrorizing the loyal population and sabotaging the economic measures ordered by the military headquarters in Smolensk. With the help of the anti-Bolshevik section of the population, the members of the Gruppe H.Q. located a group of partisans near Monastyrshchina numbering 150-200 with a large ammunition store. In cooperation with the Army, their destruction is proceeding.

At the request of the intelligence officer of the H.Q. of 2nd Army, the Sonderkommando 7b joined in the fight against the partisans.

According to information, former armed members of the Red Army are in hiding in a village near Sokhanova. They terrorize that part of the population that is willing to work. A special unit of EK 7b established that the village in question was Sharjevshtina. The special unit surrounded the village, made a surprise entry and caught six partisans who were liquidated. Loaded Russian military rifles and pistols were taken. By the way, all of the partisans were members of the CP.

Einsatzkommando 9 which is stationed in Vitebsk has accomplished four major actions against the partisans. The broad woodlands made matters particularly difficult. Anyhow, it was possible to surprise and destroy a larger number of partisans.

Sonderkommando 8 discovered among other things a Jew in Cherven who had been a school supervisor until [the outbreak of] the war. He had joined a partisan group that roamed the forests of Cherven under the leadership of a Russian lieutenant. Informed Army personnel have successfully combed the area in question. The mayor of Rzhev and his house manager were liquidated because of the same activities. In the Rzhev area a Kommando of the EK 8 has arrested and finished off 51 men because they had been active as partisans. Most of them were Red Army members wearing civilian clothes who had disposed of their identification papers. Two platoons of the police were attacked by a Red Army unit the size of a battalion. Because of their great number, the police had to retreat, losing 12 dead and two injured. A retaliatory action by the 262nd Division is in progress.

According to information received in Slutsk, strong Red forces are on their way there. The defense of the town was prepared. The entire German force was alerted as well as the sub-unit of EK 8 which was on the spot. Since the last report this sub-unit has executed 77 men who had been connected with the partisans and had been convicted of acts of sabotage.

Lately, the Vorkommando Moscow received in Smolensk more and more information about partisan activities in the surrounding villages.

. . . . . . . . . . . .

### *Actions against officials, agents, Jews, saboteurs and looters. Seizure of material.*

In Smolensk some quarters of the town were systematically searched for officials, agents, criminals, Jewish intelligentsia, etc. During this action 74 persons were arrested and liquidated. Among these were persons who had contact with partisans, as well as a member of the NKGB, who had been involved in continuous shootings in the cellar of the NKVD building and is now a leader of looting bands. The screening of the remaining parts of the town continues. However, it should be taken into consideration that Smolensk still houses only a small fraction of its former population. The building-up of a network of confidential agents was energetically promoted. The fact that only few inhabitants remained and that a series of sabotage acts have occurred lately proves the existence of active Bolsheviks. Thus, great care is necessary in the recruitment of confidential agents. In spite of these difficulties, it was possible to procure a large number of reliable confidential agents. Members of the appointed town administration were also included in the network of confidential agents.

In Mogilev, the raids seeking Communist officials were continued. Apart from the ones already liquidated, 80 more Jews were executed. Among these there was, apart from a number of arsonists, an informer of the NKGB, who had denounced numerous ethnic Germans to the Russian authorities.

In Orsha, 43 Jews were found, some of whom were actively spreading atrocity stories, while others acted as snipers. Among these were two party officials. One of them was the Communist party propagandist in Orsha. Moreover, a Pole was shot for looting. Eleven Jews were executed in the villages of Shuchari and Yasna. Some of these had been active as snipers, others carried on Communist agitation. Among the ones liquidated was an official of the Communist party who was said to have been a political Commissar. The political Commissar Valerian Sakharinkov was seized in the field, near Mogilev, and liquidated. S. was a member of the party since 1919. He was a fanatic Bolshevik who until the end exercised a strong influence on large parts of the population.

31 Jews who had been in contact with partisans were liquidated in Chashy, 60 km from Mogilev. Since neither a local nor a field command post or a town administration has as yet been formed in Chashy, the detachment operating there appointed a council. Partisans shot at the detachment during its return from Chashy and succeeded in escaping into the woods. An NKGB informer was liquidated among others in Bobruisk. This man, according to the testimony of witnesses, had about 200 persons on his conscience. A number of Jews, who agitated the population by spreading rumors, were also shot.

A secret letter was found in the Communist party building in Velish during the exmination of file materials there. It concerned an instruction of the delegate of the People's Commissariat regarding preparations for December 25, 1940, in which complete mobilization by January 10, 1941 is called for. Moreover, files on the Komsomol membership and of the Communist party could be secured in the NKVD building. The formation of a Jewish Council, the marking, and registration of the Jews were also carried out.

Eight Jews who had tried to intimidate the population by spreading false rumors and who were also members of the Komsomol were liquidated in Kolkhoz Voroshilov, 17 km from Velish. Moreover, the former head of the office of forestry development in Velish, a Jewess, was shot for sabotage. In Novo-Svienchiany, 169 and in Vilnius 612 more persons were subjected to special treatment.

In Vitebsk, the actions against the Jewish intelligentsia were continued. A Jewess insidiously asked a German soldier to open a door. As he did so the soldier's lower arm was torn off by an explosive charge. She was apprehended through investigations by the Einsatzkommando. The Jewess was then publicly hanged. Some other persons who participated in setting Vitebsk afire and who drove cattle out of the villages in compliance with Stalin's proclamation were also liquidated.

In Minsk, 615 more persons were liquidated in the course of an action in the civilian-prisoner camp there. All the executed were of racially inferior stock. Also liquidated were a Russian who shot at German soldiers, and two persons who were caught red-handed while cutting cables of the Luftwaffe. A Byelorussian was apprehended by the local command post in Minsk on suspicion of committing acts of sabotage. He was found guilty of having destroyed cables of the German Army with an axe behind the Rushkin barracks. He was liquidated. A Jew and a Byelorussian woman who, as Bolshevik agitators, carried out the lowest kind of agitation and work sabotage were subjected to the same treatment. Ten more Jews from Minsk, who until the last, had carried on anti-German propaganda among the population, were also shot. A Russian who roamed through the town in the disguise of a beggar and terrorized the population with threats of arson, also had to be executed. Furthermore, a member of the civilian order service was liquidated. He made searches of apartments in Minsk and in the village of Znianka without orders. While doing this, he looted the apartments. The liquidation was necessary, for no other reason than he told the persons concerned that he was acting by order of the German authorities. A number of other persons were shot because of sabotage, looting, and Communist propaganda. Ten Russians, who found a hide-out in the barracks at the border of Minsk, were subjected to the same treatment. According to the investigations, they were former convicts.

. . . . . . . . . . . .

*Einsatzgruppe D*
Location: Ananyev

## Operational Report from the district bordering the Dniester: From Khotin to Yambol, including Chernovtshy.

. . . . . . . . . . . .

The territory, with the exception of the Hungarian-occupied area around Svanzia, was cleared of Jews. The Rumanians had driven thousands of selected persons unfit for labor, such as invalids and children, from Bessarabia and Bucovina into the German sphere. In the vicinity of Svanzia-Mogilev-Podolski-Yampol, a total of approximately 27,500 Jews were driven back to Rumanian territory, and 1,265, partly younger ones, were shot. 3,105 more Jews and 34 Communists were liquidated in Chernovtsy in the course of search actions east of the Dniester. No terror and sabotage groups were discovered.

The Chief of the Security Police
and the SD

September 4, 1941

<u>48 copies</u>
(36th copy)

## Operational Situation Report USSR No. 73

. . . . . . . . . . . .

*Einsatzgruppe B*
Location: Smolensk

## a. Execution activity

a. *General Situation*
Execution activity continues with unmitigated severity during the period of this report. Certain rearrangements, however, have become necessary in the various branches of this task-sector as the advance eastwards continued.

As is well known, Jews were forbidden, during the tsarist regime, to settle in the central parts of Russia. The eastern border of the Jewish Zone ran along a line running through Vitebsk, Orsha, Mogilev, and Gomel. As the prohibition was lifted, in February 1917, the Jews streamed in masses into that zone and also eastwards. They were mostly intellectual Jews who, of course, settled almost exclusively in the larger towns in order to be active in politics and economics. Relatively few Jews could, therefore, be found in the villages and smaller towns of this area. The larger part of the intellectual Jews from the [provincial] capitals have managed to escape the German armies and go east. It has been also established without any doubt that the Jews who, up to this point, usually returned to their homes after fleeing into the forests, etc., do not return so soon, or not at all, to the area where the Einsatzgruppe of the Security Police is active. This proves that the activity of the Security Police has become rather well known in Jewish circles. It is, therefore, hardly possible at present to continue the number of liquidations on the same scale as before, since the Jewish elements are to a great extent missing.

. . . . . . . . . . . .

In this manner the local and field Kommandaturen could be supported more effectively than previously in accomplishing their administrative and economic aims. It has become clear that quite often these authorities need the help of the Security Police in such matters as installing new mayors, establishing ghettos, marking and registering Jews, and organizing work groups from the population. It was necessary more than once to break the intransigent behavior of hostile persons through the intervention of the Security Police.

The forces that have become available through the absence of Jewish elements can thus proceed more than before with the organization of our work in accordance with the general police. Researches and investigations could be carried out more effectively. Greater numbers of dangerous agents and officials could be rendered harmless in cooperation with secret agents.

### b. Fight against partisans

. . . . . . . . . . . .

A squad operating in Slutsk raided the villages of Ogrodniki, Kvasinitse and Novido liquidating 39 snipers, among them a Russian major who had camouflaged himself by wearing civilian clothes and taken up some employment. In the village of Oshidkoviche five persons were arrested and liquidated. It was found that they had supported partisan groups and given them information about the German forces.

The squad operating in Borisov liquidated another 118 persons. With the aid of the 10th Company of the 354th Infantry Regiment, they combed through the area north of Borisov for partisans. This purge was directed chiefly against the village of Sachistshe, about 25 km distance from Borisov, which was considered the center of the guerrilla activity. Investigations proved that the partisans had been supported by the leaders of the kolkhoz. Most of the persons liquidated were Jewish activists.

. . . . . . . . . . . .

## c. Actions against officials, agents, saboteurs and Jews

The HQ of Einsatzgruppe B succeeded in arresting three NKGB informers in Smolensk and one of the small places in the area. They terrorized the sector of the population that had no Bolshevik inclinations for years, by informing on many persons to the NKGB. The population expressed its satisfaction about the liquidation of these persons.

Sonderkommando 7a carried out another action in Nevel against the Jews, in which 74 persons were shot. This action was carried out as a reprisal for arson committed by Jews.

The action was carried out as a punitive measure for arson committed by Jews in Nevel. According to the voluntary confession of many Jews, many members of that race participated in these arsons which destroyed the center of the town which was only slightly damaged during the fighting. Further steps must be taken against the Jews after their return. An additional number of active Communists and Jewish intellectuals were executed in a number of smaller localities.

A squad of Sonderkommando 7b carried out a search action in Chautsy for Communist functionaries. They arrested four Communists who spread rumors that the German forces were beaten and were retreating. They were dealt with pursuant to orders. 20 Jews who had been active as Communists were also executed.

An NKGB agent was found in the village Isobishche and subjected to special treatment. The search in the village Novoselki led to the discovery of a Communist who was also notorious outside his home village. In addition to his activities as party official, he had been guilty of theft from ethnic Germans. He was liquidated.

The Construction Battalion 9 of Minsk handed over to Einsatzkommando 8 a Ukrainian prisoner of war who made no secret of his Communist views. While being arrested he still tried to make propaganda for Communist ideas, especially for the system of collective farms. He was liquidated. A Russian who had been active in the Communist party for many years and had been a pronounced activist and troublemaker, had also to be shot. In Minsk, another 21 persons, who spread anti-German agitation by whispering propaganda among the population, were liquidated.

The squad operating in Slutsk carried out special purges in Rzhev and in Borisov. Except for 96 Red Army soldiers who were handed over to the prisoner-of-war camp, a number of Jews were liquidated who had remained active Communists to the end. Among them were ten fugitive Jewish families who came from former Polish territory and had moved east with the retreating Russian soldiers. While searching their horse-drawn carts considerable quantities of tinned food belonging to the German Army were found.

Five members of the Soviet People's Court of Slutsk were done away with. One of them was a Jew. In the village of Komarovka they were able to arrest a former Public Prosecutor who had been denounced. The squad stationed in Slutsk liquidated 115 people in all during the time covered by this report.

Einsatzkommando 8 received information that in the ghetto of Minsk the Jews were spreading anti-German propaganda in a whispering campaign. It was especially effective with the rural population who tried to sell their products in the ghetto.

Because Jews had attacked a member of the local auxiliary police and had repeatedly destroyed German Army sign-posts, a new special action was carried out against the Jews of Minsk in which 214 persons were shot.

Einsatzkommando 9 found 149 Jews of Yanovichi to be NKGB informers and political functionaries who were handled accordingly. Some of these Jews sabotaged German projects. They stayed in hiding in order not to be drafted to gather the harvest, and for road and aerodrome construction work.

After three German soldiers were killed in the vicinity of Vitebsk a German Army pacification-action was carried out. On this occasion we seized 19 Jews and Jewesses wandering around in the forest where the murder had been committed. They were executed on the strong suspicion of having taken part in the attack and committing arson in Vitebsk.

The Vorkommando Moscow was forced to execute another 46 persons, among them 38 intellectual Jews who had tried to create unrest and discontent in the newly established ghetto of Smolensk.

The Kommandos can make the gratifying observation almost everywhere that because of the strict and fair attitude of the Security Police, the population is becoming more open all the time. Also our pacification activity is supported by reports on Communists.

. . . . . . . . . . . .

## Investigating civilian prisoners camps

The search action of the civilian prison camp of Minsk continues. Another 733 civilian prisoners were seized and all of them were liquidated.

All the persons executed were absolutely inferior elements with a predominant mixture of Asiatic blood. No responsibility could be assumed if they were left in the occupied zone.

In Vitebsk the German Army handed over to Einsatzkommando 9 (after searching through the civilian prisoners' camp) 397 Jews who had committed acts of sabotage and attacked German troops.

## *Formation of labor groups, Jewish Councils, ghettos etc.*

As in the other towns until now, Jews were also picked up in Nevel in the course of systematic search actions and were organized in labor groups that were used for town-cleaning. A Jewish Council was chosen from the more intelligent Jews. As a first task, they were ordered to register the Jews of both sexes and to mark them with a yellow star.

### b. Statistics of the liquidations

The total figures of persons liquidated by Einsatzgruppe B as of August 20, 1941 were:

1. H.Q. and Vorkommando Moscow ..................... 144
2. Vorkommando 7a ................................. 996
3. Vorkommando 7b ................................. 886
4. Einsatzkommando 8 ............................. 6,842
5. Einsatzkommando 9 ............................. 8,096

Total ............................................. 16,964

## Confiscations

A member of the local auxiliary police of Minsk, a Volga German,[1] found in a Jewish doctor's apartment 17,980 rubles which the Jew had hidden. The amount was confiscated.

On the occasion of a purge in Cherven 125,880 rubles were found on 139 liquidated Jews and were confiscated. This brings the total of

---

1. An ethnic German from the German Soviet Autonomous Republic on the Volga River.

the money confiscated to date by Einsatzkommando 8 to 1,510,399 rubles.

Einsatzkommando 9 succeeded in securing nine folders containing extracts of censured letters that were written by civilians and soldiers. The letters were confiscated and studied in the censor's office of the NKVD in Novogrudok. The NKVD was obviously interested to find out what the mood was in the area of Poland that had been under Russian occupation.

48 copies
(36th copy)

## Operational Situation Report USSR No. 74

. . . . . . . . . . . .

*Einsatzgruppe C*
Location: Novo-Ukrainka

### Behavior of allied forces[1] stationed in this area

. . . . . . . . . . . .

In Pervomaysk, an ethnic German auxiliary policeman had the task to escort Jewish laborers. In the course of this activity, he had an altercation with a Jew and was injured. Self-defense was prevented by a Hungarian soldier who, with a loaded pistol, came to the aid of the Jew. Later on the Jew was found and liquidated by the Einsatzkommando in charge.

---

1. Rumanians, Hungarians, etc.

The Chief of the Security Police
and the SD

Berlin,
September 9, 1941

48 copies
(46th copy)

## Operational Situation Report USSR No. 78

. . . . . . . . . . . .

## Situational Report in former Russian-Poland

. . . . . . . . . . . .

*Ethnic groups:*

. . . . . . . . . . . .

## Nationalities

1,308 more persons were liquidated, 760 by Einsatzkommando Lvov and 548 by [EK] Brest-Litovsk. Approximately 700 persons were arrested. Distribution of Soviet Russian pamphlets has somewhat diminished at the time of this report. Only in the area of Lutsk, larger amounts were still seized in some villages. Pamphlets of more recent dates were not found any more. Six Russian parachutists landed east of Pinsk. Searches for them so far are without result. Parachutists were dropped in the area of Kremenets, most of them were seized and liquidated by the local security division. So far, no sabotage acts have been committed. The Polish resistance movement has become more evident in the area of Brest where there is strong propaganda for General Sikorski. No arrests have been effected, so as not to interfere with further investigations. Ukrainian bands have appeared lately in the neighborhood of Pinsk. However, they were driven out by the local police.

## Operational Situation Report USSR No. 80

. . . . . . . . . . . .

*Einsatzgruppe C*
Location: Novo-Ukrainka

## Observations made and measures taken by the Security Police.

Besides the thorough liquidation of the Party organization and the operations to clear the country of Jews who constitute the most negative civilian element, the executive operations of Einsatzgruppe C at present also include: above all, the fight against all partisan activities, beginning with the well-organized bands and the individual snipers down to the systematic rumor mongers.

The rumor that the Germans shoot to kill all the Jews has advantages. This is probably the reason why all the time the EKs encounters fewer Jews. Thus, it should be noted that everywhere more than 70-90% of the original local Jews have fled. In contrast to the past, this concerns not only those Jews who once held influential positions.

Primarily in the large towns, the ever increasing security tasks cannot be solved by the Einsatzkommandos alone, since they are too small for this purpose. Mounting importance is being attached to the creation and organization of a regular police service. Well screened particularly reliable Ukrainians are employed for this purpose. Moreover, a network of confidential agents composed predominantly of ethnic Germans, has been created with great success. In the kolkhozes these tasks have mostly been conferred upon the kolkhoz managers (the starostas).[1]

At Kirovo, the development has reached a stage where the men enlisted for this purpose are already being paid by the municipality from funds seized from Jews. They obtain their rations from a small farm that has been especially allocated to them.

In Narodichi, 208 terrorists, and, in a nearby barn, nearly 60 terrorists were arrested and shot in the course of a large-scale action.

In Andrushovka 6 more Bolsheviks were rendered harmless.

In Korosten, according to reports received, numerous Jews who had previously fled had gathered together again, constituting a source of continuous unrest.

238 Jews who were rounded up and driven to a special building by the Ukrainian militia were shot.

In Fastov, where the Secret Military Police of the local command post and a Defense Battalion had already liquidated about 30 snipers and 50 Jews, order was fully restored only after Sonderkommando 4a shot a former terrorist and all the Jewish inhabitants between the ages of 12 and 60, making a total of 262 heads.

August 24, 1941, the total of executions carried out by Sonderkommando 4a has thus reached the figure of 7,152 persons.

In Lisovishi three saboteurs, one of whom had destroyed several harvesters, were arrested and liquidated.

In Tarashcha, 17 executions were carried out.

In Kamenets-Podolsk 23,600 Jews were shot in three days by a Kommando of the Higher SS and Police Leaders.

---

1. The Elders.

The Chief of the Security Police
and the SD

Berlin,
September 12, 1941

48 copies
(36th copy)

## Operational Situation Report USSR No. 81

. . . . . . . . . . . .

*Einsatzgruppe C*
Location: Novo-Ukrainka.

. . . . . . . . . . . .

## Report relating to the situation in the Ukraine submitted by Einsatzkommando 6.

. . . . . . . . . . . .

## The Jewish question

All experiences confirm the assertion made before that the Soviet state was a Jewish state of the first order. This can be ascertained in every enterprise, authority and even in the kolkhozes. Take the director, vice-director, the bookkeeper, the cashier, the manager of the depots of each enterprise: they were Jews, and the employees and workers were Ukrainians. The manager of the local labor union, the party-secretary of the same enterprise are Jews as well. This is found to be the rule in the medium and small enterprises, let alone the big ones. For these reasons, the Jewish question has become a burning problem for the Ukrainian people. Whenever this question is discussed, enthusiastic approval can be heard. The use of the word "Zhid"[1] was threatened with severe punishment and considered to be

---

1. Derogatory form of "Jew" in the Russian and Ukrainian languages.

symptomatic of an anti-Soviet attitude during the Bolshevik era. The acceptable form was that of "Yevrei."[2] The aversion of the population and the clear understanding of the Jewish problem increases when going from west to east. This means that in the districts of central and east Ukraine, where there are no long-time Jews, the Jew is rejected with even greater exasperation than in the "old-Jewish" districts west of Berdichev and Zhitomir. There, a greater passivity and an accommodation to the association with Jews took place over the course of centuries. Concerning propaganda measures for the broad masses in the Ukrainian districts it should be kept in mind that the population is always grateful for our treatment of the Jewish question. Almost nowhere could the population be induced to take active steps against the Jews. This may be traced back to the fear still prevailing in many circles that the Reds might come back again.

Time and again this intimation was made by the older people with the addition that they already had the experience in 1918 when the Germans suddenly withdrew. In order to counteract this psychosis of fear, and to break the spell which adheres to the Jews as carriers of political power in the eyes of many Ukrainians, Einsatzkommando 6 in several instances marched the Jews through the town under guard prior to their execution. It was likewise often deemed important to have men from the militia (Ukrainian auxiliary police force) participate in the execution of Jews. Word seems to have passed among the Jews on the other side of the front, too, about the fate they can expect from us. While a considerable number of Jews could be apprehended during the first weeks, it can be ascertained that in the central and eastern districts of the Ukraine, in many cases 70% to 90%, and in some cases even 100% of the Jewish population had bolted. The gratuitous evacuation of hundreds of thousands of Jews may be considered to be an indirect success of the work of the Security Police. As we hear mostly from the other side of the Urals, this is a considerable contribution to the solution of the Jewish question in Europe.

As an oddity we should like to mention the discovery of Jewish kolkhozes. Between Krivoy-Rog and Dnepropetrovsk there is a considerable number of Jewish kolkhozes which consist of Jews not only as the managers but also as agricultural laborers. As far as we could find out they are Jews of low intelligence who had been found unsuitable

---

2. Hebrew.

for important tasks and "exiled" to the country by the political leaders.

In order to be sure work was carried on [without interruption], Einsatzkommando 6 refrained from shooting the Jews in these cases, and was satisfied with the liquidation of the Jewish managers [only], replacing them with Ukrainians.

. . . . . . . . . . . .

## Some experiences

. . . . . . . . . . . .

Executions of Jews are understood everywhere and accepted favorably. It is surprising how calm the delinquents [victims] are when they are shot, both Jews and non-Jews. Fear of death seems to have been dulled by 20 years of Soviet rule.

The Chief of the Security Police
and the SD

Berlin,
September 17, 1941

48 copies
(36th copy)

## Operational Situation Report USSR No. 86

. . . . . . . . . . . .

*EInsatzgruppe A*
Location: Kikerino

### Fight against partisans

. . . . . . . . . . . .

Eight persons who have provided partisans with food and information were shot. Among them was a Jew who had been hiding his true descent. He sneaked in as a translator in a German war hospital and deliberately provided false translations.

. . . . . . . . . . . .

*Einsatzgruppe C*
Location: Novo-Ukrainka

### General situation

The Einsatzkommandos maintain contact with the fighting troops in order to arrive together with the advance infantry units in the newly occupied cities and areas. In this process they are frequently exposed to violent enemy fire.

In spite of their rapid progress, the picture has by now become the same all over and can be summarized as follows: the most important officials of the KP and the NKVD and the influential Jews have fled and destroyed all documentary material. The politically important fugitives have apparently gone over the Dnieper, while the less important, among them many Jews, are returning by and by. Therefore, next to the search for strangers in prison camps and in as many small localities as possible, particular importance is given to the search of forest areas, roads, and villages at night. For, according to our experience, fugitives and partisans show up there for provisions.

The arrival of the security Kommandos is generally made known very soon and is welcomed by the Army, especially by the local command headquarters as well as by the population. Village mayors, militia commanders, and other civilians arrive from distances as far as 20 km in order to make reports. It is remarkable that up to now the peasant has hardly ever left the borders of his village. Particularly frequent are reports on Russian parachutists that have been seen, as well as bands and hidden Bolsheviks. As all the Einsatz commanders have noticed, the actions that were subsequently taken were only partly successful because the information received from the population is exaggerated or not based on reliable facts. Exaggerated anxiety, the wish to hurt personal enemies, and the wish for weapons of the Ukrainian militia are the main reasons for such useless denunciations. Anyhow, the trust of the Ukrainian population is gratifying, particularly as it was possible to ferret out the places of Bolsheviks, Jews, and asocial elements following the reports.

The above-mentioned exaggerations come at first from an inability that can be called childish on the part of the population to express itself clearly and unambiguously and of a narrow-mindedness, particularly in the southern Ukraine. It frequently happened that persons timidly denied their strongly biased reports or they weakened them when they found out that the life of the accused was in danger.

In general, such informants are sternly cautioned in order to avoid unnecessary troubles. In one case, an especially vicious informant was shot in the hamlet of Rozhyn. He was convicted of former Communist activity and asocial behavior.

One could also observe that the Jews behave in a brazen and impertinent manner in spite of the large-scale actions against them. This is proven by the following example:

In Ushomir where the 1st SS brigade shot all male Jews, bands led by four Jews entered two hours after the brigade left and set fire to 48 houses. In Zhitomir, the unarmed Ukrainian militia was repeatedly molested by Jews and, in one case, even shot at.

The Jews wrote a threatening letter in Kotelnia to the mayor that ended with the following words, "Long live the party of Lenin and Stalin! Long live the Jewish Communists! Death to the German bandits."

In Cherniakov, a Jewish woman managed to pose as an ethnic German in front of the mayor in the presence of a member of the SD by presenting a forged German document. Referring to this so-called proof she demanded a plot of land from the local commander.

Smuggling flourishes among the Jews in Zhitomir. They hoard the products which the peasants exchange for looted goods.

The Jews use work certificates that were given them by the Army offices for short-term occupations and do not return them. They also occupy themselves with forging documents. Thus, certificates were found like those used by the local Kommandatur in Zhitomir. Although the 6th Army HQ stamps were forged, the forms appeared to be real. They stem probably from an Army printing shop where Jews had been employed as auxiliary workers.

## Operations

266 Jews were liquidated as further reprisal measures against the rebellion of the Zhitomir Jews. They even sabotaged the black-out regulations at night and lit up their windows during Russian air raids.

In the vicinity of the town, it was possible to disarm and arrest a parachutist with the aid of the militia after a rifle skirmish. He was equipped with explosives.

160 persons were shot in Korosten; during the course of the actions 68 persons were executed in Byelatserkiev and 109 in Tarashcha, mostly Jews.

Thus the Sonderkommando 4a has exterminated 6,584 Bolsheviks, Jews, and asocial elements. In two cases, ethnic Germans had to be arrested. They were active in the Communist sense, participating actively in the preparations for the deportation of ethnic Germans and Ukrainians. The investigations against these have not yet been concluded.

For the time being, Einsatzkommando 5 has been divided into platoons covering a larger territory, and is systematically combing the villages of this area. Among others, several Bolshevik mayors and kolkhoz representatives were taken care of. Besides that, several mentally retarded persons who were ordered to blow up bridges and railroad tracks and to carry out other acts of sabotage, were rendered harmless. It seems that the NKVD favored mentally retarded persons in allocating these kinds of tasks; they, in spite of their inferiority, mustered enough energy for their criminal activities. Four executions were carried out in Ulianov, 18 in Uledovka.

It was possible to take care of 229 Jews in the clean-up action carried out in Khmielnik. As a result, this area, which suffered especially from Jewish terror, is extensively cleaned up. The reaction of the population here to their deliverance from the Jews was so strong that it resulted in a Thanksgiving service.

Einsatzkommando 5 took care of 506 Bolsheviks and Jews in the course of 14 days.

In the south of the Einsatzgruppen area, there still exists an empty area with respect to security police work because military operations do not take place sufficiently far away. So far, the return of the fugitives has not started in sufficient measure. Therefore, the number of actions naturally increases in the area which lies further back [from the front].

The remaining units of Einsatzkommando 6 shot about 600 Jews in Vinnitsa.

Up to now, 140 politically tainted persons were arrested in Kirovo and 48 of these were shot. Among these were heads of unions, Komsomol leaders, lay judges, and leaders of other Bolshevik central offices.

In Krivoy-Rog, 39 officials, 11 saboteurs and looters, and 105 Jews were taken care of.

Several actions for the seizure of officials, terrorists, and migrating Jews were carried out by the Einsatzgruppen HQ in Novo-Ukrainka and vicinity. Among others, a caravan of Jews, which was taking along a wagon of loot, was stopped. The Jews were shot and the goods distributed to the population. It was possible to find and to take care of two leading Communists during a night action in Zlinka. On the basis of individual reports and of road blocks on streets in the course of official travels, several Jews or Bolshevik agents were shot.

The office of the Higher SS and Police Leader took care of a total of 511 Jews in actions in Pilva and Stara-Sieninva.

. . . . . . . . . . . .

## The Jews

Even if an immediate hundred percent exclusion of the Jews were possible, this would not remove the political source of danger. Bolshevik work depends on Jews, Russians, Georgians, Armenians, Poles, Latvians, and Ukrainians. The Bolshevik apparatus is very limited in scope, identical with the Jewish population. In this situation, the goal of the political security police would be missed if the main task of the destruction of the Communist machine were to become a second or third choice in favor of the practically easier task of the exclusion of the Jews. Furthermore, concentrating on the Bolshevik official robs the Jews of their most able forces. Thus, the solution of the Jewish problem becomes more and more a problem of organization.

In the western and middle Ukraine, the Jews are almost identical with the city workers, artisans, and the tradesman class. *If the Jewish labor force is entirely discarded, an economic reconstruction of the Ukrainian industry and the extension of the administration centers of the cities are almost impossible.*

There is only one possibility, which the German administration in the General Gouvernement has not sufficiently understood for a long time, *the solution of the Jewish problem by extensive labor utilization of the Jews.* This will result in a gradual liquidation of the Jews, a development which corresponds to the economic conditions of the country.

The Chief of the Security Police
and Security Service

Berlin,
September 19, 1941

48 copies
(36th copy)

*Operational Situation Report USSR No. 88*

. . . . . . . . . . . .

*Einsatzgruppe A*
Location: Posje

## Liquidations

a) Operations were carried out by the Sonderkommando of the Einsatzkommando 3 in conjunction with the Lithuanian Kommando in the districts of Raseiniai, Rokiskis, Sarasai, Perzai and Prionai. Eleven districts are now free of Jews. These executions bring the number of persons liquidated by Einsatzkommando 3, together with Lithuanian partisans, to 46,692. The total number of executions is approximately 85,000.

b) After scrutiny of the Daugavpils (Dünaburg) prisons, a total of 279 persons (against whom there was no reason for detention) were discharged. 21 persons were liquidated.

c) Of the inmates in the lunatic asylum Aglona, a total of 544 insane persons were liquidated on August 22 with the assistance of the Latvian self-defense unit. Ten males who could be regarded as partially cured were discharged by the governor of the institution, Dr. Borg, after steps for their sterilization had been taken. After this action, the asylum no longer exists. The question of the re-employment of the nursing staff (about 150 persons) to care for the troops or in connection with the establishment of a hospital is being discussed with Military Headquarters.

## Operations in Riga

In Riga, 223 searches and check-ups were carried through during the period under review. In the prisons, there are at present 3,857 persons among them 3,569 Communists, 172 Jews and 116 persons against whom various charges are pending. The prison is being continually cleared.

## Operation in the Town and District of Dorpat

Since the occupation of the town by German troops, approximately 1,200 cases of arrest were dealt with up to the present. Most of these concern people arrested for Communist activities. 504 individuals were set free after the conclusion of the investigation and registration. 150 persons were released as there was obviously no reason for their detention. 291 prisoners were taken to the detention camp set up and supervised by the Dorpat Military Headquarters. The total number of persons executed in Dorpat is 405, among them 50 Jews. There are no more Jews in prison.

*Einsatzgruppe C*
Location: Novo-Ukrainka

## Locations

The Vorkommando 4b, which was previously stationed in Koryukov, has since moved to Kremenchug. Work in Kremenchug, which was heavily damaged by the actions, was begun at once. Headquarters will move into the town on completion of the bridge over the river now under construction.

The Einsatzgruppe, too, will effect a change of location these days, presumably to Poltava.

## Measures in the sphere of the Security Police

On September 6, 1941, Kommando 4a carried out an action against the Jews in Radomyshl. There, Jews from all over the district had been assembled. This led to an overcrowding of Jewish homes. On the average, 15 persons lived in one room. Hygienic conditions became intolerable. Every day several Jewish corpses had to be removed from the houses.

It was impossible to supply food to the Jews as well as the children.

In consequence, there was an ever-increasing danger of epidemics. To put an end to these conditions, 1,107 Jewish adults were shot by Kommando 4a, and 561 juveniles by the Ukrainian militia. By September 6, 1941, Sonderkommando 4a has liquidated a total of 11,328 Jews.

Between August 23 and September 5, 1941, Vorkommando 4b carried out a total of 519 executions by shooting, among these 56 officials and agents of the NKVD, 28 saboteurs and looters, and 435 Jews.

Between August 24 and August 30, 1941, Einsatzkommando 5 carried out 157 executions by shooting comprising Jews, officials and saboteurs.

On September 1 and 2, 1941, leaflets and inflammatory pamphlets were distributed by Jews in Berdichev. As the perpetrators could not be found, 1,303 Jews, among them 875 Jewesses over 12 years, were executed by a unit of the Higher SS and Police Leaders.

Owing to the halt of military operations, the Kommandos were restricted to their locations for longer periods than before. The time thus gained could be used for an intensification of work in the area. This partially very successful work was rendered possible by the creation of an excellent network of confidential informers. In the first place ethnic Germans and reliable Ukrainians were selected for these jobs.

It is with a view to the later period that an efficient communications network in the whole country is of particular importance. For this reason, it is intended to set up message centers all over the country which will be in charge of particularly reliable informants. These informants, then, will maintain communication with the others and collect the incoming messages. At longer or shorter intervals, these message centers will be visited by the Kommandos or by command headquarters to pick up the accumulated information. This may afford a possibility to keep check on this vast area, so as to discover early and suppress by surprise potential dangers. Finally, a certain political alignment of the population could be achieved through the message centers. While headquarters have not been stationed yet, these talks will be carried out as far as possible by the group itself.

. . . . . . . . . . . .

*Einsatzgruppe D*
Location: Nikolayev

**Russian administration in Bessarabia**

. . . . . . . . . . . .

*General*

. . . . . . . . . . . .

The Jews are concentrated in camps in the district of Tighina and are used for all kinds of work. Part of them count on being shot. In general, a strong anti-Jewish tendency can be observed among the Rumanian population.

The Chief of the Security Police
and Security Service

Berlin,
September 20, 1941

48 copies
(36th copy)

## *Operational Situation Report USSR No. 89*

. . . . . . . . . . . .

*Einsatzgruppe D*
Location: Kikorino
Work areas of the Kommandos have been freed of Jews. From August 19 to September 25, 8,890 Jews and Communists were executed. The total number is 13,315.

Presently the Jewish question in Nikolayev and Kherson is being solved. In each place about 5,000 Jews were seized. In this location there are hardly any Communists since almost all of them retreated with the Soviets. In addition to a few Party officials, eight NKVD officials in Anayev and fourteen in Nikolayev were rendered harmless.

. . . . . . . . . . . .

After interrogations any denunciations concerning terror organizations proved to be unfounded.

Jewish partisan group removed in . . .

. . . . . . . . . . . .

Reconstruction work until now:

a) Organization and training for German self-defense. Continuation of furnishing guards, road blocks, assistance to relatives of banished persons. Assistance in house-to-house searches.

b) Marking of German villages, including the exterior of all houses with posters and sign boards in German, Rumanian and Ukrainian languages. Ethnic Germans were issued certificates signed by the Commander-in-Chief.

c) Freeing of settlements from Jewish and Communist elements.
d) Influence on Rumanian offices regarding self-administration of German communities.
e) Concentration of settlements was started. Farmers, physicians, teachers, etc. who had lived in scattered places brought into German settlements.

f) Economic protection, distribution of loot, cattle, harvesting machines to the people, distribution of Jewish houses, belongings, etc.

g) Reviving cultural life by starting German instruction in most of the communities on September 9. Some hospitals opened. Influence on German behavior through lectures on Germany and the Führer.

h) Preparatory work for the inclusion of all ethnic Germans. Forty communities were included in the Beresany area. All the ethnic Germans were registered. In Nikolayev and Kherson they were also registered in card indexes. Selecting of the best for further reconstruction work, etc.

The Chief of the Security Police
and Security Service

Berlin,
September 21, 1941

48 copies
(36th copy)

## Operational Situation Report USSR No. 90

. . . . . . . . . . .

*Einsatzgruppe B*
Location: Smolensk

. . . . . . . . . . .

Cooperation with the police and Army headquarters has been extremely gratifying without any friction, as well as during the period of this report.

Security police is generally in great demand by the German Army. They willingly utilize our assistance, our experience, and suggestions. In the course of some larger operations carried out by us, Army units have been placed under our command. The economic offices as well as the military administration in general ask for our advice and gladly accept our suggestions. As was already mentioned repeatedly, the mutual steady information flow between the Einsatzgruppe and the Army Group on the one hand, and the commander of the Rear Area Headquarters of the various armies, and the field and local commanders on the other, produced extremely fruitful results. Until now, our requests have been granted every time.

### Information activity

*General situation and mood of the population*
The situation in the newly-occupied areas:
Following the military operation on the northern and southern flanks of Army Group Center, the area of Veliki-Luki on one hand, and Gomel-Chernigov on the other, matters concerning information

service could now be handled for the first time. There is a general impression that in these towns, occupied in the course of the new military operations, a systematic *evacuation* has been planned and actually carried out by the Soviet Russians to a far greater extent than before. Particularly striking is the fact that in towns like Gomel and Chernigov which formerly held quite significant numbers of Jews (for instance in Gomel: of 100,000 inhabitants, 50% were Jews), hardly a single Jew can be found. As was learned, the Jews were given preference in the evacuation of the population that started some weeks ago. This happened because Communist propaganda pointed out that all the Jews would be shot immediately upon the German occupation of the towns.

The day fixed for the evacuation of Gomel was July 6. Jews, Communist officials, as well as the skilled laborers were evacuated first. At the same time, a systematic removal of all the essential factories and their staffs was started. As far as is known, the evacuation was carried out first of all toward Moscow, a smaller part also to the East Ukraine. In some cases, the evacuation took place directly to Siberia.

The remaining population in town which had tried to avoid evacuation was usually subjected to violent oppression by the Red Army, which, as in Gomel, burned the homes of the inhabitants. The inhabitants who wanted to escape evacuation therefore fled into the surrounding villages and forests gradually to return after the towns had been occupied. Almost all valuable assets, insofar as they had not been evacuated, were looted and destroyed by the Red Army. The Bolsheviks have even removed the railway lines and sleepers in Veliki-Luki.

While Veliki-Luki was relatively only slightly damaged, the towns on the southern flank were very badly disrupted (particularly Gomel and Chernigov) by Bolshevik self-destruction as well as by German air attacks. In Chernigov, the entire center of the town with the important government buildings was allegedly destroyed by German air attacks.

## The mood of the population

. . . . . . . . . . . .

There is, of course, no change in the attitude of the population that had been against the Bolsheviks. But a certain nervousness cannot be ignored, which, at least at this moment, cannot be relieved through the obvious singular successes of the German occupation authorities, within the framework of the economic reconstruction, and by certain advances in the revitalization of commerce and trade.

On top of this, the civilian population, for instance of Smolensk, complains constantly to military headquarters about burglaries and rapes committed by members of the German army. They point out that they had been promised in various proclamations good treatment and protection.

. . . . . . . . . . . .

## Church matters

. . . . . . . . . . .

From this side, one maintains that F. [Finkovski] was not an "honest Byelorussian" but that he harbored Great Russian sympathies. One maintained also that F. had hoped to become bishop of Byelorussia. Finkovski actually displays extraordinary energy and distinguishes himself in his whole personality from other Greek Orthodox priests. He is also the only Greek Orthodox priest here who is active outside his hometown Minsk, also conducting services in neighboring towns. At the same time, he is presently the best propagandist for the German cause. His services are actually thanksgiving services for the "Führer" whose ardent admirer he appears to be [in fact and] not only outwardly. A picture of the "Führer" hangs in his room, and his many visitors seem to cross themselves in front of it. Finkovski has also declared that, according to his conviction and that of his many believers, Byelorussia should never become an independent state but that it should remain forever under German sovereignty. The desire to become bishop might, of course, be a strong motivation. In any case, Finkovski is presently the man who actually influences the population more effectively than German propaganda. We learn about his position among Greek Orthodox Byelorussians through the petition of the Greek Orthodox Church Council of Minsk to the General Commissar of Byelorussia which asks that Finkovski be appointed bishop or archbishop of Byelorussia.

The Chief of the Security Police
and Security Service

Berlin,
September 27, 1941

48 copies
(36th copy)

*Operational Situation Report USSR No. 91*

. . . . . . . . . . . .

*Political survey*

. . . . . . . . . . . .

The internment of the Jews of Bialystok into a ghetto is in effect. Preparations for internment in other towns can be considered completed. As agreed between the German mayor of Bialystok, the Einsatzkommando of the Security Police, and the Chief of the Police, a plan has been drawn up to deport the Jews of Bialystok to Pruzhana, except for 3,000 that are required as skilled workers. The deportation of 20,000 Jews is to start this month. It is intended to make of Pruzhana a totally Jewish town.

. . . . . . . . . . . .

In the period August 25 to September 9, 1941, 595 persons were executed. This number is composed of Jews, Communist officials, members of the JBV, and dangerous mentally ill persons.

The Chief of the Security Police
and Security Service

Berlin,
September 23, 1941

48 copies
(36th copy)

*Operational Situation Report USSR No. 92*

. . . . . . . . . . . .

*Einsatzgruppe B*
Location: Smolensk

. . . . . . . . . . . .

*National groups*

. . . . . . . . . . . .

*Single Operations against Partisans*
SK 7b arrested and executed a Jewish partisan in Rogachev. Three Communists from the same place were also found to be partisans and arsonists, and were liquidated. The villages Nosovichi and Antolovka, southeast of Gomel, were also searched for partisans.

A group of 37 male persons who were arrested in Bolshevik near Minsk were treated as partisans by EK 8 since they extracted food from the population. Two Russian women from Vishniovka near Minsk were executed because they had willingly extended every possible help for an extended period of time to a group of partisans who had killed an SS man on July 28, 1941, in the forest near Vishniovka.

In the area north of Borisov, a pacification operation was carried out by a platoon of EK 8 with the support of the Army.

*Operations against officials, agents, saboteurs, and Jews*

The former chairman of the district council of the district

"Stalinski" in Smolensk, Georgi Belov (not Benov), born on August 16, 1898, in Anat-Kassy, was arrested in his apartment. Belov had been excluded from the KP(B) [Byelorussian SSR] and arrested by the Soviets on July 5, 1941. He was accused of not having mobilized the population of Smolensk and instead demobilizing them [encouraged Byelorussian nationalistic feelings], and of having committed acts of sabotage and demonstrating his hostility against the people. As a result of those charges, at a session of the Court Martial, he was condemned to death by shooting on July 8, 1941, and was imprisoned pending execution. The sentence was not carried out as Belov was freed and discharged by the German Army. During his interrogation Belov appeared open and talkative and gave information to the best of his knowledge on all pertinent questions. Thus 132 leading Bolshevik officials of Smolensk became known and whose whereabouts are at present being investigated. Since Belov made a good impression at the interrogation and seemed to have seriously broken with the ideology of Bolshevism, he was set free and at his own request made a confidential agent.

Repeated complaints had been voiced alleging that the Jews in Monastirshchina and Khoslavichi had shown an impudent and provocative attitude. A Kommando of the Vorkommando caused all Jews in these villages to be marked [identified with a Jewish star or yellow badge], transferred into a ghetto, forced to work and registered by name. It also shot the existing Jewish Council and another 20 Jews.

Sonderkommando 7 arrested 21 Jewish economic saboteurs and looters and subjected them to special treatment. A search for all Jewish economic saboteurs and looters was carried out in Zhlobin by a detachment of the same Kommando.

The mayor accused the Jews especially of continually sabotaging his measures. Two Jews were caught while they beat up a Russian family and drove them from a house in order to install themselves and their families.

The persons described above and 31 more Jewish saboteurs, arsonists, and looters were apprehended and treated according to orders.

The looted goods found with the Jews were distributed on the spot to the needy population.

In the course of operating in Zhlobin, it was observed that the German Army had employed Jews for board and wages, whereas the Russian part of the population is still unemployed and suffers great want. These measures can very easily be interpreted as preferential treatment of the Jews. A change was effected through contacts with the local Army agencies.

In Gomel, it was possible to apprehend another ten Jews who were suspected of having carried out acts of sabotage and of having been active as partisans. A Communist was also apprehended, who, during the evacuation of the town, had driven the occupants out of their houses with a pistol in his hand. He was shot.

In Novozybkov, an elderly Jew and a former NKVD militia man who had maintained constant communications with and had transmitted information to the partisans were treated in accordance with orders.

A secret agent of the NKVD who happened to have returned to the town was taken prisoner by surprise and liquidated.

Not far from Novozybkov, twenty unarmed Red soldiers in uniform and one officer were taken prisoner without resistance. They explained that they were tired of the fighting. They were handed over to the garrison commander.

In Slyka, 27 Jewish terrorists were apprehended and executed. In Klimov, 27 Jewish Bolshevik agents and terrorists and a local leading official were apprehended and subjected to special treatment.

In Minsk, ten persons were shot for trying to intimidate the population by announcing that the Bolsheviks were about to return and by carrying out anti-German propaganda.

Eleven Asiatics and two Jews found by members of the Army at a bridge under suspicious circumstances were executed as highly suspect of having planned acts of sabotage. A further number of Party officials, convinced Communists, former NKVD agents, and Jews were shot by Einsatzkommando 8.

In Lohoysk, nine males were liquidated by the Einsatzkommando, eight of them because they had carried out Communist propaganda among the population until recently.

Moreover, a half-Jewish person, a Party member of many years' standing, was transferred from the prisoner-of-war camp to Minsk. He had been a Politruk and a political unit commander in the Red Army. He was liquidated together with three other Jews who had been active in the NKVD at the time of the Bolshevik regime. He had refused to wear the identification marks prescribed for Jews.

A Jewess was shot in Minsk. She had worked as an interpreter in the German Field Command Headquarters, passing herself off as a Pole in order to get this job. After a thorough interrogation, she stated that she had repeated sexual intercourse with a non-commissioned officer of the Field Command Headquarters, unknown by name, and a non-commissioned officer of the Luftwaffe. She had also told them that she was Polish.

In the district town Ivinits, it was necessary to carry out a special action against the Jewish population as only a small number wore the prescribed identification patch. Besides this, they did not surrender looted goods in spite of repeated public proclamations, and supported partisan groups in every way. In carrying out this measure, a part of the looted goods were procured. Fifty male Jews were shot for not observing German decrees and for terrorizing the Byelorussian population.

In Bobruisk, a number of Jewish adherents of the Communist Party were apprehended. Among them was a Jewish non-commissioned officer of the medical corps. He, according to his own confession, poisoned two wounded German officers and four wounded German soldiers.

In addition, the head of a collective farm in the vicinity of Bobruisk was arrested because he had intentionally disorganized production by ordering the farmers to cease their work, and by giving instructions to hide the harvested products in the forests.

A total of 600 persons were arrested in Bobruisk and vicinity by a detachment of Einsatzkommando 8. Out of these, 407 persons were liquidated. The executed comprised in addition to the above mentioned, Jews and elements who had shown open resistance against orders issued by German occupation authorities, or had openly incited to acts of sabotage.

In Borisov, 176 more Jews were liquidated because they opposed the establishment of the ghetto.

A large-scale anti-Jewish action was carried out in the village of Lahoysk. In the course of this action, 920 Jews were executed with the support of a unit of the SS Division "Reich." The village may now be described as "free of Jews."

In Mogilev, a Soviet-Russian prisoner-of-war, Nikolai Gusev, was turned in by the Army. This prisoner had been the assistant to the head of the Third Department of the Staff of Division 110 (Riflemen). The interrogation by the 2nd Army HQ revealed his activity and the tasks of the Soviet-Russian troop commissars in general as well as of their organizational duties.

While searching a village for arms, Einsatzkommando 9 arrested a Bolshevik teacher who was found to have concealed a loaded revolver. At the same time a military radio receiver set was found in a hayloft. He claimèd to have found the set near Polotsk. The set is no longer serviceable.

. . . . . . . . . . . .

Furthermore, three more Jews were shot for not moving into the ghetto, i.e. for concealing their Jewish racial origin when applying for a pass.

In the Nevel ghetto which was set up approximately 3 km outside the city and which comprised several wooden houses, scabies broke out according to the diagnosis of a German doctor. In order to prevent further contagion, 640 Jews were liquidated and the houses burned down.

In Janovichi, approximately 15 km south of Surash, a contagious disease accompanied by fever had also broken out. The doctor, the Elder of the Jews, and the mayor urgently requested help. Since it was feared that the disease would spread to the city and to the rural population, the inmates of the ghetto, totaling 1,025 Jews, were subjected to special treatment. This operation was carried out solely by a commander and 12 men.

## Screening operation of the ghetto in Minsk

According to reports received, the telephone cables of the German Army were repeatedly cut in the ghetto in Minsk.

In addition, the Jewish inhabitants started a whispering campaign of a rumor that the Red troops would soon return to Minsk.

Finally, members of the civil police forces had repeatedly been threatened with violence and had even been shot at in the ghetto, although they were engaged in the legitimate performance of their duties there. The perpetrators could not be seized. In numerous cases, Jews were also caught not wearing the prescribed badge.

Furthermore, refusals to work on the part of the Jews were an everyday occurrence. In order to check the aggressive behavior of the Jewish population, the severest defense measures had to be taken.

In combination with the order police and with the support of the field police, a major operation was carried out in the ghetto. Close to 2,500 Jews, among them a number of women, were arrested. Out of these, in the course of three days, a total of 2,278 persons were executed. The executed were comprised exclusively of saboteurs and Jewish activists. Among them were many who did not wear the prescribed badge on their clothing.

## Measures against criminals and looters

EK 8 shot eleven male persons who roamed and looted in the environs of Minsk and could not identify themselves.

This concerns exclusively Jews, Tartars and Kalmucks.

Further, 13 male and ten female Gypsies were delivered by the local Kommandatur Lepel, district of Minsk, and given special treatment for having terrorized the population of the countryside and committed numerous thefts.

Five Russians who had previously been repeatedly convicted by the Soviet authorities banded together in the town district of Minsk in order to steal and loot. They were caught red-handed and shot.

A Russian who mastered the German language pretended to be a German police official and demanded under threats and acts of violence that persons who passed by identify themselves. He was also given special treatment.

Various other persons who had attacked people for food and other usable objects were executed.

EK 9 liquidated a Russian who stole and slaughtered a head of cattle in a kolkhoz. Clothing was also found in his possession (from looting and thefts) which was secured.

As was made known in our last report, the population reacted in a gratifying way to an appeal in Vitebsk that they should hand over objects that were plundered. They satisfactorily delivered the looted objects, first of all usable objects. This is doubtless proof of the recognition by the Russian population of the authority of the German offices.

The Teilkommando Surash of EK 9 arrested grenadier Welzel of the 28th Infantry Regiment. He had defected from his troop near Vitebsk on July 12, 1941, and settled down in the village Brigitpolie near Surash. K. declared in the course of his interrogation that he wanted to settle in Russia as a farmer. He was handed over to the GFP who passed him on to the relevant military law court.

## Search of civilian prisoner camps

2,000 more civil prisoners were examined in the civilian prisoner camp Minsk during the period of this report. Most of the persons were recognized as fit for construction work. Altogether 377 men were handed over and shot. All the executed persons were inferior elements whose presence here could not be advocated.

## Confiscated material

Army Group Center has handed over various files and documents mostly with military political content that were found in the church of Staroslup. This material mainly concerns the activity of the political organs of a military unit.

During a search in the present army railway office in Minsk by EK 8, one could find, hidden under old files, information on all of the GPU, respectively NKVD agents that had been employed by the Byelorussian government. The list is being utilized.

## Confiscated money

Einsatzkommando 8 has confiscated in the period of the report 111,962 more rubles. Also 43 gold rubles were cashed in. The sum total of Russian paper-money that was secured by EK 8 so far amounts to 1,739,052 rubles. EK 9 has confiscated 3,639 more rubles.

## Organizational measures

In all the places that were recently occupied by the Sonderkommando and Einsatzgruppen during the period of the report, police service was immediately installed and Jewish ghettos established. Also, Jewish Councils were appointed in all the larger localities that are to carry out the orders issued by German offices. Even if the Russian police service does not at first meet the expectations concerning personal dedication, poise, and character, nevertheless, through cooperation with the police and a regular exchange of ideas, the commanders could offer valuable suggestions and receive valuable information.

## Balance of liquidations

The sum total of the liquidations is, according to the state of affairs on September 13, 1941:

a) Stab and VKM (advanced commando) .............. 312
b) SK 7a ........................................ 1,011
c) SK 7b ........................................ 1,153
d) EK 8 ........................................11,354
e) EK 9 ........................................ 9,974
   Total ......................................23,504

The Chief of the Security Police
and Security Service

Berlin,
September 25, 1941

48 copies
(36th copy)

## Operational Situation Report USSR No. 94

\* \* \*

*Einsatzgruppe A*
Location: Kikerino

### I. Partisans

. . . . . . . . . . . .

Within the area of the civil administration, Einsatzkommandos 2 and 3 found at various localities an intensified propaganda activity of the Jewish population for the Bolshevik cause. Wherever such propaganda activity appears, the severest measures are taken and as far as possible the localities are entirely purged of Jews. As this Jewish propaganda activity has been particularly intensive in Lithuania, the number of persons liquidated within the area of Einsatzkommando 3 has increased to approximately 75,000.

For specific tasks, special Kommandos had to be sent repeatedly into the rural districts and were assigned to certain localities for several days. Thus, for example, one Kommando had to be sent to Plyusa as reports about large-scale looting were received from there. 47 persons were arrested and questioned. Seven persons were shot for looting, two more were publicly escorted through the streets of the locality, while the inhabitants were told that these persons had been looting food to the detriment of the population. Another Sonderkommando had to be sent to Mugotovo where 87 insane persons armed themselves and roamed the countryside looting. It was ascertained that these inmates were incited by eleven Communists,

-156-

part of whom presumably belonged to a partisan group. The eleven agitators, among them six Jews, and the insane were liquidated.

In the vicinity of the headquarters of Group Staff Posye, Kikerino, and Meshno, the whole male population was regularly screened immediately on arrival of the units. This repeatedly resulted in the arrest of partisans, Jewish and Communist agitators, looters, etc. Since the locations of the Einsatzgruppe are always near the headquarters of Armored Group IV, appreciation for this systematic and successful screening of the neighboring area was repeatedly voiced by Armored Group IV.

## II. The Jewish problem in Ostland

The first actions against the Jews in the Reichskommissariat Ostland (besides in the capacity of the administrative police) were undertaken by the Security Police. After the civil administration had taken over, the Einsatzkommandos transferred all anti-Jewish actions in the administrative police field, whether completed or only initiated, to the civil administration agencies. The establishment of ghettos has already begun everywhere and is being continued by the civil administration. Only in Vilnius, which was taken over by Einsatzgruppe A at a later date, preparations were not as yet made for the confinement in a ghetto of the 60,000 Jews living there. Einsatzkommando 3 now has suggested the establishment of a ghetto and will at the same time initiate the necessary pacification actions against the political activity of the Jews.

In Riga, the so-called Moscow quarter of the town was designated as a ghetto even before the civil administration took over and a council of Jewish elders had been appointed. The removal of the Jews into the ghetto is being continued.

The Jews in the cities are being employed by all German agencies as unpaid manpower. Difficulties with employing agencies are everyday occurrences. If and when they occur the Security Police must take steps against Jewish workers. Economic agencies have repeatedly filed applications for exempting Jews from the obligation to wear the Star of David and to authorize them to patronize public inns. This concerns mostly Jews who are designated as key personnel for certain economic enterprises. Such efforts are, of course, suppressed by the agencies of the Security Police.

In the old Soviet-Russian territory, Jews were found only sporadically, even in the cities. Most of the Jews who had been living there had fled. At present, and since the old Soviet-Russian territories have been occupied, the Wehrmacht itself usually issues orders for the marking of Jews. Thus the Commander-in-Chief of the 18th Army has ordered, for example, that Jews must be distinguished by white armbands with the Star of David to be worn on both arms.

## III.

*Einsatzgruppe C*

### *Measures taken and observations made by the Security Police*

During the preparation period for the military offensive now underway [the attack on Moscow], the operations of the Einsatzkommandos were continued intensively and on a broad basis.

In the southern region of the operational area, because of the sparseness of the Jewish population, the main effort had to be directed toward individual investigations and search actions. However, particularly in the region of Zhitomir and Berdichev, there was an opportunity for actions on a larger scale.

This also explains the difference in the number of executions reported by the individual Kommandos.

Sonderkommando 4a has now surpassed the number of 15,000 executions. Einsatzkommando 5, for the period August 31-September 6, 1941, reports the liquidation of 90 political officials, 72 saboteurs and looters, and 161 Jews. Sonderkommando 4b, in the period September 6-12, 1941, shot 13 political officials and 290 Jews, primarily of the intelligentsia, whereas Einsatzkommando 6, in the period September 1-13, 1941, executed 60 persons. Group Staff was able to liquidate during the last days four political officials and informers of the NKVD, six asocial elements (Gypsies), and 55 Jews. The units of the Higher SS and Police Chiefs, during the month of August, shot a total of 44,125 persons, mostly Jews.

. . . . . . . . . . . .

As already mentioned, the procedure against the Jews is necessarily different in the individual sectors, according to the density of their settlement. Especially in the northern sector of Einsatzgruppe C, a great many Jewish refugees have returned to the villages, and now present a heavy burden with respect to the food situation. The population neither houses nor feeds them. They live partly in caves, partly in overcrowded old huts. The danger of epidemics has thus increased considerably. For that reason alone, a thorough clean-up of the respective places became necessary.

The insolence of the Jews has not diminished. Apart from the fact that on the occasion of raids they like to pass themselves off as Russians, Ukrainians, and even ethnic Germans, they are often in the possession of passports which, though showing their names correctly, give a false nationality. Concealment of their Jewish descent has been made easier for them by the russification of their names which took place to an ever-accelerating pace during the past years.

At Kirovograd, it became known that Jews tried to obtain all of the registry office's identity papers with a false nationality. Several Jews, on the basis of forged papers, even succeeded in obtaining various posts with the administration. They also performed such acts of "rebaptism" through a system of patronage as had been the old custom.[1] The Ukrainian population, for fear of revenge by the Jews, often does not dare to report this situation to the authorities. The most severe measures are taken here in dealing with such cases.

Difficulties have arisen because Jews are often the only skilled workers in certain trades. Thus the only harness-makers and the only good tailors in Novo-Ukrainka are Jews. At other places also, only Jews can be employed for carpentry and locksmith work. The cause of this shortage of skilled workers is to a large extent to be found in the unlimited compulsory evacuation of skilled Ukrainians by the Soviets. In order not to endanger reconstruction as well as repair work for the benefit of passing military units, it has become necessary to exclude, provisionally, from execution, the older Jewish skilled workers especially.

---

1. i.e., bribing the local priest to declare a Jew a bona fide born Christian.

The Chief of the Security Police            Berlin,
and Security Service             September 26, 1941

48 copies
(36th copy)

## Operational Situation Report USSR No. 95

*Einsatzgruppe A*
Location: Kikerino

. . . . . . . . . . . .

### Situation in Estonia

The mood of the population has improved considerably. The circles that had until now played with the idea of a free Estonian state or of a Finnish-Estonian Union have given up this idea and are now resigned to the facts. It has become clear in general that the future of the Estonian people is to be envisaged only in the closest connection with the Great German Reich. In general, there is not much concern as to the structure and form. Circles of the intelligentsia are, in many cases, of the opinion that it will be in the form of a protectorate.

. . . . . . . . . . . .

A Jewish question in the German sense did not exist until the Soviet occupation. The year under the Soviet regime has caused a deep change here. The realization of the role played by the Jews, particularly in the NKVD, has utterly shattered the slogan about equality of the Jews in a democratic Estonia and has turned into bitter hatred. The Estonian people, not merely in Reval but in the whole country, have adopted an attitude towards Judaism that encompasses all the preconditions for an involvement in the final solution of the Jewish question. The Jewish population in Reval numbered only 2,000. The Jews that had come into the country together with the Soviets had, without exception, also fled together with them.

\* \* \*

. . . . . . . . . . .

*Einsatzgruppe D*
Location: Nikolayev
Two areas of activity were in the foreground:
1) To free the area where work goes on of Jews, Communists, and groups of partisans.
To protect and care for ethnic German settlements.
1) Territories of Kommandos have been cleared of Jews: 8890 Jews and Communists were executed from August 19 to September 15. Sum total: 13,315 at this time. The Jewish question is being solved in Nikolayev and Kherson. About 5,000 Jews were involved. There are hardly any leading Communists. They have left, almost without exception, together with the Soviets, except for some scattered party officials. Eight NKVD officials were rendered harmless in Ananyev and 14 in Nikolayev. Searches of NKVD buildings and other buildings have yielded little results. Material was either evacuated or destroyed. Some printed material that had been found in half-packed suitcases was secured. Some military newspapers (Naval) have been transferred by the counter-intelligence to headquarters. . . . Upon closer examination, many indications about terrorist organizations have turned out to be unfounded. Jewish partisan groups were done away with in Voletsovulovo. Inquiries confirmed that some of the released prisoners of war had been active in propaganda in that place and had distributed Communist posters. Inquiries continue.

. . . . . . . . . . .

An Einsatzkommando was installed in the area of Beresander and in the area of Dubosari to protect and care for ethnic German settlements.
The Einsatzkommando posted outside of Odessa took over the protection of ethnic Germans in that area.

. . . . . . . . . . .

Reconstruction work

. . . . . . . . . . .

c) Freeing the settlements of Jews and Communist elements.
d) Influencing the Rumanian administration with the aid of self-administration of German communities.

e) [Ethnic German] farmers, physicians, teachers etc. who had lived dispersed in the country were gathered into German communities.

f) Economic security, distribution of loot, cattle and harvest machines for the population, houses and possessions of Jews were put at their disposal, etc.

The Chief of the Security Police
and Security Service

Berlin,
September 26, 1941

48 copies
(36th copy)

## Operational Situation Report USSR No. 96

*Einsatzgruppe A*

*Executions*

In the period from August 30 to September 5, the following were executed:

in Riga [Latvia] ............................... 186 persons
in the area of the field office Siauliai [Lithuania] ... 44     "
in the area of the field office Liepaja [Latvia] ...... 38     "
in other areas ................................. 191     "
sum total: .................................... 459     "

Included among those executed were 237 mentally ill Jews from the mental institutions in Riga and Liepaja.

The present total [of executed] in Keinsatzkommando 2 territory is now 29,246 persons.

. . . . . . . . . . . .

## Quartering in Riga prisons

In the Riga prisons there are at present 3,777 persons including:
3,452 Communists
195 Jews
103 criminals.

The Chief of the Security Police
and Security Service

Berlin,
September 28, 1941

48 copies
(36th copy)

*Operational Situation Report USSR No. 97*

. . . . . . . . . . . .

*Einsatzgruppe C*
Location: Kiev

Vorkommando 4a [operates] directly with the combat troops in Kiev since September 19. Einsatzgruppe HQ came up on September 24. Office Building NKVD, October 24th street, assigned and commandeered as seat of Einsatzgruppe HQ. Building evacuated this morning to move into emergency quarters in the one-time Tsar's castle. Town almost destroyed upon entry of troops. Numerous barricades and tank traps put up in main street. In addition, other strong defensive installations in the town area. On September 20, the citadel blew up and the Artillery Commander and his chief of staff were killed. On September 24, violent explosions in the quarters of the Feldkommandatur; the ensuing fire has not yet been extinguished. Fire in the center of the town. Very valuable buildings destroyed. So far, fire-fighting practically without any effect. Demolitions by blasting being carried out to bring the fire under control. Fire in the immediate neighborhood of this office. Had to be evacuated for this reason. Considerable damage done in and around the building by blasting. Blasts continuing. Also, fire breaking out. Up to now, 670 mines detected in buildings, according to a mine-laying plan which was discovered: all public buildings and squares are mined, among them, it is alleged, also the building assigned to this office for future use. Building being searched most assiduously. In the course of this search, 60 Molotov cocktails of explosives were detected and removed. In the Lenin Museum, 70 hundredweights[1] of dynamite dis-

1. 8,000 lbs.

-164-

covered which were to be touched off by wireless. It was repeatedly observed that fires broke out the moment buildings were taken over. As has been proved, Jews played a pre-eminent part. Allegedly 150,000 Jews living here. Verification of these statements has not been possible yet. 1,600 arrests in the course of the first action, measures being evolved to check the entire Jewish population. Execution of at least 50,000 Jews planned. German Army welcomes measures and demands drastic procedure. Garrison commander advocates public execution of 20 Jews. A larger number of NKVD officials, political commissars, partisan leaders and partisans arrested. According to reliable information, demolition battalion of the NKVD and considerable number of NKVD men in Kiev. This morning, enemy plots detected. Contact established with German Army and authorities. Participated pre-eminently in setting up town administration. Informants posted. Vorkommando of the Higher SS and Police Leaders arrived. Detailed reports to follow.

The Chief of the Security Police  Berlin,
and Security Service  October 1, 1941

48 copies
(36th copy)

## Operational Situation Report USSR No. 100

. . . . . . . . . . . .

*Einsatzgruppe D*
Location: Nikolayev

### Situation in the District of Ananyev

*General*

The situation in Ananyev is characterized at this time by the transfer of the administration to Rumanians. This fact is generally regretted by the population. One regards the Germans as friends who leave and the Rumanians as the enemy who enters the country. The reason for this phenomenon may be ascribed to the following:

Apart from the different behavior shown by the German and the Rumanian troops at the time of their appearance, the German soldiers soon elicited trust from the population, who very soon instinctively grasped that the war conducted by the German people is not against the peoples of the USSR but exclusively against Jewish Bolshevism. Thus, they now regard the Germans, almost without exception, as the liberators from the Bolshevik yoke.

The attitude towards the Rumanian army is quite different. The Rumanian people does not regard this war as ideological, [a war against] Bolshevism, but, as Rumanian circles admit, as a national revenge against Russia for their annexing Bessarabia and North Bucovina in the summer of 1940.[1]

---

1. Most of this territory became the Moldavian SSR; the rest was added to the Ukrainian SSR.

This conception of the war is expressed also in the attitude of the Rumanian soldiers towards the population, and is recognized by the population even if only by part of them subconsciously. In any case, the Ukrainians regard the Rumanians not at all as liberators as they regard the Germans, but as a momentarily victorious enemy. The Ukrainians and Rumanians share this point of view and thus no mutual trust is possible.

. . . . . . . . . . . .

*Economy*

. . . . . . . . . . . .

Large gaps have been formed in trade that can hardly be closed, especially in regard to reconstruction because of the flight and the extermination of the Jews. Rumanian circles point to the fact that not even a single glazier exists in Ananyev, since all the members of this trade used to be Jews. Also in the other building trades almost all the artisans, like carpenters, cabinet makers, etc., were formerly Jews. In general, the Jewish sector of this trade is estimated at 80%.

Chief of the Security Police
and Security Service

Berlin,
October 2, 1941

## *Operational Situation Report USSR No. 101*

*Einsatzgruppe C*
Location: Kiev
Sonderkommando 4a in collaboration with Einsatzgruppe HQ and
two Kommandos of police regiment South, executed 33,771 Jews in
Kiev on September 29 and 30, 1941.

*Einsatzgruppe D*
Location: Nikolayev
The Kommandos continued the liberation of the area from Jews
and Communist elements. In the period covered by the report, the
towns of Nikolayev and Kherson in particular were freed of Jews. Remaining officials there were appropriately treated. From September
16 to 30, 22,467 Jews and Communists were executed. Total number,
35,782. Investigations again show that the high Communist officials
everywhere have fled to safety. On the whole, leading partisans or
leaders of sabotage detachments have been seized.

The Chief of the Security Police
and Security Service

Berlin,
October 4, 1941

48 copies
(36th copy)

## Operational Situation Report USSR No. 103

. . . . . . . . . . . .

*Einsatzgruppe D*
Location: Nikolayev
*Volksdeutsche settlements between Bug and Dniestr*

. . . . . . . . . . . .

Also otherwise, some families were very poor so that often, the more important household utensils like beds, etc. are lacking. The most desperate need was eliminated by the Einsatzgruppe D by placing at their disposal flats or furniture of Jews. Children's beds and other essential objects were brought in.

The Chief of the Security Police
and Security Service

Berlin,
October 5, 1941

48 copies
(36th copy)

*Operational Situation Report USSR No. 104*

. . . . . . . . . . . .

*Einsatzkommando D*
Location: Nikolayev

. . . . . . . . . . . .

The attitude of the [ethnic] Germans of Beresany toward the Jews, for instance, is mostly indifferent. In this matter it is characteristic that the ethnic Germans did not take any measures against the remaining Jews. After the German troops marched in, they declared that Jews were harmless and not dangerous.

. . . . . . . . . . . .

The Jews had little influence in the village councils. Only in some cases, like, for example, in Rohrbach,[1] where a Jew had been the chairman of a collective farm, he influenced the life in the village, [in particular] education. A Jewish activist was director of the Ukrainian school in Waterloo. In all the other settlements, Jews were merely grocers and tradesmen and had no political power. According to the information provided by the ethnic Germans, the Jews were informants of the NKVD.

---

1. The German invaders promoted a policy of German colonization by means of settling ethnic Germans in the Soviet Union. The (new) settlements were given German and non-Slavic names.

Berlin,
October 7, 1941

48 copies
(36th copy)

## Operational Situation Report USSR No. 106

. . . . . . . . . . .

*Einsatzgruppe B*
Location: Smolensk

. . . . . . . . . . .

## Mood and general conduct of the population

. . . . . . . . . . .

It can be observed that, just as before, the population in the area of our activities abstains from any self-defense action against the Jews. True, the population reports uniformly about the Jewish terror against them during Soviet rule. They also complain to the German offices about new attacks from the side of the Jews (like unauthorized return from the ghetto to their previous homes, or hostile remarks against the Germans made by the Jews). However, in spite of our energetic attempts, they are not ready for any action against the Jews. The decisive reason here seems to be the fear of Jewish revenge in case of a return of the Reds. Even very active elements who help us find Jewish Communists and members of the intelligentsia and show themselves very efficient in their cooperation prefer to remain invisible and anonymous in the decisive moments.

Reports on a stable, good mood in the population can be found only in those areas where economic life is somewhat normal, as, for instance, in the town Klintsy that has not been destroyed at all; also in Vitebsk.

. . . . . . . . . . .

*Einsatzgruppe C*
Location: Kiev

## *I. Kiev*

. . . . . . . . . . . .

As a result of [war] destruction, especially of houses, and the forced order to evacuate endangered streets, about 23,000 persons became homeless and were forced to spend the first days of the occupation in the open. They accepted this inconvenience quietly and did not cause panic.

Meanwhile, locked and empty apartments, insofar as they had not been burned and damaged, were put at the disposal of the population. A corresponding number of apartments have also become available through the liquidation, thus far around 36,000 Jews on September 29 and 30, 1941. The housing of the homeless is assured and has also been taken care of in the meantime.

The population of Kiev before the start of the war numbered around 850,000. For the time being, no exact indication concerning its national composition can be given. The number of Jews is said to have been about 300,000. The total number of ethnic Germans living in Kiev is presently being counted by a Kommando. The final results will be available in ten days. The temporary appointed city administration has begun immediately to register all the inhabitants of Kiev. As a first measure, all males aged 15-60 must report.

Except for a small part, the non-Jewish population, as far as can now be established, seems to welcome the German Army, or at least to display loyal behavior. During the first days of the occupation, serious unrest could be detected within the population because of rumors that the German Army was leaving the city. These rumors were successfully squelched with proper official announcements. The population cooperates very readily by furnishing information on explosives or secret membership in the NKVD, the Party and the Red Army. Unlike the first days, one could note that this information was 90% correct. The reason for this is that the city inhabitants are less frightened than is the rural population, since they do not fear the possibility of a return of the Bolsheviks. The supply situation in Kiev is extremely poor. There are no food stocks and these must be provided. A staff in charge of economic affairs was created by the appointed city administration. Its main task was, for the time being, the supplying of the most vital food. This economic staff supplied the required transportation and, thus, the most urgent needs could be met by bringing in supplies from the nearby collective farms.

## *II. Executions and other measures*

The population was extremely infuriated against the Jews because of their preferential economical status under Soviet rule. It could also be proved that the Jews had participated in arson. The population expected adequate reprisals from the Germans. For this purpose, in agreement with the city military command, all the Jews of Kiev were ordered to appear at a certain place on Monday, September 29, by 6 o'clock. This order was publicized by posters all over the town by members of the newly organized Ukrainian militia. At the same time, oral information was passed that all the Jews of Kiev would be moved to another place. In cooperation with the HQ of EGC and two Kommandos of the police regiment South, Sonderkommando 4a executed 33,771 Jews on September 29 and 30.[1] Gold and valuables, linen, and clothing were secured. Part of it was given to the NSV (National-Sozialistische Versorgung = Nazi Welfare) for the ethnic Germans, and part to the appointed city administration for distribution among the needy population. The action was carried out smoothly and no incidents occurred. The population agreed with the plan to move the Jews to another place. That they were actually liquidated has hardly been made known. However, according to the experience gained so far, this would not meet with any opposition. The army has also approved the measures taken. The Jews that have not yet been caught or who will return will be treated accordingly. At the same time, a number of NKVD men and commissars were arrested and finished off.

The Bandera members lost power with the arrests made by the Kommandos. Their activity was restricted to the distribution of leaflets and posters. Three arrests were made; more are pending.

The HQ of EGC as well as Sonderkommando 4a and Einsatzkommando 5, both stationed in Kiev, have made connections with the proper offices. Constant cooperation with these offices was achieved, and imminent problems are discussed daily. Because of the

---

1. This took place in the ravine of Babi Yar outside Kiev.

vast amounts of information, each time [with each action] detailed operation reports must be submitted about the activity of the Einsatzkommandos.

## III. Zhitomir, actions against the Jews

The Militia headquarters, according to a suggestion of Sonderkommando 4a, arranged a temporary, local concentration of the Jews in Zhitomir. This resulted in a quieter atmosphere, for example, in the markets, etc. At the same time, obstinate rumors diminished and it seemed that together with the concentration of the Jews, the Communists, too, lost much ground. However, it became obvious after a few days that concentration of the Jews without building a ghetto did not suffice, and that the old difficulties emerged again after a short while. Complaints about the impertinence of the Jews in their various places of work stemmed from several quarters. It was noted that strong propaganda activity among the Ukrainians, claiming that the Red Army would return very soon into the areas that had been taken away from them, had their origin in the Jewish quarter. The local militia was shot at, at night, and even in daytime from an ambush. It was also established that Jews exchanged their belongings for money in order to move into the Western Ukraine where a civil administration already exists.

All these phenomena could be observed. However, it was possible to get hold of the involved Jews only in the rarest cases, as they had sufficient opportunities to evade arrest. Therefore, a conference was called together with military H.Q. on September 10, 1941. The resulting decision was the final and radical liquidation of the Jews of Zhitomir, since all the warnings [threats] and special measures [punishments] had not led to any perceptible change.

On September 19, 1941, from 4 o'clock [a.m.], the Jewish quarter was emptied after having been surrounded and closed the previous evening by 60 members of the Ukrainian militia. The transport [deportation] was accomplished in 12 trucks, part of which had been supplied by military headquarters and part by the city administration of Zhitomir. After the transport had been carried out and the necessary preparations made with the help of 150 prisoners, 3,145 Jews were registered and shot.

About 25-30 tons of linen, clothing, shoes, dishes, etc. that had been confiscated in the course of the action were handed over to the officials of the NSV in Zhitomir for distribution. Valuables and money were conveyed to the Sonderkommando 4a.

The Chief of the Security Police
and Security Service

Berlin,
October 8, 1941

<u>50 copies</u>
(36th copy)

*Operational Situation Report USSR No. 107*

. . . . . . . . . . . .

*Einsatzgruppe B*
Location: Smolensk

. . . . . . . . . . . .

Oral Bolshevik-oriented propaganda continues as before. It is obviously systematically carried out by enemy agents and partisans as well as by the Jewish population. Together with the continually growing rumors and, due to the lack of effective counter-propaganda, this oral propaganda has the effects desired by the Bolsheviks.

*Einsatzgruppe D*
Location: Nikolayev
A small Vorkommando had entered Kherson on August 20, 1941, together with the army, and reported that the town was free of enemies. Consequently, a Kommando consisting of two officers and 13 men was sent to Kherson on August 22, 1941, in order to accomplish the task of Sonderkommando 11a. After the first two days, initial steps were taken towards the solution of the Jewish question, the protection of the ethnic Germans, and the fight against Bolshevism. Then, a change occurred in the situation in this town of some 100,000 inhabitants. Artillery fire began on August 24, 1941, at about 15 o'clock, and lasted, with some interruptions, until September 6, 1941, reaching on some days extraordinary force. Because of that situation, a number of German officers left Kherson again.

. . . . . . . . . . . .

The work of the Kommando from August 22 to September 9, 1941, reveals the following picture:

I. The first part of the Jewish question was solved. On August 23, 1941, the Jews were ordered by a summons to carry the Jewish star and to register. The registration was carried out on the instructions of the Kommando and by the Council of Elders appointed for the purpose. These measures of marking and registering the Jews made it easier to guard them in a few streets where they were concentrated and confined. As a result of the registration, the Wehrmacht demands for Jewish labor could be fulfilled from the second day on. Jewish labor groups of all kinds were made available daily, the strength of which started at 120 and rose, toward the end, to a thousand persons.

. . . . . . . . . . . .

III. An Ukrainian self-defense unit was organized to assist in the keeping of peace and order, to safeguard the important plants and stores, and to enable the extension of our activities. The Kommando found in Kherson a so-called "Ukrainian Security Service" which was provided with certificates given by the city Kommandatur.

IV. The Kommando performed the following executions: 400 Jews and 10 Jewesses were shot as reprisals for acts of sabotage and passing of information. 11 political criminals (GPU-Chief Kaminski, a prison director, a Commissar, and three partisans, etc.) were executed. One partisan leader whom the Kommando itself had taken, was hanged publicly. Further, 17 Jews were shot for not wearing the Jewish star.

Chief of the Security Police
and Security Service

Berlin,
October 9, 1941

50 copies
(36th copy)

## Operational Situation Report USSR No. 108

*Einsatzgruppe B*
Location: Smolensk

### Police activity

1) *General Situation*

In general, the situation at the front is unchanged, except for the southern part of the area of Einsatzgruppe B. This permitted, at the time of this report, the conduct once more of intensive searches in many areas and localities. General organizational measures were also continued, like the introduction of the Order Service,[1] marking of the Jews, registration, putting up ghettos, planting of informants, and calling upon the population to cooperate with the police. We are also concerned with the fight against partisans and agitators who were hostile toward the Germans. The actions that were required were difficult because of the streets and roads that had turned into mire due to the bad and wet weather.

. . . . . . . . . . . .

In any case, the endeavors and the attempts that were made to convert the partisan movement into a real popular movement to be used against German operations and plans have failed. This is without a doubt due to the enthusiasm of the German Security Police and the SD, the alertness of the Army, and the systematic approach to these problems on the part of the Army and the Security Force. This is by no means to belittle the danger of the partisan movement. First of

---

1. Ordnungsdienst — Police.

all, attention will have to be paid to the effect of partisan activity on the feelings of the population. Partisans, Jews, and other Communists constantly try to intimidate the friendly population through Bolshevik pamphlets or whispering campaigns. They threaten that, as soon as the Reds return, they will take revenge on everyone who has rendered the smallest service to the Germans. Troop movements away from the front line cause the population to worry and to ask the German offices if they must really count on a return of the Red Regime.

## 2. Fight against the Partisans

The Vorkommando was urgently called to Khoslavichi by the local commander, since partisans were said to have invaded the place. After having shot a German soldier, the partisans retreated when the Kommando arrived. Confidential information showed that several hundred partisans had committed their evil deeds in the localities and forests around Khoslavichi. Because of extremely bad road conditions, only two smaller places could be searched. In each of them two partisans were caught and liquidated.

SK 7a has repeatedly reported that a large number of partisans have carried out plunderous attacks from the dense forests south of Demidov. They caused considerable anxiety in the area as well as endangering the roads. According to reliable reports, one had to reckon with 800 to 2,000 partisans. The 9th Army headquarters supplied two divisions for a thorough search of the area. Each male between the ages of 15 and 55 was sent to the Demidov prison camp for an interrogation. The examination was conducted during several fire fights with the partisans. They resulted in the arrest of 493 people; 438, most of them kolkhoz farmers free of suspicion, were released. 72 former Red Army members who lived in the area of the action, with no proven connection to the partisans, were brought into the prisoner-of-war camp. SK 7a uncovered 183 partisans and Communists. Interrogations revealed that they had repeatedly carried out attacks on members of the German Army. Five partisans admitted killing a total of 14 German soldiers. One German soldier was strangled as he fetched eggs; the others were shot. They had also thrown hand grenades into trucks and cars.

In response, several kolkhoz farmers that had supported the partisans, even if only under duress, and five partisans who murdered

14 German soldiers were hanged in the market-place in the presence of about 400 Kolkhozniki farmers. The other partisans were shot.

The Sk 7a, in cooperation with a unit of the 9th Army headquarters, conducted, on different days, actions against the partisan groups that were known in the area of Trosty, Shitiki, Shlyki, Novi-Masyolok, Kupioly, Yanki, and Buly, some 20 km northwest of Velish. Also, the areas of Osinovka, Doroshkino, Prudok, Burshchina and Shility, about 20 km north of Velish, were thoroughly combed. In these actions, a total of 27 partisans were arrested and liquidated.

After careful investigations, eight partisans were taken by surprise as they were having their supper in the village of Mikhailovo. They were arrested and hanged together on the following morning in the place that was particularly infested with partisans.

Kommando 7b stated that "sabotage units" were posted prior to the occupation of Koseletz. Parts of these units were still in the surroundings of Koseletz at the time of the police activities. Systematically conducted searches led to the arrest of five persons belonging to these units according to concurrent testimonies.

. . . . . . . . . . . .

## Actions against functionaries, agents, saboteurs and Jews

. . . . . . . . . . . .

In Khoslavichi, the Jews living in the ghetto there, according to reports of the Russian population, tried to create panic by spreading false rumors to the effect that the Bolsheviks were supposed to be advancing. Furthermore, they threatened to take revenge after the return of the Bolsheviks. Thereupon, the Vorkommando sent a Kommando and liquidated 114 Jews.

. . . . . . . . . . . .

SK 7a also reports of juvenile Communists who were liquidated. They intended to blow up a railway bridge nearing completion. Explosives had already been supplied and were at hand.

In Velikye Luki a group of juveniles intending to blow up a railway bridge was also rendered harmless. The ringleader of the group had persuaded the others to participate.

Sonderkommando 7a executed a local leading Bolshevik official and 21 Jewish plunderers and terrorists in Gorodnia. In Klintsy, 83 Jewish terrorists and three leading Party officials were likewise liquidated. At another check, three Communist officials, one Politruk, and 82 Jewish terrorists were dealt with according to orders.

In Chernigov, 19 Jews who were under suspicion of having either been Communists or of having committed arson were given special treatment. During the search operations in Beresna, east of Chernigov, eight Jews who had committed Bolshevik acts, that is to say, had sabotaged the regulations of the German authorities, were seized and shot. In Gomel, 41 Jews and nine Russians were liquidated; they were equipped with firearms and carried out acts of sabotage and looting. In addition it was ascertained that two women started fires in houses by igniting wood shavings. The accused were shot after confessing their deeds. In Rechiza, 216 Jews were liquidated for having committed acts of sabotage and for refusing to work. They had, in addition, accommodated partisans and provided them with food.

Special stress is given to the fact that, according to information given by SK 7b, evacuated Jews in the towns where they were located reported that the Jews from Koseletz informed the remaining Ukrainians that they could plunder their [the Jews'] homes, since they would not return.

In Mogilev, 18 persons who had been political functionaries, politruks, and guerrillas were liquidated by Einsatzkommando 8. One of them was found at a Dnieper bridge with four Russian handgrenades in his pocket. The village of Krugloye, approximately 50 km west of Mogilev, was checked. While carrying out these operations, we were struck by the fact that practically the whole of the male Jewish population was missing. According to reports by the local Russian population, they were supposed to have left with the retreating Russian forces, that is to say, they are hiding in the surrounding woods. The Jewish women were extremely restive and not one was wearing the prescribed badge. In the course of the operations, 28 Jewish women and three men were liquidated. In Mogilev as well, an increased resistance on the part of the Jews was noticeable, so that energetic measures, such as the shooting of 80 Jews and Jewesses, had to be taken. When even these measures did not suffice and the Jews continued to spread false rumors and sabotage the regulations of the German Occupation authorities, 215 Jews and 337 Jewesses were shot. In Minsk, at the city check points, 142 Jews were arrested and shot for loitering outside the ghetto without the prescribed identification badges.

According to reports received, large numbers of Jews of the district of Marina-Borka are supposed to have taken refuge in the woods, cooperating with the partisans and plundering in the vicinity of Marina-Morka. In some cases even Byelorussian mayors have been shot by these gangs. The mopping-up operations carried out in this area resulted in the arrest of 70 Uzbekis, Kirghizes, Tartars, and Jews. After a short interrogation, the arrested were liquidated; it had been proved that they had participated in the aforementioned acts of terrorism and violence.

Various acts of sabotage committed by Jews in Borisov were confirmed. At a mopping-up operation there, a total of 321 Jews were liquidated. Near Smolovich, the Jews were under suspicion as well of having several times, together with the partisans and other criminal elements, blown up the Minsk-Smolensk railway line. In conjunction with the Kommando from Minsk, 1,401 Jews were shot during large-scale operations carried out in Smolovich. After these mopping-up operations, there were no more Jews left north, south, and west of Borisov. In Borisov itself, a further 118 Jews were liquidated because of sabotage at work and for having been engaged in plundering. In Bobruisk and its vicinity, about 1,380 persons were liquidated during the time of this report, 20 of them while escaping. The persons executed were mainly Jews, persons engaged in sabotage, and those who until the last minute were engaged in spreading hate propaganda against the German Occupation authorities.

. . . . . . . . . . . .

## 5. *Measures against criminals and marauders*

According to information obtained by SK 7b, the Red troops had, before leaving Chernigov, opened the door of the Asylum for the Insane and had armed part of the inmates. These were marching down the streets marauding. 21 of them were caught in the act and liquidated. Others left the town for the surrounding villages, probably in order to live there. The population, however, is cooperating with regard to the capture of these insane persons. Soon again there will be quite a few in the asylum. Then, they will be treated according to the usual procedure. In Minsk, 632 mentally deficient people and, in Mogilev, 836 were accorded special treatment.

. . . . . . . . . . . .

## 8. Liquidation

The liquidations carried out during the time of this report up to and including September 28, 1941, increased the final figures as follows:

a) Staff and VKM ................................. 2,029
b) Sk 7a ........................................... 1,252
c) SK 7b ........................................... 1,544
d) EK 8 ...........................................15,000
e) EK 9 ...........................................10,269
Total ................30,094 persons liquidated by the group.

. . . . . . . . . . . .

*Einsatzgruppe D*
Location: Nikolayev

## *Construction work achieved so far by the Kommandos of Einsatzgruppe D*

1) *Protection*

. . . . . . . . . . . .

f) Strengthening of German consciousness in the different villages by bringing back the deported inhabitants [Germans]: removing Ukrainians and replacing them as far as possible with Germans mostly from Ukrainian communities.

. . . . . . . . . . . .

2) *Economic Safeguarding*

. . . . . . . . . . . .

. . . Distribution of Jewish possessions and Jewish property, in the first place to widows and families of deported persons.

The Chief of the Security Police
and Security Service

Berlin,
October 12, 1941

50 copies
(36th copy)

## Operational Situation Report USSR No. 111

*Einsatzgruppe* A: Sonderkommando 1a
Location: Reval

### Reports: Jews in Estonia

At the beginning of 1940, about 4,500 Jews were living in Estonia, of these, 1,900 to 2,000 lived in Reval; larger Jewish communities were in Dorpat, Narva, and Pernau, while only a few Jews lived in the countryside.

The deportations carried out by the Russians, as far as they concerned Jews, quantitatively cannot be established. According to inquiries made so far, the Jews were hardly affected by them.

With the advance of the German troops on Estonian territory, about half of the Jews prepared to flee. As these Jews collaborated with the Soviet authorities, they left the country with them, going east. Only a few of them were seized in Reval because their escape route had been cut off. After the occupation of the country, there were probably still about 2,000 Jews left in the country.

The Estonian self-defense units which were formed when the [German] army marched in, immediately started to arrest Jews. Spontaneous demonstrations against the Jews did not take place because there was no known reason for the population to do so.

The following orders were therefore issued by us:

1) The arrest of all male Jews over 16;

2) The arrest of all Jewesses fit for work between the ages of 16 and 60, to be utilized to work in the peat bogs;

3) Collective billeting of female Jewish residents of Dorpat and vicinity in the synagogue and a tenement house in Dorpat.

4) Arrest of all male and female Jews fit for work in Pernau and vicinity;

5) Registration of all Jews according to age, sex, and fitness for work and billeting in a camp which is at present being built.

All male Jews over 16, with the exception of physicians and the appointed Jewish Elders, were executed by the Estonian self-defense units under supervision of the Sonderkommando. As for the town and country district of Reval, the action is still underway since the search for the Jewish hideouts has not yet been completed. So far, the total number of Jews shot in Estonia is 440.

When these measures are completed, about 500 to 600 Jewesses and children will still be alive.

The village communities are by now free of Jews.

For the Jews residing in Reval and vicinity, a camp is at present being prepared at Harku [Reval county], which, after receiving the Jews from Reval, will be expanded to contain all Jews from Estonia. All Jewesses fit for work are employed in farming and cutting of peat on the property of the nearby prison. Thus, the questions of feeding and financing are answered.

As an immediate measure, the following order was issued:

1) Marking of all Jews over six with a yellow star at least 10 cm large, to be attached to the left side of the breast and on the back;

2) Prohibition to engage in public trade;

3) Prohibition to use sidewalks, public communications, and to frequent theaters, cinemas and restaurants;

4) Seizure of all Jewish property;

5) Prohibition to attend schools.

. . . . . . . . . . . .

*Einsatzgruppe C*
Location: Kiev

## Security police measures

Sonderkommando 4a has now reached a total of over 51,000 executions. Apart from the special action in Kiev of September 23 and 29, in which two Kommandos of the Police Regiment South were involved, all executions carried out so far were made by that Sonderkommando without any outside assistance. The executed persons were mainly Jews; a small number were political officials as well as saboteurs and plunderers.

In the period between September 7 and October 5, 207 political officials, 112 saboteurs and plunderers, as well as 8,800 Jews were liquidated by Einsatzkommando 5.

Sonderkommando 4b, in the period between September 13 and 26, executed 103 political officials, 9 saboteurs and plunderers, and 125 Jews.

Einsatzkommando 6, in the period between September 1 and 27, executed 13 political officials, 32 plunderers and saboteurs, as well as 26 Jews.

These were the reasons for the executions carried out by the Kommandos: political officials; plunderers and saboteurs; active Communists and political representatives; Jews who gained their release from prison camps by false statements; agents and informers of the NKVD; persons who by false depositions and witness influencing were instrumental in the deportation of ethnic Germans; Jewish sadism and revenge; undesirable elements; partisans; politruks; danger of plague and epidemics; members of Russian bands; armed insurgents; supplying Russian bands; rebels and agitators; drifting juveniles; Jews in general.

On September 26, the Security Police took up its activities in Kiev. That day, seven interrogation Kommandos of Einsatzkommando 4a started their work in the civilian prisoner camp, in the prisoner-of-war camp, in the Jewish camp, and in the city itself. Thus, among other things, in the camp for civilian prisoners and prisoners-of-war, ten political commissars were discovered and interrogated in detail. Conforming to the old Communist tactics these guys denied all political activity. Only when confronted with trustworthy witnesses, five commissars relented and confessed, that is, they admitted the position they had held, but did not make any statements beyond this. They were shot on September 27. In one case, a Jewish politruk tried to ransom himself by offering gold. The man was taken to his apartment where he pried loose a few floor tiles, dug about 50 cm deep and produced a counter-weight of a clock. That weight contained 21 gold coins. The Jew was shot.

Furthermore, 14 partisans were found, among them leading persons. They, too, adhered to their tactics of silence during the interrogation. Again, their status was proven by testimony. In some cases, a confession was obtained. A partisan leader who had made propaganda for the defense of Kiev also attempted to ransom himself by offering gold. In this case gold watches and Rubel notes were hidden behind a stove. All accused were shot.

Three Jewish party officials who also tried to ransom themselves by offering gold were liquidated. The gold was seized.

. . . . . . . . . . . .

## Kremenchug

A Vorkommando of SK 4b entered Kremenchug together with the fighting troops. Controls were carried out by all the other authorities. The city contains about 89,000 inhabitants, 40% of them Jews. All the persons of interest have, as usual, fled, among them a large part of the Jews. Searches have been initiated in the town as well as in the surrounding areas and were partly successful. A number of officials of lesser importance were arrested and finished off. Without exception, the offices were emptied. Some material of local interest was secured.

## Poltava

The same conditions generally existed also in Poltava. Only material of local importance was secured. People of any interest had fled.

As the German troops quickly advanced and, together with them the Kommandos, it is particularly inconvenient that there is not a larger rear Kommando that could follow up and do the intensive work. According to police and security experience, there exists a vacuum. Greater success in the intensive work can be expected only within 10-14 days. This concerns particularly the Jewish problem. Also in the area of Poltava most of the Jews fled. It is certain that, in time, Jews and other people of interest [to us] can be expected to return [from hiding].

The Chief of the Security Police
and Security Service

Berlin,
October 13, 1941

50 copies
(36th copy)

*Operational Situation Report USSR No. 112*

. . . . . . . . . . . .

*Einsatzgruppe C*
Location: Kiev

## Bolshevism and Jewry

The population's attitude towards these two problems in the areas of Kiev, Poltava, and Dniepropetrovsk is the same as has been observed elsewhere in the Ukraine. The population rejects Bolshevism almost without exception, since there is practically no family which has not lost one or more members through Bolshevik deportation or killing. Also, the Ukrainians had been free farmers and independent in ancient Russia and have not forgotten that everything was taken from them when forced into the collective farms. The number of Ukrainians who joined the Communist Party out of conviction is surprisingly low.

Only the young people who have neither seen nor heard of anything else but Communism and its "successes and achievements" allow themselves to be captivated by the Communist ideology. Yet even in this group one finds few fanatics and really convinced fighters. German propaganda will not have difficulty in promoting a complete change in this attitude. In order to begin the process of such a re-education, and as long as the powerful battle is still fresh in the minds of the Ukrainians, propaganda, lectures, performances, films, radio, and periodicals should be introduced.

The Ukrainian rejects Judaism together with Communism, as it was mainly Jews who were officials of the Communist Party. The

Ukrainians had the opportunity to discover that practically only the Jews enjoyed the advantages connected with membership in the Communist Party, especially in its leading positions. The population is, however, unaware of real anti-Semitism based on rural and ideological principles. There are no leading personalities and no spiritual impetus within the Ukrainian population to trigger off persecution since all remember the harsh punishments inflicted by the Bolsheviks against anyone who attacked the Jews. For instance, whoever called the Jews "Zhid" (Yid) (which was at that time a curse word) and not "Evrei" (Hebrew), was sent to prison. However, if an impulse comes from any side and should the population be given a free hand, an extensive persecution of the Jews could result.

The Chief of the Security Police                    Berlin,
        and the Security Service

                                                   50 copies
                                                   (36th copy)


*Operational Situation Report USSR No. 113*

. . . . . . . . . . . .

*Einsatzgruppe D*
Location: Nikolayev

. . . . . . . . . . . .


*Superstructure, organization, and work of the partisan*
*groups, sabotage troops, and Party groups in the area of*
*Nikolayev*

. . . . . . . . . . . .


*Special cases*
*a) Partisan movements*

1. In the course of identification work in the municipal hospital in
Nikolayev, the Jew Hershko Salomon, who had reported there for
treatment of an injured jaw, was identified. The thorough interrogation of Salomon revealed that he had been a member of a parachute,
counter-intelligence and assault battalion that had to destroy German
parachutists. Prior to the occupation of Nikolayev by German troops,
the battalion was dissolved and broken up into separate partisan
groups according to the instructions for partisan war from the commander of the Russian northwestern front. One of these groups to
which Salomon belonged retreated in the direction of Kherson and
fought German troops, in the course of which 43 German soldiers
were killed. Salomon was injured in the jaw in that battle.

. . . . . . . . . . . .

3) During the examination of so-called prisoners-of-war, it became clear that the Jews Pinchovsky, Shoichert, and Shoshelevsky had been members of a partisan company numbering 120 men who operated between the Red Army and the German lines near Novy-Bug and had been scattered. The members of the partisan company did not wear uniforms but were equipped with guns and one MG. The three persons named above were equipped with one gun and 45 rounds of ammunition. They had been hiding together, apparently with the intention of establishing contact with other scattered partisans.

The Chief of the Security Police
and Security Service

Berlin,
October 17, 1941

50 copies
(36th copy)

## *Operational Situation Report USSR No. 116*

. . . . . . . . . . . .

*Einsatzgruppe A*
Location: Krasnogvardeisk
*Security Police Work*
The cooperation of security police work in the pacification of the area behind the front and in the Rear Army area continued at the time of this report. As to details, the activities of the Einsatzgruppe can be summarized as follows:

1) Partly in collaboration with the Field and Local Military Commanders the population was recently checked on the basis of security police standards. Unreliable elements blocking efforts to pacify the region were segregated and either transferred to military and civilian prisoner camps or executed by the Kommandos. Between October 2 and 12, 260 persons in all had to be executed.

2) Owing to the change-over to trench warfare and, in compliance with requests from our side, the Army evacuated a strip next to the front line. The respective orders of the various army corps differed in their basic approaches (some ordering complete evacuation, others the evacuation of all men, others again to transfer to definite quarters in towns, etc.). Upon the request by the Army, Security Police investigations were carried out in the transient camps.

3) As partisans were still alive behind the fighting troops, special measures became necessary in this matter as well. In the first place, the intelligence work had to be broadened by dispatching our own spies, by drawing in the village elders, and the population in general. The results of this preparatory intelligence work served as the basis

of various operations actively combatting partisans. For the rest, a partisan report which was intercepted indicates that because of the imminent cold season, the partisans do not expect to be able to hold out beyond the middle of November.

Actions for combatting sabotage followed the same lines as with the cooperation in combatting partisans. For instance, on October 6, ten people had to be shot in Slutsk, the population being informed thereof by the following announcements:

"Notification: On October 6, 1941, ten people were shot in Slutsk because a Wehrmacht telephone line was cut with the intent to commit sabotage. Should further acts of sabotage of the same kind be committed, twenty people will be shot in future. The German Security Police."

4) During the time covered by this report, one of the main tasks of the Einsatzgruppe was setting up the organization to secure information from Petersburg.[1] In general, the information is being collected in the following ways:

a. By Russian deserters (either caught by our own Sonderkommandos or delivered by the fighting troops or local military commanders;

b. By prisoners (methodical searches and clearing of military prisoner-of-war camps; this way proved to be exceptionally successful);

c. By dispatching our own agents (owing to the increasing rigidity of the fronts and the development of stable lines with trenches, entanglements and mine-fields, it is extremely difficult to get an agent through the lines and back. Moreover, every reasonably healthy man is being enlisted at once in the workers defense force in Petersburg. At any rate, only agents with good Bolshevik identification papers can be sent out).

Although our intelligence work originally aimed at the collection of information concerning the general political climate, the questions of general mood, supply conditions, important persons and offices, from the outset information of a purely military character was forwarded in great quantities. Therefore, the military circles were extremely interested in reports on the situation. In some cases, this went so far that the results of our intelligence service regarding military targets were used by the HQ of the 10th Army for giving orders

1. Leningrad.

to the artillery. According to our investigations, the targets of military and war-economic importance in Petersburg tally with the statements of the Army, as laid down in the military-geographical plan.

The Chief of the Security Police
and Security Service

Berlin,
October 18, 1941

50 copies
(36th copy)

## Operational Situation Report USSR No. 117

. . . . . . . . . . . .

*Einsatzgruppe D*
Location: Nikolayev
*Working report by E[insatzgruppe] D for 1-15 October 1941*
During the time to which the report relates, the settlement of the Jewish question was tackled, particularly in the territory to the east of the Dnieper. Investigations concerning followers of Bandera and partisans are next in importance.

1. The districts occupied by the Kommandos were cleansed of Jews. 4,091 Jews and 46 Communists were executed during the time span covered by the report, bringing the total to 40,699.

. . . . . . . . . . . .

3. On the Odessa front, a partisan leader of a five-man group was arrested after offering violent resistance. His tasks included fixing artillery positions and reporting them to a Soviet command stationed on the east bank of the Suchoi-Liman; carrying out attacks on German soldiers; destroying telephone cables. Names of members of the group were established. House searches yielded weapons and munition. It is remarkable that partisan groups had no support whatsoever from the population.

4. Concerning Bandera members: 16 arrests in searches in Nikolayev. Three leaders under arrest, among others Machilynsky and Martynok. The rest were given appropriate warning. Political material confiscated.

Members were gathered in small groups at the beginning of the

-194-

campaign in Lvov or in Sanok where they received short training, propaganda material, and money. Martynok took over the leadership of Lvov group. Machilynsky was in charge of these groups from Sanok. On the way, under the pretext of performing police duties, they continued political work such as installing mayors, organizing military units, and finishing off Jews and Communists, etc. The two immediately took up leading positions with the militia. Their participation in murder in Zhitomir is not confirmed. They declared, however, that they would remove rivals.

5) Ethnic German settlements east of the Dnieper were taken under protection; part of them were passed on to the command of VOMI.[1] Concerning the preservation of German nationalism, the observations are similar to those between the Bug and the Dniester. In some areas, situation substantially better.

6) In the course of the work in Nikolayev, Party instructions concerning work in the navy were seized.

---

1. Volksdeutsche Mittelstelle — Liaison Office for Ethnic Germans.

## Operational Situation Report USSR No. 119

*Einsatzgruppe C*
Location: Kiev

### Security Police measures

According to observations made by Einsatzkommando 5, the last few weeks a large number of Jews from the near and far have gathered in Uman. The population of Uman before the outbreak of the war was about 55,000; about 10,000 of these were Jews. In spite of large departures of Jews originally living in Uman after the outbreak of the war, due to [new] migration, the number has been reported at about 8,000. A good intelligence net was discovered among the Jews of Uman. Information about the events at the front and behind was passed by the Jews not only to their coreligionists, but also to the Ukrainian population. They received very quickly information about actions against Jews in the vicinity. A two-day action was agreed upon in order to combat this source of danger in Uman.

On September 21, 1941, contrary to the plan, excesses were perpetrated against the Jews by members of the militia with participation of numerous German soldiers.

During these events, Jewish apartments were completely demolished and robbed of all utensils and valuables. In this action, German soldiers also participated. Spot checks of the apartments of militia members which were undertaken immediately after arrival in Uman of a platoon of Einsatzkommando 5 were without any result.

Naturally, the systematic action of Einsatzkommando 5 suffered greatly by these planless excesses against the Jews in Uman. In particular, a large number of the Jews were now forewarned and escaped from the city. Besides numerous Jews, many of the Ukrainian officials and activists still living in Uman were warned by the excesses, and only two co-workers of the NKVD were found and liquidated. The results [i.e., damage] of these excesses were cleaned up immediately by Einsatzkommando 5 [shortly] after its arrival.

In the remainder [of the action], 1,412 Jews were executed by Einsatzkommando 5 in Uman on September 22 and 23, 1941. The South Armies Group was informed about the part played by the Wehrmacht in the anti-Jewish excesses.

. . . . . . . . . . . .

13 Ukrainian members of the Communist Party and 35 Jews, among them the village council, who continuously spread rumors about the retreat of German troops, frightening and alarming the population, were shot by Einsatzkommando 5 in Yustungrad on September 19, 1941.

. . . . . . . . . . . .

Two Ukrainians who asked the population to destroy all machines, to drive off cattle, and to destroy grain supplies, were arrested by the militia in Volodarka and handed over to Einsatzkommando 5 and executed. One of these Ukrainians was a leader of the village council and a party member since 1939. The other was a schoolteacher, candidate for the Party, and agitator from the county economic office.

Two more Ukrainians (both candidates for the Party), who actively participated in the destruction of farm-machinery and the driving off of cattle (which took place before the entry of the German troops), were executed in Tychy-Chutor by Einsatzkommando 5 on September 23. One more Ukrainian in the same town, who kept the population under continuous pressure by rumors that the Red troops were likely to return soon, was likewise taken care of.

On September 14, 1941, in Cherepin, the same Einsatzkommando executed two kolkhoz leaders (Ukrainians), and a half-Jew, a member of the Komsomol. After the departure of the Red Army and under threat of the death penalty, they ordered the other kolkhoz workers to destroy machines and grain supplies.

The leader of the village council (Ukrainian) in Shuralivka, who, according to his own testimony, deported 15 persons to Siberia during his time in office, was executed. Furthermore, the former mayor of the town and 13 more male Jews and three Jewesses were finished off.

In Tsybulov, where there are 3,000 inhabitants, the Jews comprise about 3% of the population. They were particularly insolent to the Ukrainian population. Therefore, on September 25, 1941, 78 Jews were shot.

An action against the Jews was carried out on October 4, 1941, in Pereyaslav by the Vorkommando of Sonderkommando 4a with the aid of reliable Ukrainian men. A total of 537 Jews (men, women and adolescents) were apprehended and liquidated. The Ukrainian population and the Wehrmacht looked upon this action with satisfaction.

On October 8, 1941, the town of Yagotin was searched by Sonderkommando 4a for suspicious elements. In this action 125 Jews were apprehended and liquidated.

An action was carried out in Ivankov on September 19, 1941, by Sonderkommando 4a with the aid of the militia, in which 168 persons were apprehended and liquidated. In the same town, a search for Communists took place on September 21, 1941. One woman Communist, the leader of a "secret department," was arrested and executed. On the same day, 29 more Jews were shot.

The local military command in Korosten reported that meetings of farmers in surrounding villages were interrupted or dispersed, and the perpetrators are mainly Jews. In the following action by Sonderkommando 4a, a total of 177 Jews were checked and then executed because it was demonstrated conclusively that they caused a series of unbearable disturbances.

On September 13, 1941, three adolescents aged 13, 14 and 17 were apprehended in Radomyshl by Sonderkommando 4a and accused of active espionage. By order of a Russian captain, they were to penetrate the German lines in order to determine the strength and type of troops, their equipment, and their weapons. They reported their observations to the Russian captain stationed in Irpin.

. . . . . . . . . . . .

On the trip from Vyrna to Dederov, a Gypsy band of 32 persons was stopped by Sonderkommando 4a. During the search of their wagons German pieces of equipment were found. Since this band did not have any [identification] papers, and since they did not have any explanation for the origin of the goods, they were executed.

On September 15, 1941, Einsatzkommando 5 performed another

action in Boguslav because, according to reliable reports, partisans and parachutists were cared for by Jews. As a result of the execution of 322 Jews and 13 Communist officials, the town is now free of Jews.

Also, in Koshevatoye, partisans and parachutists were allegedly sheltered by Jews. Thus, all the Jews of this town were also liquidated by Einsatzkommando 5.

. . . . . . . . . . . .

## Kiev

. . . . . . . . . . . .

On October 1 and 2, 1941, the men of Kiev who were fit for army service were registered by the city Kommandatur. In order to examine their personal data, etc., the Einsatzkommando 5 put suitable men at the disposal of the interrogators. Thus, a total of 15 persons were arrested, of these one Jewess, one politruk, and 13 members of the Russian army. The Jewess and the politruk were executed after intensive investigation. The 13 Russian soldiers were handed over to the field gendarmery for transfer to a prisoner-of-war camp.

The Chief of the Security Police
and the Security Service

Berlin,
October 21, 1941

30 copies
(18th copy)

## Operational Situation Report USSR No. 120

*Political Survey*
Occupied Territories
Serbia

. . . . . . . . . . . .

## *Extraordinary occurrences*

Until the installation of the authorized commanding general in
Serbia, ruthless action by the troops was bound to fail because of the
lack of adequate and unequivocal orders. Then an entirely clear line
of action was established at the command of General B. According
to this [policy], for each [German] soldier shot 100 Serbians are to
be executed, and for each soldier wounded, 50 Serbians. Based on
that formula, for example, 2,200 Serbians and Jews were shot as reprisal for an attack on the escorting train near Topols when 22 members of the Army lost their lives. 1,738 inhabitants and 19 Communist
women from Kraljovo were executed for the soldiers who fell in the
battle of Kraljovo.

. . . . . . . . . . . .

# Military events

## Greece

Two villages near the Strymen estuary that were proved to have given support to [partisan] bands were burnt down. All the male inhabitants (202) were shot. At the time of the burning, ammunition and also some explosive material exploded in every house.
Telephone cable Athens-Saloniki cut.

50 copies
(36th copy)

## Operational Situation Report USSR No. 122

*Political Survey*
The Reich

. . . . . . . . . . . .

Evacuation of the Jews to from Bialystok to Pruzhana continued. Because of transportation difficulties, only 9,000 Jews could be transported [deported] so far. Following a consultation with the Regierungspräsident [government president], an improvement of the means of deportation can be expected in the near future.

During the time of the report, a total of 63 persons have been executed, all of them Communists.

The Chief of the Security Police
and the Security Service

Berlin,
October 24, 1941

<u>50 copies</u>
(36th copy)

## *Operational Situation Report USSR No. 123*

. . . . . . . . . . .

*Einsatzgruppe B*
Location: Smolensk

*Police activity General Situation*

. . . . . . . . . . .

The flight and the systematic evacuation of the Jews to the east clearly assumes bigger dimensions all the time. Thus, Vorkommando Moskaw, which is on the march to Moscow, reports that the localities which they have reached so far are free of Jews because the Jews were previously evacuated by the Bolsheviks.

. . . . . . . . . . .

*Fight against partisans*

. . . . . . . . . . .

EK 9 was informed that six partisans are in Lemnitsa, some 15 km west of Surash. A 15-man Kommando was immediately dispatched to Lemnitsa. It was established that on the same day, six men equipped with automatic rifles were seen there. Amongst other things, they had spread the rumor that the war would soon come to an end in favor of Russia. As it had already become dark, that group managed to escape into the vast forests.

In the Ostova district, three Jews who had been informers for the partisans were arrested and liquidated.

The Chief of the Security Police        Berlin,
and Security Service        October 25, 1941

<u>50 copies</u>
(36th copy)

## Operational Situation Report USSR No. 124

. . . . . . . . . . . .

*Einsatzgruppe B*
Location: Smolensk

### Actions against functionaries, Agents, Saboteurs and Jews

Group HQ and Vorkommando Moskau undertook an action against the Jews in Tatarsk. The Jews began to leave the ghetto on their own initiative returning to their old homes, in the meantime trying to expel the Russians living there. The place was combed systematically and the Jews were herded into the market square. Some of them fled and had to be driven out of the nearby woods. As punishment for not following the orders of the German Security Police, all male Jews and three women who were in Tatarsk at that time were shot.

During the period being reported on, Sonderkommando 7a gave "special treatment" to another 63 Communist functionaries, NKGB agents, and agitators.

In one of the actions, a man was liquidated for arson. It was proved that he participated in the burning down of Sloboda, and was also strongly suspected of having killed German soldiers.

The Jews resisted somewhat turning the village of Boloshchina into a ghetto for the Jews of Sadrudubs.[1] Consequently, 272 Jews and Jewesses were liquidated. Most of them were members of the Communist Party, publicly dangerous elements and political agitators. Am-

---

1. Mistake in the original; the name is Starodubs.

ong them there was a political commissar who encouraged the Jews in their opposition.

In Mogilev, the Jews also tried to sabotage their removal into the ghetto by fleeing en masse. Einsatzkommando 8, with the help of the Order Police, blocked the roads leading out of town and liquidated 113 Jews.

In the vicinity of Shklov, about 50 km north of Mogilev, acts of sabotage were constantly committed, chiefly the destruction of the German Army's telephone communication lines. An inquiry showed that Jews of Shidov[2] had taken part in these acts of sabotage; thus, 627 Jews were liquidated. In a further action, another 812 male and female persons were given "special treatment," all of them racially and mentally inferior elements.

A subunit raided the village of Kuyachiche, liquidating all 32 Jews living there, because of proof they had widely supported the partisans.

Six Russians were shot for illegal possession of arms and for threatening arson.

In Mogilev, two more Jews were liquidated for kicking wounded German soldiers and for not wearing the [yellow] badge as ordered. Ten more Jews and Russians, Communist officials and agents, were liquidated. They attempted to influence the population along Communist lines. Some of them had in their possession hate-propaganda literature and German army-maps which they obviously had intended to hand over to Bolshevik agents. One of those liquidated had played an important part in the deportation of Russian peasants to Siberia.

Four Jews were liquidated for instigating others to refuse to work. During the period covered by the report, 23 individual cases of execution of Jews took place because they did not wear the [yellow] badge while residing in the town.

A rearguard squad of Einsatzkommando 8 stationed in Minsk until October 3, 1941, executed another 42 persons in Minsk. Most of them were Jews who had not moved into the ghetto or who had refused to wear the badge against orders.

At the request of Gauleiter Kube, the area of the Marina-Gorka district was raided. This action concentrated chiefly on the village of Talka where 222 Jews were liquidated. They made persistent anti-

---

2. Probably mistaken; should be Shklov.

German propaganda among the inhabitants of Talka and continuously terrorized them. The action against the Jews in Marina-Gorka carried out immediately afterwards became necessary because the Jews were sabotaging all the instructions issued by the occupying authorities. The work assigned to them was done with great reluctance. 996 Jews and Jewesses were given "special treatment" in order to break this spirit of resistance.

In Borisov, another 83 persons were shot individually during the time of this report. They were seditious Jews, former NKGB agents, and Communist functionaries.

Two large-scale actions were carried out by the platoon in Krupka and Sholopaniche: 912 Jews were liquidated in the former, and 822 in the latter. The Krupka district can now be considered free of Jews. The complete liquidation of all Jews in the two villages was deemed necessary in order to deprive the numerous partisans and parachutists in these parts of any assistance which the Jews in particular had given most persistently.

In Bobruisk, during the time under report, a platoon of Einsatzgruppe 8 executed 418 persons. Among them were rebellious Jews and persons who had shielded former Red Army soldiers or who had acted as spies for the partisans. Some of those executed had committed anti-German agitation, conducting whisper campaigns and distributing leaflets.

Einsatzkommando 9 arrested the elder of the collective farm in the village of Tromkavichi. The interrogation of four witnesses proved that in 17 cases he had reported people to the NKGB in Lepel; besides, 17 persons were deported at his instigation; they have not returned yet. He was shot for that reason.

In Vitebsk, there were four more cases of liquidating Jews for loitering outside the ghetto and earning their living by begging for food; they, too, had removed their badges. One of them had also made insulting remarks about members of the German Army.

On October 8, 1941, began the complete liquidation of the Jews in the Vitebsk ghetto owing to the imminent danger of epidemics. The number of Jews who came under "special treatment" amounted to about 3,000.

During the pacification [action] in Borovyany, a Jewish family of five living in the local kolkhoz was also executed for spreading anti-German rumors.

In connection with another tour of inspection in the vicinity of

Ostrovno, it was discovered that the local Jews had repeatedly betrayed hostile conduct and had not followed the orders of the German authorities. Thus, 163 Jews were shot in Ostrovno.

On October 1, 1941, Einsatzkommando 9 gave "special treatment" to 52 Jews who fled from Gorodok to Vitebsk where they made the population restive by spreading rumors.

The Chief of the Security Police
and Security Service

Berlin,
October 26, 1941

50 copies
48th copy
(handwritten)

## Operational Situation Report USSR No. 125

. . . . . . . . . . . .

*Einsatzgruppe B*
Location: Smolensk

### Confiscation of funds and other objects

Sonderkommando 7b secured 46,700 rubles in cash which were in the possession of a number of Jews brought in for liquidation.

During the time reported, Einsatzkommando 8 confiscated another 164,061 rubles. They were formally recorded and transferred to the administration of Einsatzkommando 8. The total sum of rubles so far secured by Einsatzkommado 8, therefore, amounts to 2,019,521 rubles.

During the time reported, Einsatzkommando 9 seized 43,825 rubles for the administration, as well as various valuables in gold and silver.

. . . . . . . . . . . .

*Organizational Measures*

. . . . . . . . . . . .

Einsatzkommando 8 completed the establishment of a ghetto in Mogilev. The Jewish Council was ordered to set up in the ghetto a Jewish Order Service [Ghetto Police] of about 15 men to assist it. Moreover, it was directed to separate the ghetto from the rest of the town with a barbed wire fence. The number of Jews remaining in the ghetto barely amounts to 1,000 persons, including women and children.

## Enemy intelligence service

. . . . . . . . . . . .

*Liquidations*
The liquidations which took place during the time under report increased the final figures to the following:

a) Staff and Vorkommando Moskau . . . . . . . . . . . . . . . . . . . . 2,457
b) Sonderkommando 7a . . . . . . . . . . . . . . . . . . . . . . . . . . . 1,344
c) Sonderkommando 7b . . . . . . . . . . . . . . . . . . . . . . . . . . . 1,822
d) Einsatzkommando 8 . . . . . . . . . . . . . . . . . . . . . . . . . . . 20,108
e) Einsatzkommando 9 . . . . . . . . . . . . . . . . . . . . . . . . . . . 11,449
Total: . . . . . . . . . . . . . . . . . . . . . . . . . . . . . . . . . . . . . . . 37,180
persons liquidated so far by Einsatzgruppe B.

. . . . . . . . . . . .

*Einsatzgruppe D*
Location: Nikolayev
On October 22, at 18.10 hours, the NKVD building, residence of the commander of the 10th Rumanian division, who is also the town commander of Odessa, was dynamited. The following were killed: the commander and his staff, the German harbor-captain (Captain Reichert), Captain Schmidt, other German officers, and SS-Unterstürmfuehrer Güldner of the VOMI. Obviously the dynamiting was prepared a long time ago. The way in which the NKVD building was installed and maintained appears to indicate a trap. The Commander, who was also the town commander, had been warned on various occasions. If the purpose of such dynamiting was to cause confusion, then it was achieved. On October 24, it was impossible to tell where in Odessa the new town commander or any other Rumanian authority resided. As a counter-measure, the Rumanians seem to be preparing to shoot the Jews in Odessa. To date, about 10,000 have been shot.

The Chief of the Security Police
and Security Service

Berlin,
October 27, 1941

50 copies
(38th copy)

## Operational Situation Report USSR No. 126

. . . . . . . . . . . .

### Political Survey

### Occupied Territories

*General Gouvernement*

The Commander of the Security Police and the SD in Lvov reports:

In a letter signed OUN (Organization of Ukrainian Nationalists) sent to the Secret State Police in Lvov, the Bandera Group again advocates the political independence of the Ukraine.

It is stated in the letter that Hitler cheated the Ukraine and that America, England, and Russia would create an independent Ukraine reaching from the River San to the Black Sea. "Long live greater independent Ukraine without Jews, Poles and Germans. Poles behind the San, Germans to Berlin, Jews to the gallows." Moreover, the letter expresses doubts in Germany's victory in the war, stating that Germany could not win the war without the Ukraine.

It is also demanded that Ukrainians under arrest be released.

*Execution activity*

As for the executions to date, about 80,000 persons have been liquidated by the Kommandos of the Einsatzgruppe.

Among them, about 8,000 persons were convicted, as a result of interrogations, on the grounds of activity against Germans or for being Communists.

The remaining have been finished off as reprisal measures.

Several reprisal measures were carried out within the framework of Grossaktionen [large-scale actions]. The most extensive of these actions took place immediately after Kiev was taken; it exclusively concerned Jews with their entire families.

The difficulties in carrying out such a large action — first of all with respect to sowing disunity [among the Jews] — were overcome in Kiev by a call via posters to the Jewish population that they were to move.

Although at the start, one could [reasonably] count on the participation of about 5,000-6,000 Jews, more than 30,000 Jews turned up who, due to extraordinarily skillful organization, believed in the transfer [ruse] right up to the moment of their execution.

Thus, even if about 75,000 Jews had been liquidated so far, it has already become clear that a solution of the Jewish question will not be possible in this way. True, we have succeeded in bringing about a total solution to the Jewish problem, particularly in smaller towns and also in the villages. However, in bigger towns it was observed that all the [remaining] Jews have disappeared after such an execution. Yet, if a Kommando returns after a period, a number of Jews is always found that is significantly larger than the number of executed Jews.

*Cooperation with army and the Secret Field Police[1]*
This concerns the relationship of the Einsatzgruppe and its Kommando to other offices and authorities. The relation to the Army deserves special attention. The Einsatzgruppe has managed to establish an excellent relationship with all Army offices. It was thus possible for the Einsatzgruppe never to remain in the rear of the Army from the start of its activity. The Army has again and again made the request that the Einsatzgruppe should move up to the front as far as possible. In very many instances, the fighting troops asked for the support of the Einsatzkommandos. In every larger military action, there always were Vorausabteilungen [advance units] of the Einsatzgruppe who entered the newly conquered places together with the fighting troops. Thus, maximal support was given in all instances. In this respect, it is worthwhile mentioning the support during the capture of Zhitomir, where, immediately after the first tanks [entered], three cars of Einsatzkommando 4a moved into the town.

The successful work of the Einsatzgruppe has also resulted in the

---

1. GFD —Geheime Feldpolizei.

fact that the Security Police enjoys great respect, especially with Army staffs.

The Verbindungsfürer [liaison officers] who have been stationed at the headquarters are loyally kept informed about all the military operations, and, in addition, receive extensive support. The commanding officer of AOK 6, Brigadier General von Reichenau, has also repeatedly expressed his appreciation of the work of the Einsatzkommando and has, accordingly, represented the interests of the SD *vis-à-vis* his staff. The complete success of the Kommandos have contributed to this: for instance, the capture of Lieutenant General Sokolov, the report of the imminent blasting of a bridge by parachutists, and the transmission of other militarily important information.

Only in the Jewish question has there not been an absolute understanding with the junior Army officers, until most recently. This revealed itself in particular during the thorough search of prisoner camps. A particularly blatant example is the behavior of the camp commander in Vinnitsa who absolutely refused to deliver 362 Jewish prisoners of war through his representative. He even initiated a court martial against him and two other officers. The Einsatzkommando was exposed too frequently to more or less veiled accusations because of their persistent attitude with respect to the Jewish question. Another aggravating factor was the fact that the SD was completely forbidden by order of Army headquarters to enter the camp. These difficulties are likely to be removed by a new order of the OKH, since this order clearly states that the Army, too, must contribute towards the solution of these problems and, in particular, that the SD should be given maximum authority. During these last days it has been noted, however, that this basic order has not yet reached the lower ranks. Further support and readiness to help on the parte of the Army is expected in the future as far as the competence of AOK8 is concerned. This is due to Brigadier General von Reichenau's order issued on October 10, 1941, stating unambiguously that the Russian soldier is to be regarded as an exponent of Bolshevism and is to be treated accordingly by the Army.

Cooperation with the Secret Field Police did not meet with any difficulties. True, one could note that the Secret Field Police mainly took care of security police matters, obviously because there were no other tasks; however, these irregularities have been stopped each time after they were discussed. Furthermore, the most recent order of the Chief of the Field Police must have removed any remaining doubts. Exchange of documents between the SD and the Secret Field Police took place without any friction, and the initial fears that the G.P. would sometimes withhold information seem not to have been justified. Besides, pressure was put on the AOKs and their staffs that matters concerning the Security Police would be passed on directly to the Kommandos.

Work has progressed smoothly on the counter-intelligence positions established in the rear area. On the one hand, counter-intelligence officers regularly visit [EG HQ] and its Kommandos in order to report on their work; on the other hand, they come to receive advice.

Since the work of the security police has been carried out without a hitch and has gained unanimous respect, it can be as sumed that this useful association [between the EG and the German Army] will continue unchanged in the future.

The Chief of the Security Police
and Security Service

Berlin,
October 31, 1941

55 copies
(36th copy)

## Operational Situation Report USSR No. 127

. . . . . . . . . . . .

*Einsatzgruppe C*
Location: Kiev

## Work carried out to date by the Security Police

Around July 1, 1941, Einsatzgruppe C started to go into action in Galicia together with its Kommandos. It is located in the area of Army Group South. As agreed with the commanding officer of the rear area of the Army Group, General von Roques, the Einsatzkommandos, as well as the staff of the Einsatzgruppe itself, were to move as close as possible to the fighting troops.

Two broad areas of activity became evident during the work itself: first, the occupied territory of Galicia, that is, the area that has been under Russian rule for only one year and nine months; secondly, the Ukraine proper, which had to suffer twenty-three years of Bolshevik rule.

In Galicia, particularly in Lvov, the German-speaking element was predominant. This made matters easier in practical terms since one was hard put to find any Bolshevik influence in the country. Measures were, therefore, mainly directed against the Jewish part of the population for they had used the short period of Bolshevik rule for a brutal display of power against the rest of the population. The country here still had a markedly West European character which also significantly facilitated the work of the Security Police.

The deeper, however, the Einsatzgruppe advanced into Ukrainian territory, the more the traces of former Bolshevik rule became evident. The country was particularly characterized by the lack of bigger towns. The surrounding area had a decidedly rural character.

First, very little industry was found. Through the confiscation of all private property and the installation of kolkhoz and sovkhoz farms, the entire population had been subjected to such a strong Soviet suppression and exploitation that the appearance of the Security Police Kommandos elicited deep satisfaction everywhere. In conclusion, it may be stated today that the entire Ukrainian population has remained free of any Bolshevik ideology. In the beginning, as the German troops rapidly advanced, only superficial control was required in that area since hardly any Bolshevik seditious elements were found there.

After the advance of the German troops had come to a standstill and larger towns like Zhitomir, Berdichev, Kirovograd, and Krivoy-Rog in the southeast were reached, the work of the Security Police assumed a different character. Again, lack of pronounced Bolshevik influence could be noted. Industry in these areas and the halt of military operations caused more intensive work in the interior areas of the newly [conquered] territories.

While it could be noted that in the Galician part, all those circles that were of interest to the Security Police were uncovered except for the Bolsheviks, the situation changed significantly later on. This concerned the Jews initially, who thanks to information rapidly transmitted, learned that the measures of the Security Police were directed mainly against them. One could observe, for example, in the course of further advances into the Ukraine, that, from a Security Police point of view, the Kommandos arrived in evacuated areas. The part of the population hostile to the Germans and sympathetic to the Soviets retreated in order to return later, if only partly. Therefore, in the beginning, the Kommandos changed their tactics, abstaining from Security Police measures in order to gain an overview of the situation, and [instead] installing a network of informants. Deceived by this apparent inactivity, the elements in question, in this instance, first of all the Jews, slowly returned, and a high percentage of them could [then] be caught.

Following this procedure, the Kommandos greatly depended on the cooperation of the population. In this respect, very strong support was given by the ethnic Germans who live scattered all over the area. In most cases in the beginning it was not easy to gain the cooperation of the Ukrainian population. The population that had lived for many years under the terror of the NKVD at first lived in fear that the Russians might return and then take their revenge.

Through skillful propaganda on the part of the German Army, [though] mainly, however, by the Einsatzkommando itself, it was possible to win over these circles to gradual, active support. It was, however, observed that the Ukrainian is able to provide any real cooperation only in a limited way: first, because of his indolence, and also because of years of suppression. He is still indifferent to such an extent that often we Germans simply do not understand. As a result of years of terror and suppression, he has become resigned to his fate and is satisfied if he has work and bread for the future.

Security Police has found two large groups of enemies in this area. They are:

1) the Jews;

2) active members of the former Soviet regime.

It must here be stated that in the Ukraine, a high percentage of the circles sympathizing with the Soviets is composed of Jews.

It can be stated positively today that the Jews without exception served Soviet Bolshevism. Again and again, mainly in the towns, the Jews were named as the actual Soviet rulers, exploiting the people with indescribable brutality and delivering them to the NKVD. About 10,000 interrogations have been conducted by the Kommandos during these four months. Repeatedly it has become clear that the Jews especially worked for the Soviets, if not in responsible positions, then as agents or informants. The large number of mass graves do not contain Jewish corpses, not even in one single instance. It is, however, established that the Jews in particular share maximum responsibility for the slaughter of the Ukrainian population and the ethnic Germans.

Thus, the Security Police saw the necessity for special measures against the Jews.

The Chief of the Security Police                    Berlin,
and Security Service                    November 2, 1941

50 copies
[50th copy]

*Operational Situation Report USSR No. 128*

. . . . . . . . . . . .

*Einsatzgruppe C*
Location: Kiev

### Execution activities

As to purely execution matters, approximately 80,000 persons have been liquidated by now by the Kommandos of the Einsatzgruppe.

Among these are approximately 8,000 persons convicted after investigation of anti-German or Bolshevist activities.

The remainder was liquidated in retaliatory actions.

Several retaliatory measures were carried out as large-scale actions. The largest of these actions took place immediately after the occupation of Kiev. It was carried out exclusively against Jews and their entire families.

The difficulties resulting from such a large-scale action, in particular concerning the round-up, were overcome in Kiev by requesting the Jewish population to assemble, using wall-posters. Although at first only the participation of approximately 5-6,000 Jews had been expected, more than 30,000 Jews arrived who, until the moment of their execution, still believed in their resettlement, thanks to extremely clever organization [propaganda].

Even though approximately 75,000 Jews have been liquidated in this manner, it is already evident at this time that this cannot be the best solution of the Jewish problem. Although we succeeded, particularly in smaller towns and villages, in bringing about a complete liquidation of the Jewish problem, nevertheless, again and again it has been observed in the larger cities that after such an action, all Jews have indeed been eradicated. But, when after a certain period of time a Kommando returns, the number of Jews still found in the city always surpasses considerably the number of the executed Jews.

Besides, the Kommandos have also carried out military actions in numerous cases. On request of the Army, separate platoons of the Kommandos have repeatedly combed the woods searching for partisans, and have accomplished successful work there.

Besides, prisoners-of-war marching along the highways were systematically overtaken [by the Kommandos of the EG]. All those elements were liquidated who did not possess identification papers and who were suspected, once set free, of [possibly] committing acts of sabotage against the German Army, the German authorities, or the population. In numerous cases, systematic searches for parachutists were carried out, with the result that approximately 20 parachutists were captured, among them a Russian who, at his interrogation, supplied extremely important information to the Army.

Finally, it should be mentioned that prisoners-of-war were taken over from the prisoner assembly points and the prisoner-of-war transit camps, although, at times, considerable disagreements with the camp commander occurred.

. . . . . . . . . . . .


## Collaboration with the Wehrmacht
## and the Secret Field Police

This concerns the relation of the Einsatzgruppe and its Kommandos with other offices and authorities. Its relation to the Army is especially noteworthy. From the outset, the Einsatzgruppe succeeded in establishing excellent terms with all Army headquarters. This made it possible for the Einsatzgruppe never to operate in the rear of the military zone. On the contrary, the request was frequently made by the Army to operate as far on the front as possible. In a great number of cases, it happened that the support of the Einsatzkommandos was requested by the fighting troops. Advance detachments of the Einsatzgruppe also participated in every large military action. They entered newly captured localities side by side with the fighting troops. Thus, in all cases, the utmost support was given. For example, in this connection, it is worth mentioning the participation in the capture of Zhitomir, where the first tanks entering the city were immediately followed by three cars of Einsatzkommando 4a.

As a result of the successful work of the Einsatzgruppe, the Security Police is also held in high regard, in particular by the HQ of the German Army. The liaison officers stationed at Army HQ are loyally briefed of all military operations, and, besides, they receive the utmost cooperation. The Commander of the 6th Army, Generalfeldmarschall von Reichenau, has repeatedly praised the work of the Einsatzkommandos and, accordingly, supported the interests of the SD with his staff. The extraordinary success of the Kommandos was a contributing factor: for example, the capture of Major-General Sokolov, then information concerning a plan by parachutists to blast a bridge, and the transmission of other important military information.

Only with respect to the Jewish problem could a complete understanding with junior Army officers not be reached until quite recently. This was most noticeable during the taking over of prisoner-of-war camps. As a particularly clear example, the conduct of a camp commander in Vinitsa is to be mentioned. He strongly objected to the transfer of 362 Jewish prisoners-of-war carried out by his deputy, and even started court martial proceedings against the deputy and two other officers. Unfortunately, it often occurred that the Einsatzkommandos had to suffer more or less hidden reproaches for their persistent stand on the Jewish problem. Another difficulty was added by the order from the Army High Command prohibiting entry by the SD into the POW transit camps.[1] These difficulties have probably been overcome by now due to a new order from the Army High Command. This order clearly states that the Wehrmacht has to cooperate in the solution of this problem, and, in particular, that the necessary authorizations must be granted the SD to the fullest extent. However, it became evident in the past few days that this policy-making order still has not reached lower [military] authorities. In the future, further cooperation and assistance by the Wehrmacht authorities can be expected. As far as the province of the 6th Army HQ is concerned, Generalfeldmarshall von Reichenau issued an order on October 10, 1941, which states clearly that the Russian soldier has to be considered in principle to be a representative of Bolshevism and thus has to be treated accordingly by the Wehrmacht.

---

1. Durchgangslager.

No difficulties whatsoever resulted from the cooperation with the Secret Military Police. To be sure, it was noted that the Security Military Police preferred to handle matters concerning the Security Police only, evidently because of a lack of other duties; however, these defects were always eliminated following consultation. Besides, the latest order of the Chief of the Military Police has probably eliminated any remaining doubts. The exchange of informational material between the SD and the GFP took place without any disagreement. The original doubts whether the GFP would not retain some of the cases were not justified. Besides, it has already been ordered by Army HQ and its staff that matters concerning the Security Police have to be immediately transferred to the Kommandos.

As for the counter-intelligence offices in the rear, the work there is running smoothly. Counter-intelligence officers regularly visit [EK Hqts] and Kommandos in order to transfer files, as well as to receive orders.

Since the work of the Security Police has been carried out smoothly and has won high recognition, it can be assumed that this pleasant relationship will also be maintained in the future.

The Chief of the Security Police          Berlin,
and Security Service          November 5, 1941

55 copies
(51st copy)

## Operational Situation Report USSR No. 129

. . . . . . . . . . . .

*Einsatzgruppe D*
Location: Nikolayev
During the last two weeks, the activity of the Kommandos and Einsatzgruppen consisted mainly in searches and in finishing off partisan groups. Besides, more places were freed of Jews, and inquiries were made concerning Bandera followers. During the time under report, 11,037 Jews and 31 Communist officials and saboteurs were executed. In all: 31,767.

The Chief of the Security Police
and Security Service

Berlin,
November 6, 1941

55 copies
(51st copy)

## Operational Situation Report USSR No. 130

*Einsatzgruppe A*
Location: Krasnogvardeisk

. . . . . . . . . . . .

## Activity of Einsatzgruppe A

The activity of the front line unit of Einsatzgruppe A reported in the preceding complete report continues. On the whole, the following tasks were carried out:

Interrogation of the population behind the front took place again, partly in cooperation with the military administration headquarters and the town headquarters and with the help of Security Police measures. For instance, a stretch of coast near Strelna was searched. All those elements which constituted a danger to the rear of the German troops were executed after they had been arrested and had confessed. Four village elders were appointed by the Army to stabilize the situation.

On October 20, 1941, at 8 o'clock, in Tosno, in cooperation with the Second SS-Brigade as well as the Field Police, a screening of all persons in this locality took place. All of Tosno was surrounded by units of the SS-Brigade and all houses searched according to a pre-arranged plan. The men were led to a large square and screened by a Kommando of the Security Police. Altogether 156 persons had to be executed in the period from October 15 to October 23.

## Attitude of the Polish clergy in the Vilnius area

3) A priest, Jonas Gylys, said during his sermon: "Like the hangmen they hit innocent people, pushed old men and pregnant women. Innocent persons suffered like Christ from Judas. The blood did not yet have time to dry, and already they rob their property."

These words of the priest were apparently meant for those who had participated in the liquidation of the Jews.

This is particularly characteristic of Gylys. Without permission, he went to the synagogue to the arrested Jews in order to console and encourage them.

The Chief of the Security Police
and Security Service

Berlin,
November 10, 1941

55 copies
(51st copy)

*Operational Situation Report USSR No. 131*

. . . . . . . . . . . .

*Einsatzgruppe A*
Location: Krasnogvardeisk

. . . . . . . . . . . .

*Executive operations*

. . . . . . . . . . . .

*Arrests*
1) Arrested were:
45 Communist officials or members of Communist organizations;
5 Jews;
3 persons who had contact with Russian prisoners-of-war;
22 escaped prisoners-of-war.
2) Several scattered Red Guards were seen on October 13, 1941,
in Tukum county, who had reached the coast of Kurland in boats from
Ösel. Energetic searches carried out together with the Auxiliary Police and the Volunteer Police Reserve made it possible to capture the
fifteen Red Guards. One Red Guard who wanted to avoid arrest by
escaping was shot.
3) The Jew Max Wulfson was arrested in his apartment in Riga on
October 20, 1941. He is suspected of being the liaison man of the
teacher Karl Bühndorff who had emigrated from Germany in 1933
and was associated with Soviet-Russian and English agents.
Bühndorff himself was arrested on March 27, 1941, by officials of the

NKVD. Nothing could be established so far about his whereabouts. It is likely that he was deported to Russia.

## Executions

During the period of October 18-25, 1941, the following executions took place:

In Riga ................................. 115 Communists
........................................... 6 Jews
In the area of the Field Office:
Volmar................................. 56 Communists
........................................... 15 Jews
Libau.................................... 13 Communists
    Total .................................. 15 Jews
........................................... 220
The estimated total in the area of Einsatzkommando 2, therefore, amounts to 31,598.

## Miscellaneous
### Reports of field offices

a) Volmar

During the week under survey, the files of persons arrested by the Latvian Auxiliary Police were examined.

On October 23, 1941, the following executions took place:

in Wenden .............. 9 Communists ............ 3 Jews
in Volmar .............. 12 Communists ........... 10 Jews
in Valk ................. 15 Communists .................
in Smilton .............. 7 Communists .................
in Marienburg .......... 12 Communists .................
total .................. 55 Communists ........... 13 Jews
With the exception of Madon, it will not be necessary to carry out any further executions in this area.

b) Libau

In the period under review, 15 members of Communist organizations have been arrested in Libau and in the surrounding rural districts. The Libau prisons at present contain 693 political prisoners. Searches and checks have been carried out in 14 localities.

In Libau, four juveniles were arrested who tried to form an illegal group. They were former members of the Red Pioneers [Communist youth organization]. They intended to get hold of arms in order to organize partisan warfare against the German Army either in case of a possible Russian return or a revolution which they were expecting to take place in Germany. Investigations have not yet been concluded. Some of the perpetrators confessed. When one Libau Jew was arrested, a quantity of strychnine sufficient to poison 1,000 people was found in his apartment. The poison had been for some time in the hands of the Jew in question. His statement concerning its origin cannot be believed. He will be executed.

Two Latvians were arrested in the act of looting Jewish apartments, having identified themselves as German Security Police men. Both were executed. As looting is becoming too common of late, the execution of the two Latvians was publicized in the local newspapers.

At present, investigations are in progress concerning the ambushing of a naval orderly. Suspicion is centering more and more upon certain persons. It is to be expected that the investigations will be successful.

During the period under survey, 30 persons, 18 Jews and 12 Communists, were executed.

The Chief of the Security Police
and Security Service

Berlin,
November 12, 1941

<u>55 copies</u>
(51st copy)

## Operational Situation Report USSR No. 132

. . . . . . . . . . . .

*Einsatzgruppe C*

. . . . . . . . . . . .

Dniepropetrovsk

. . . . . . . . . . . .

### Execution activity

The number of executions carried out by Sonderkommando 4a has meanwhile increased to 55,432.

Among those executed by Sonderkommando 4a in the latter half of October 1941 until the date of this report, in addition to a comparatively small number of political functionaries, active Communists, people guilty of sabotage, etc., the larger part were again Jews. A considerable part of these were Jewish prisoners-of-war handed over by the German Army at Borispol, at the request of the Commander of the Borispol POW camp. On October 14, 1941 a platoon of Sonderkommando 4a shot 752 Jewish prisoners-of-war, among them some commissars and 78 wounded Jews were handed over by the camp physician.

At the same time, the platoon executed 24 partisans and Communists arrested by the local commander at Borispol. It should be noted that due largely to the energetic help of the German Army authorities in Borispol these activities in Borispol were carried out smoothly.

Another platoon of Sonderkommando 4a was active at Lubny.

Without any opposition, it executed 1,363 Jews, Communists, and partisans, among them 53 prisoners-of-war and a few Jewish rifle-women. Before the war, Lubny had 35,000 inhabitants, among them 14,000 Jews. A recent census undertaken by the local municipal administration showed that of 20,000 inhabitants allegedly only 1,500 Jews can be listed.

. . . . . . . . . . . .

Sonderkommando 4b is stationed in Poltava, according to a report dated October 16, 1941. Slaviansk is to be its next location. The work of Sonderkommando 4b, influenced partly by weather and road conditions, was mainly limited to the area of Poltava. In the week from October 4, 1941, to October 10, 1941, a total of 186 persons were executed, among them 21 political functionaries, four people guilty of sabotage and looting, and 161 Jews. In addition, the task of the Sonderkommando included searches and pursuits of former leading Communist functionaries and members of the executive committee of the Poltava district.

Everywhere in the area of Sonderkommando 4b, full understanding was shown by the German Army for the activity of the Sonderkommando in connection with the security service of the police.

The number of people executed by Einsatzkommando 5 amounted to 15,110 on October 20, 1941. Of this number, 20 political functionaries, 21 people guilty of sabotage and looting, and 1,847 Jews were shot between October 13, 1941 and October 19, 1941. On October 18, 1941, 300 insane Jews from the Kiev lunatic asylum were liquidated. This represented a particularly heavy psychological burden for the members of Einsatzkommando 5 who were in charge of this operation.

A large part of the work of Einsatzkommando 5 is dealing with denunciations which are reported daily in great numbers by all classes of the population. These necessitate subsequent interrogations and investigations.

Between September 26, 1941 and October 4, 1941, Einsatzkommando 5 executed eight political functionaries and two people guilty of sabotage in Krivoy-Rog. Between September 23, 1941 and October 4, 1941, 85 political functionaries, 14 people guilty of sabotage and looting, and 179 Jews were executed in Dniepropetrovsk.

137 trucks full of clothes made available as a result of the campaign

against the Jews of Zhitomir and Kiev were put at the disposal of the National Socialist People's Welfare Organization[1] for further disposal. The greater part of these articles, after having been disinfected, were distributed among ethnic Germans. From this supply, a field hospital of the Waffen-SS, among others, was also able to meet its requirements of woolen blankets, etc. [for the bitter cold winter months].

---

1. Nationalsozialistische Wohlfahrtspflege (NSW).

The Chief of the Security Police　　　　　Berlin,
and Security Service　　　　　November 14, 1941

60 copies
(57th copy)

## Operational Situation Report USSR No. 133

. . . . . . . . . . . .

*Einsatzgruppe A*
Location: Krasnogvardeisk

### Partisans in Riga
### Organization

In the last days partisan groups were uncovered in Riga. 56 arrests have been made so far. More are to follow. So far, one mortar with 15 shells, pistols, munitions, and a wireless-transmitter were seized. Members of a group dressed in army uniforms of army deserters have, among other acts, attacked an army truck on the Riga-Madohn highway. It is very probable that partisans have connections with the ghetto and German deserters. Informants connected to the individual groups are assured. Inquiries are not yet concluded. They promise further success.

. . . . . . . . . . . .

*Einsatzgruppe B*
Location: Smolensk

### Intelligence Activity

1) *Situation in the newly-occupied area*
In the course of the advance of Army Group Center, a number of newly-occupied towns like Briansk, Ordzhonikidzegrad, Uritski, Gzhatsk, Rzhev were also treated according to SD methods by the

Kommandos of the Einsatzgruppe. Once again one can state generally that the civilian population of the towns that are now occupied by our troops were systematically evacuated [by the Soviets] quite a while ago. At the time of occupation there is usually only a fraction of the former population in the towns. They are mostly such persons who have managed to avoid evacuation by running into the surrounding villages. The Jewish population, as well as the Communist party members and the skilled workers, however, have all escaped, as far as could be ascertained. According to available reports, the population was exhorted by a steady stream of propaganda to move, if possible, to the Volga and the Ural areas. Transport trains were put at their disposal and thus a large part of the population was gradually evacuated in this direction.

. . . . . . . . . . . .

2) *Morale and general conduct of the population*

. . . . . . . . . . . .

The public execution of a partisan leader and of three Bolshevik terrorists had a quieting effect on the civilian population of Mogilev. Numerous civilian inhabitants were present at the execution by hanging. It appeared to make a deep impression on them that, from the German side, measures which they themselves can also witness, will now be taken against partisans and Bolshevik functionaries. At any rate, this action is proved to have made far more of an impression on the civilian population than some executions announced by poster. On the other hand, the population exhibited more indifference to the total liquidation of Jews, as in the Vitebsk ghetto, for example. They soon became used to the absence of the Jews without being influenced in either a positive or negative way.

## Executions

1) *General situation*

. . . . . . . . . . . .

Resistance among the masses has visibly slackened since the recent German military successes and, in particular, in those areas where the Jews, well known for leading resistance movements, have been completely removed. If the Russian segment of the population had any tendency towards resistance, our very harsh and strict measures (executions by hanging and shooting) have not failed in their effect. The flight of the Jews towards the east goes on, as could be ascertained at the time of the report. Thus, EK 9, which is marching towards Moscow, reports that in the town Yartsevo where 7,000 Jews used to live, not a single one has remained. It was much the same in Rzhev, Gzhatsk, Mozhaisk, Izichnov, and Briansk.

. . . . . . . . . . . .

Generally, the cooperation of the peace-loving population, particularly the Byelorussian circles, can be felt. In particular, one meets with understanding of how the Jewish question is dealt with. The Jews are regarded as a pest, particularly in the rural areas. The population has already repeatedly asked that the various local military commanders carry out measures against the Jews. Unfortunately, the population can not even decide to take up auxiliary measures on its own against the Jews. The reasons, which are purely psychological, have been referred to before.

2) *The fight against the partisans*

When a partisan organization in Mogilev was uncovered, it was noted that its leader, the former Soviet Russian Lieutenant Moktseev, had already managed to recruit 39 men as well as 15 women (mainly adolescents), to serve as spies and to transmit information. Among the 55 persons, there were, all told, 22 Jews who worked with fanatical zeal to further strengthen the organization. Moktseev received strong support from a vegetable dealer who put at his disposal his storeroom in which to carry out the work. The 55 persons were liquidated and, in addition, collective measures were carried out against the Jews.

. . . . . . . . . . . .

3) *Operations against Party functionaries, agents, saboteurs, and Jews*

In Mogilev, the female worker Nina Lisunova was arrested. She has an elementary school education (up to fourth grade) and worked in a silk factory in Mogilev. She was a deputy to the Soviet Supreme Council and had participated in eight meetings of the Soviet Council in Moscow.

On October 11, 1941, the Russian Feodor Karyago from Shklov and three more Russians were shot for Communist agitation.

On the same day, the Russians Vasily Bertyev, Vladimir Berendovsky, and Andrei Siniakov were shot. They had attempted to build up an organization for Communist activities and had already acquired pistols.

On October 14, 1941, the Russians Michael Sokishevsky, Vasily Terisov, Maxim Rudakov, Georgi Charsevu, and Makar Amsalovich were shot. Under the Soviet regime, they had been active Party functionaries and had handed large numbers of people over to the NKVD, as well as assisting in the deportations.

On October 16, 1941, the Russian girl Anna Garbusov was shot for particularly violent expressions of hostility against Germany while a member of the NKVD [that is, prior to the arrival of the Germans].

On the same day, the Jews Stanislaus Borsky and Tolia Akhonin were liquidated for being former NKVD agents. The Jews Simen Alexandrovich, Shuster Peiser, and Mikhail Saki were shot for being in possession of explosive ammunition.

On the same day the Jewess Kadin Orlov was executed for being found without a Jewish badge and for refusing to move into the ghetto. On October 18, 1941, the Jews Lova Wasman, Fama Birkman, Yakob Saravo, Abraham Linden, Abraham Baraniche, Salomon Katzman, and Ber Katzman, as well as the Jewess Fania Leikina were liquidated for refusing to wear the Jewish badge and for spreading inflammatory propaganda against Germany. On October 20, 1941, the Jew Stanilov Naum and the Jewish couple Alter were liquidated. They had hidden themselves in Mogilev outside the ghetto.

On October 14, 1941, the Jew Isaak Piaskin was shot by the Vorkommando of Einsatzkommando 9. He had been a political functionary of the Red Army and was found on the road to Viasma in suspicious circumstances.

On October 17, 1941, the woman Maria Spirina was shot for sniping.

On October 21, 1941, the Jew Yoel Liubavin was shot after he was found not far from Viasma in a Russian bunker in possession of firearms.

. . . . . . . . . . .

4) *Measures against criminals and looters*
The Jew Samuel Goffman was shot on October 17, 1941. He was convicted of having falsified his identity card in order to hide his Jew-

ish origins. The Russian, Emil Stubin, was shot on the same day after having been convicted of repeated arson.

Six Russians were shot in Mogilev on October 20, 1941. They had been wandering about the town and lived by committing criminal acts, including extortion.

Twelve persons were shot on October 21, 1941. They were convicted of criminal theft.

Two Jewesses who set fire to two houses in Bobruisk during the air attack on the night of October 13, 1941, were liquidated.

A larger number of persons were shot in Bobruisk for looting and other criminal acts.

. . . . . . . . . . . .

### 5) "Sonderaktionen"

83 of the several hundred inmates from the forced labor camp in Mogilev were liquidated on October 15, 1941, for being racially inferior elements of an Asiatic strain. The responsibility for their retention in the Rear Army area could no longer be taken.

According to a report by Infantry Regiment 691, the Jews of Asmony in every way possible supported the partisans still holding out in the immediate area. On October 9, 1941, during a mopping-up operation in that area 81 Jews were shot for breaking the regulations of the German occupying forces. Russian uniforms were found in several Jewish dwellings.

As a result of numerous complaints about their provocative behavior in Gorki (northeast of Mogilev) as well as in the surrounding area, a total of 2,200 Jews of all ages were liquidated in mopping-up operations in eight localities. They were, for the most part, Jews who had immigrated from the district of Minsk. Like the rest, they committed offences against the regulations of the German [occupation] forces. The operation was carried out in close cooperation with the Military Police.

In Mstislavl, about 80 km east of Mogilev, 900 Jews were liquidated for breaking regulations of the German forces, harboring partisans in transit, and providing them with food and clothing.

On October 19, 1941, a large-scale operation against the Jews was carried out in Mogilev with the aid of the Police Regiment "Center." 3,726 Jews of both sexes and all ages were liquidated by this action. These measures were necessary because, ever since the town of Mogilev was occupied by German troops, the Jews ignored the authority of the Occupying forces. In spite of previous measures taken against them, they not only failed to desist but continued their anti-German activities (sabotage, support of partisans, refusal to work, etc.) to such an extent and with such persistence that, in the interests of establishing order in the rear areas, it could no longer be tolerated.

On October 23, 1941, to prevent further acts of sabotage and to combat the partisans, a further number of Jews from Mogilev and the surrounding area, 239 of both sexes, were liquidated.

Sonderkommando 7a carried out 173 liquidations during the period covered by this report.

. . . . . . . . . . .

7) *Confiscation of money and other belongings*
During the period covered by this report, Einsatzkommando 8 confiscated a further 491,705 rubles as well as 15 gold rubles. They were duly recorded and passed on to the Administration of Einsatzkommando 8. The total amount of rubles seized so far by Einsatzkommando 8 now amounts to 2,511,226 rubles.

8) *Organizational measures*
Mogilev can be considered practically free of Jews after the last operations. The area of the ghetto built in Mogilev by Einsatzkommando 8 could, for the main part, be returned to the city administration. The few remaining Jews are accommodated in a forced labor camp and are ready to be used as skilled artisans.

Sonderkommando 7a has set up an Order Service and a Judenrat in Rzhev.

9) *Liquidations*
According to the reports at hand, the reports of Sonderkommando 7b and Einsatzkommando 9 and VKM[1] have yet to follow. The liquidations during the period covered by this report have reached the following figures:

a) Staff and VKM ................................3,457
b) Sonderkommando 7a ............................1,517
c) Sonderkommando 7b ............................1,822
d) Einsatzkommando 8 ...........................28,219
e) Einsatzkommando 9 ...........................11,452
Total: ........................................45,467

persons liquidated to date by Einsatzgruppe B.

---

1. Vorkommando Moskaw.

. . . . . . . . . . . .

*Einsatzgruppe C*
Location: Kiev

. . . . . . . . . . . .

## II. Nationality problems

. . . . . . . . . . . .

4.) *Jews*

It need not be particularly stressed that Communist agitators received very warm support from the Jews. Under the prevailing conditions, it is important to stop the activity of the Jews in Volhynia and to remove thereby the most fertile soil from Bolshevism. The extermination of the Jews, who are, without any doubt, useless as workers and more harmful as the carriers of the bacillae of Communism, was [unavoidably] necessary.

. . . . . . . . . . . .

## V. Mood of the population

Following a thoroughly hopeful mood within the population at the time of the entry of the German troops, under the impact of the liberation from the Bolshevist blood terror, there can now be felt considerable ill-humor because of the aforementioned conditions. Even though Bolshevik propaganda is ineffective within wider circles, the propaganda activity of the Ukrainian political parties does not contribute towards improving trust in the German troops. This is particularly so with Bandera's propaganda, but also in Melnyk's. It was apparently not yet possible to present the German administration as the [supreme] power above all [Ukrainian] parties, having the best of Ukrainian interests in mind. The ill-humor is also nourished by Jewish activity, whose influence in economic matters cannot at all be regarded as broken. Also the events and measures which have been mentioned above under Section II — Nationality problems, affect the mood. Though the question of the Church has not yet been solved, it seems to be of little importance with respect to influencing the opinion of the Ukrainian people. This problem will probably be tackled only after a decision has been reached here.

The Chief of the Security Police
and Security Service

Berlin,
November 19, 1941

60 copies
(60th copy)

*Operational Situation Report USSR No. 135*

. . . . . . . . . . . .

*Einsatzgruppe A*
Location: Krasnogvardeisk

*The political basis for Germanization activity*

. . . . . . . . . . . .

The improved mood of the Estonians towards the Germans is observable and can be described as follows:

a) active cooperation of the Estonian Self Defense in the fight against partisans and scattered parts of the Red Army in Estonia;

b) active cooperation of the Estonian Self Defense and the Estonian police authorities in the fight against Bolsheviks and Jews;

c) appointment of Estonian officials in towns and rural communities by the field and local military commands;

d) rapid revival of cultural work in the towns, supported in part or, at least, not interfered with by the German authorities;

e) organization of a central ethnic self-administration, cautious, reserved, but, nevertheless, successful propaganda activity on the part of that self-administration body in favor of a firm anti-Bolshevik stance and for all-out support of the German Army against Bolshevism.

. . . . . . . . . . .

*Einsatzgruppe C*
Location: Kiev

*Mood and situation in Kiev*

. . . . . . . . . . .

The population would hardly dare to express its admiration for the Germans had it not gradually become convinced that the Bolsheviks would never come back. The capture of Kharkov has had an extraordinarily wholesome effect on the mood. At the same time, however, a gradual change occurred in the attitude of the people towards the Bolsheviks. The animosity against Communists and Jews finds expression not only in increased denunciation but also in conversations among the population. The returning deportees and war prisoners are, on the one hand, bearers of information against Bolshevism; on the other hand, and much more effectively, they are witnesses of the [positive] steps taken up to now in the occupied areas.

. . . . . . . . . . .

*Executions*

In the course of the systematic mopping-up operations and the complete rounding-up of all Jews and Communists in the neighborhood of Kiev, Sonderkommando 4a dispatched a number of Teilkommandos who were able to complete their assignments without any difficulties in cooperation with the local commanders of the German Army. Thus, on October 22, 1941, at Koselets, apart from 11 Communists and partisans who were handed over by the German Army, 125 Jews were executed. They were the survivors of a population which, before the war, had numbered over 2,000. On this occasion, the Ukrainian militia, recruited at Koselets, made itself useful in the round-up by recruiting the required manpower to dig mass graves.

On October 23, 1941, a Teilkommando of Sonderkommando 4a arrived in the town of Chernigov which, before the war, had a population of 70,000 of which only 40,000 remain today. Of more than 10,000 Jews, not more than 260 have stayed behind. The town itself was a scene of almost complete destruction. It is said that the inner part was set afire by the Jews before the German troops entered the town. Apart from eight Communists and partisans who again were handed over by the local military commander, the Kommando shot 116 Jews on October 23, 1941, and 144 the following day. The same Kommando again passed through Chernigov on October 23, 1941. 49 Jews were arrested who, after the executions on October 24, 1941, believed that the danger had passed and returned from their flight. On the same day, too, the request of the director of the mental asylum in Chernigov to liquidate 270 incurables was complied with.

On October 29, 1941, in Oster, 215 Jews, partisans as well as a few functionaries of the Communist Party were arrested and executed.

The attempt by Sonderkommando 4a to take action against Nieshin, where approximately 325 Jews are living, failed three times since it was impossible to reach on roads made impassable for motor vehicles by the mud following the rain.

For the same reason, the plan of Sonderkommando 4a to strengthen the Vorkommando already sent to Kharkov had to be deferred for the time being.

Further arrests were made by Sonderkommando 4a in the course of the investigations made in Kiev in connection with the closing of the illegal Party machinery of the Communist Party. The arrest of the Ukrainian Michael Chernish, a member of the Secret Kyrov-Rayon Party Committee, led to the discovery and seizing of approximately 50 kilos of leaflets and propaganda pamphlets. These were intended for illegal activities of the Communist Party in the Ukraine.

From October 22 to 24, 1941, Sonderkommando 4b carried out 205 executions. These were:

11 political functionaries,
13 saboteurs and looters,
and 181 Jews.

During the period October 25 to 30, 1941, Sonderkommando 4b executed:

7 political functionaries,
2 saboteurs and looters,
and 381 Jews.

According to a report by Sonderkommando 4b, there is a mental asylum in Poltava with 865 inmates; attached to it is a 1250 acre farm. Its produce is used to feed the insane and the staff living there. The food situation in Poltava is extremely critical. For example, there is no whole milk available for the three large military hospitals. Thus, the commander of Sonderkommando 4b, with the approval of the

High Command of the 6th Army and the local military commander, contacted the woman doctor in charge of the asylum with the object of reaching an agreement on the execution of at least part of the insane.

The woman doctor in charge understood quite well that the problem should be solved in this manner. However, she objected because the measure would cause unrest among the population, which ought not to be disregarded, especially since the Soviets, naturally for propaganda reasons, gave every conceivable assistance to this asylum. A way out of this difficulty was found. It was decided that the execution of 565 incurables should be carried out in the course of the next few days under the pretext that these patients were being removed to a better asylum in Kharkov. It could then be taken for granted that the remaining 300 patients (light cases) will be released from the asylum shortly. A commissioner appointed by the local military commander will care for the vacated parts of the building, [including] the furniture, linen and clothing, while a district leader will take over the farm.

The work of Sonderkommando 4b in Poltava was severely handicapped by extremely unfavorable weather and road conditions since a number of neighboring villages, where the appearance of partisans and Communist elements had been reported, could not be reached with any of the available motor vehicles. Activities, therefore, had to be confined to the area of Poltava itself. Cooperation with the German Army and the Ukrainian police ran smoothly.

As to the activities of the Bandera group, no observations of importance could be made in the area of Sonderkommando 4b. On the other hand, the Melnyk group is beginning to become rather active. Obviously, attempts are being made to exclude German influence and to establish a free and independent Ukraine. For the time being, however, [more] detailed reports cannot be made.

On November 2, 1941, the total number of executions carried out by Einsatzkommando 5 was *21,250*.

Included in this number are

36 functionaries,

32 saboteurs and looters,

and 4372 Jews

who were shot between October 20 and 26 inclusive. In the week of October 26 to November 1, 1941, inclusive, Einsatzkommando 5 executed

40 political functionaries,
16 saboteurs and looters,
and 2658 Jews.

Included in this number are
1) 414 hostages, shot in reprisal for various incendiary crimes, 2) 1,391 executions carried out by a Teilkommando of EInsatzkommando 5 which had returned from the area of Skvira-Pogrebishche-Plyskiv.

Since October 5, 1941, Einsatzkommando 6 has been busy in the district of the Dnieper Bend. Apart from [covering] extensive rural districts, the following towns, all of a definitely industrial character and densely populated, were dealt with: Dniepropetrovsk, Dnieproderzhinsk (150,000 inhabitants), Vorkhnedpeprovsk (30,000 inhabitants), Novo-Moskovsk (30,000 inhabitants), Zaprozhye (350,000 inhabitants), and Nikopol (60,000 inhabitants). In the area of Einsatzkommando 6, the total number of town dwellers is around 1.2 million, not including those of smaller places. Naturally the amount of work to be accomplished is proportionally high and can hardly be accomplished with the forces available. Apart from the cases which are really of interest to the Security Police, there is the work, unfortunately unavoidable, to be done in connection with the immense number of denunciations with which the Einsatzkommando is simply swamped. Here, the low level of the moral character of the population becomes apparent. Almost everyone of the inhabitants considers it necessary and laudable if, for selfish interests, he denounces to the German police his relatives, friends, etc. as having been Communists.

During the time covered by the report, Einsatzkommando 6 was able to find out about a number of [Soviet] functionaries. However, again and again it appeared that here, too, the most active people had escaped in time. On October 26, after a long search, an NKVD murderer of the worst kind was arrested. Lately, partisans and saboteurs have caused Einsatzkommando 6 more trouble than ever. Five different arms caches, including two of considerable size, were discovered and destroyed. A large-scale operation, which took place on October 22 against partisans in a forest district on the other side of the Dnieper, ended with the arrest of nine partisans, some of whom were armed and others had buried their weapons. The execution by shooting of these partisans contributed considerably to the pacification of this district.

On October 24, 1941, a similar action was carried out by Einsatzkommando 6 in cooperation with the Military Police in a large forest district. The only result of this was the discovery of some arms and other partisan supplies.

Of approximately 100,000 Jews originally living in Dniepropetrovsk, about 70,000 escaped before the German troops entered the town. Of the remaining 30,000, approximately 10,000 were shot on October 13, 1941, by a detachment of the Higher SS and Police Chiefs.

To date, during the period of the report, a further 1,000 Jews were shot by Einsatzkommando 6. In spite of the shortage of skilled workers, it was impossible to avoid sparing, for the time being, the lives of Jewish artisans who were urgently needed for repair work, etc. Steps are being taken for the extermination of 1,500 inmates of the provincial lunatic asylum.

Finally, it is important to pass on a report of the commander of Einsatzkommando 6, according to which the behavior of Italian and Hungarian troops has often caused annoyance to the German authorities. It was noticed, for instance, that Italians and Hungarians had abundant supplies of German cigarettes which they sold at exorbitant prices to our soldiers. For instance, Italians selling them in the street are demanding 2 RM for six cigarettes.

The Chief of the Security Police
and Security Service (SD)

Berlin,
November 21, 1941

60 copies
51st copy

## Operational Situation Report USSR No. 136

. . . . . . . . . . . .

### Activities of Einsatzgruppe A

The advanced units of Einsatzgruppe A continued their security measures and activities as security police.

As a result of an investigation in the area around Krasnoye Selo, which took place from October 18 to 28, 1941, 70 suspicious persons were arrested and thoroughly interrogated. Seven persons were convicted of being members of partisan groups and of the Communist Party, as well as for participating in acts of sabotage. They confessed and were executed. The remainder of the arrested persons was released. The provisional mayor appointed by the local military commander in Krasnoye Selo and some of his assistants were objectionable from a political point of view. With the agreement of the local military commander, they were discharged and two of them were executed, since they had previously been active in the Communist Party. In all, 118 persons were executed in the period October 24 to November 5, 1941, 31 of these because of their activities as agents.

. . . . . . . . . . . .

*Einsatzgruppe D*
Location: Simferopol

### General remarks

The Kommandos of Einsatzgruppe D are proceeding in two main directions. Two commandos are proceeding via Taganrog, Rostov, and

Stalino in the direction of the northern Caucasus. Two Kommandos are assigned to the Crimea. As far as the kommando is concerned proceeding in the direction of the northern Caucasus, the Jewish problem has been solved. The cities of Mariupol and Taganrog are free from Jews. In the cities of the Crimea, actions are in preparation.

In Mariupol, 60 persons who were active Communists were liquidated. 26 corpses of men who had been killed by the NKVD were exhumed, made available for an inquest, and publicly buried.

In Taganrog, it was learned that plans had been made to set up communications with the Reds with carrier-pigeons. In Taganrog, 20 Communist officials were liquidated. Ten of them were shot publicly in accordance with martial law.

The Chief of the Security Police
and Security Service

Berlin,
November 24, 1941

<u>60 copies</u>
(51st copy)

*Operational Situation Report USSR No. 137*

. . . . . . . . . . . .

*Einsatzgruppe A*
Location: Krasnogvardeisk

. . . . . . . . . . . .

*Petersburg* [Leningrad]

1. *Population*

. . . . . . . . . . . .

Dismissals from various destroyed and closed factories have taken on such dimensions that about a third of the population is said to be unemployed at present. This concerns mainly women, as most of the men in any case are in the army. Many Jews were evacuated at the beginning of the war, though, according to an intelligence man, not more than 15,000 to 20,000. Nevertheless, Jewish influence on various bureaus and institutions is said to be stronger than ever. One has learned that only a short while ago there were cases where Jews replaced Russians in such responsible positions as the railway.

The Chief of the Security Police
and the Security Service

Berlin,
December 1, 1941

65 copies
(57th copy)

*Operational Situation Report USSR No. 140*

. . . . . . . . . . . .

*Activities of Einsatzgruppe A*

. . . . . . . . . . . .

In all, 67 people were executed between November 6 and 20, 1941. In the course of a special action on November 20, 1941, 855 persons were killed, and 6,624 Jews were shot by Sonderkommando 1b in Minsk between November 7 and 11, 1941.

At the request of the 18th Army, the Kommandos of the Security Police and the Security Service took part in the registration of persons of German blood. It was carried out by the troops and the command posts of the Security Police. The problem of registering and providing better treatment to the racial Germans scattered throughout Ingermanland[1] has been referred to the military command posts by the Security Service.

Large-scale acts of sabotage have not been confirmed. In isolated cases, Russian wooden houses in towns and villages went up in flames for unexplained reasons.

---

1. Area to the southwest of Leningrad.

65 copies
(57th copy)

## Operational Situation Report USSR No. 141

. . . . . . . . . . . .

*Einsatzgruppe A*
Location: Simferopol

### Cultural situation in the area around Mariupol
### The Ethnic Situation

While 242,000 people lived in the region of Mariupol before the campaign in the East, there were 220,000 citizens in Mariupol proper. The distribution of ethnic groups was as follows: 47% Ukrainians, 34% Russians, 11% Greeks, 4% Jews, 1% Germans, 1% Byelorussians, and 2% from various other nationalities.

Regarding the ethnic German settlements, the following has to be stated: until 1930, there existed an independent German district within the territory of the city of Grunau, 50 km north of Mariupol. With the liquidation of the Soviets, the district was dissolved as a German settlement and annexed to the Russian district of Kribishevno. There, the former German district was named Rosa Luxemburg. Apart from this district that is exclusively settled by ethnic Germans, there are fifteen more German settlements scattered throughout the Mariupol region.

A short time before the German Army arrived in the town, between September and the beginning of October 1941, the majority of Germans residing in this area were gathered at assembly points in Mariupol. There, they were lined up in columns and deported by rail to the north. The whereabouts of these ethnic Germans is unknown.

There was no difference in the behavior of the various ethnic groups living in Mariupol. However, the German group, consisting today of not more than 1,000 ethnic Germans in the Mariupol district, live in extreme poverty and keep apart from the other ethnic groups. The low percentage of intermarriage contrary to strong Russification efforts among the other ethnic groups accounts for this attitude of the ethnic Germans. The one common trait of the ethnic groups as a whole is their strong hatred of the Jews.

The Chief of the Security Police
and Security Service

Berlin,
December 5, 1941

65 copies
(57th copy)

## Operational Situation Report USSR No. 142

. . . . . . . . . . . .

*Einsatzgruppe C*
Location: Kiev

### The Ukrainian people's mood in Kiev

. . . . . . . . . . . .

There are almost no intellectuals among the population of Kiev.
The intellectuals came as a rule from the ranks of the party functionaries and the NKVD. The Jew was the dominant and vitalizing factor
in the face of whom Ukrainians felt inferior and subordinate. For this
reason until today, Ukrainians resent not having been able to formu-
late a concrete view concerning the Jewish question. They merely regard the Jewish question as a religious conflict and not as a race problem.

. . . . . . . . . . . .

*Einsatzgruppe D*
Location: Simferopol

. . . . . . . . . . . .

### Work in Yevpatoria/Crimea, in particular the fight against partisans

. . . . . . . . . . . .

Regarding the registration of ethnic Germans and of Jews at the same time, it became clear that the Germans had been totally deported only from the villages. However, some of them managed to remain in the town.

During the registration of the Jews, the question concerning non-Jewish inhabitants of Jewish faith had to be clarified when the question of the Karaites and the Krimchaks was dealt with. The following facts were established:

According to their own testimony, the Karaites have nothing in common with the Jews apart from their religion. They are said to originate from a group of Mongols who lived in former times around the Black Sea.

The Karaites had, contrary to the Jews, full citizens' rights during the time of the Tsar, of which they are proud to this day.

According to the statement of the Jews, the Krimchaks are Jews who emigrated from Italy about 400 years ago. They arrived in the Crimea and adopted the Tartar language as their everyday language. The Krimchaks themselves maintain that they are a branch of the Tartar people. It can be assumed that both are right. They are Jewish emigrants from Italy who, in the course of the centuries, intermarried with the Tartars whose language they adopted. They kept their faith, however.

The Chief of the Security Police
and Security Service

Berlin,
December 8, 1941

65 copies

## Operational Situation Report USSR No. 143

. . . . . . . . . . . .

*Einsatzgruppe C*
Location: Kiev

. . . . . . . . . . . .

### Security police measures of the Einsatzkommandos

On November 9, 1941, the number of people executed by Sk 4a amounted to 97,243.

On November 7, 1941, a Teilkommando of SK 4a shot 385 Jews after summary proceedings in Gornostaipol. The Jews had mostly been rounded up from the surrounding villages. On their way back to Kiev, the same Kommando on the same day shot 120 Jews in Dymer and 30 Jews and partisans in Oster. In cooperation with the German Army, this action was carried out without incident.

From October 31, 1941 to November 5, 1941, the SK shot a total of 740 people after summary proceedings, among them:

3 political officials
1 saboteur
137 Jews
599 mentally ill persons.

This Aktion was carried out without difficulties due to the advance preparations. The farm freed after the greater part of the inmates of the Poltava lunatic asylum had been shot is primarily used by the local field hospitals. Underwear, clothing, and household articles have also been placed at the disposal of the field hospitals. The remaining 200 inmates of the asylum, who are curable, have been set to work in the agricultural plant.

A Teilkommando of SK 4b has started to purge the prison camp in Losovaya.

The total number of persons shot after summary proceedings by Einsatzkommando 5 on November 10, 1941, amounted to 2,514.

Between November 2 and November 18, 1941, EK 5 shot
15 political officials
21 saboteurs and looters
10,650 Jews
and 414 hostages.

The hostages were shot by agreement with the Military Commander of Kiev in retaliation for increased incidents of arson and sabotage. In a proclamation to the population of Kiev, the City Commander publicized the shooting of the hostages. He also stressed that for every new case of arson and sabotage, a large number of people would be shot. Furthermore, he stressed that it was the duty of all the inhabitants to report immediately to the German police any suspicious thing they observe.

Since November 9, 1941, 1,509 people were shot after summary proceedings by the EK 5; this number includes:
57 political officials
30 saboteurs
1,422 Jews.

On November 6 and 7, 1941, an action against Jews that had been prepared for some time was carried out in Rovno, where about 15,000 Jews were shot. According to the orders of Higher SS and Police Chiefs, the organization of this action was in the hands of the German Order Police. Aussenkommando Rovno of Einsatzkommando 5 participated substantially in carrying out this Aktion.

From October 26, 1941 to November 11, 1941, EK 6, after summary proceedings, shot:
26 political officials
10 saboteurs and looters
43 Jews;
in the period November 3 to 9, 1941:
20 political officials
3 saboteurs
113 Jews;
and from November 10 to 16, 1941:
4 political officials
10 saboteurs and looters

and 47 Jews.

The total number of people whom EK 6 executed between November 17 and 23, 1941, amounts to 105, including

24 political officials

20 saboteurs and looters

61 Jews.

The Chief of the Security Police          Berlin,
and Security Service          December 10, 1941

65 copies
(51st copy)

*Operational Situation Report USSR No. 144*

. . . . . . . . . . . .

*Einsatzgruppe B*
Location: Smolensk

## General situation in the newly-occupied territories

In the course of the operations of Armies Group Center, the newly-occupied towns and surrounding areas of Kalinin, Borovsk, Maloyaroslavetz, Orel, and Karatchev were taken care of with SD methods. In contrast to the towns of Bryansk, Ordzhonikidzegrad, Uritzki, Vyazma, and Rzhev, which had been systematically evacuated some time ago, and where only a fraction of the original population was encountered when German troops occupied them, only a small part of the population was evacuated or has fled. Thus, for example, of 120,000 citizens in Orel, 100,000 have remained; in Karatchev, of 15,000, about 10,000 remain; in Borovsk, of 7,600, about 5,000; in Maloyaroslavetz, of 6,000, about 4,000. Those evacuated were mostly skilled workers, while party officials and clerks joined the withdrawing Red troops at the last moment. It was observed again and again that Communist Party members without any particular function, and those who joined the Party only a short while ago, remain behind and show themselves willing to continue working under the Germans. The entire Jewish population left this area. The number of Jews who lived here was, in any case, very small.

The Chief of the Security Police
and Security Service

Berlin,
December 12, 1941

<u>65 copies</u>
(65th copy)

## *Operational Situation Report USSR No. 145*

. . . . . . . . . . . .

*Einsatzgruppe B*
Location: Smolensk

. . . . . . . . . . . .

## *Ethnic questions*
## *General*

A first statistical evaluation of the composition of the ethnic groups in the town of Smolensk shows the following:

| | | | | |
|---|---|---|---|---|
| 23,110 | Russians | = | 90.7 = | % |
| 1,026 | Byelorussians | = | 4.1 = | % |
| 488 | Poles | = | 1.9 = | % |
| 312 | Ukrainians | = | 0.8 = | % |
| 189 | Latvians | = | 0.5 = | % |
| 106 | Germans | = | 0.4 = | % |
| 118 | Lithuanians | = | 0.5 = | % |
| 23 | Gypsies | = | 0.1 = | % |
| 27 | Tartars | = | 0.1 = | % |
| 10 | Estonians | = | 0.05 = | % |
| 41 | other | = | 0.2 = | % |

Conditions in the areas surrounding Smolensk are probably similar.

. . . . . . . . . . . .

## School matters

. . . . . . . . . . . .

4) As a matter of policy, only elementary schools are to be opened; no higher or private schools.

5) Jewish children receive no instruction.

These preparatory actions aim at coordinating the measures to be taken for the civilian population and at organizing the rear area of the German Army, in order not to make it necessary to rearrange the administration when the area is taken over by a civilian administration at a later stage.

There will be difficulties in organizing the school system, particularly because of the problems of space, salaries for the teachers, and the question of school books.

. . . . . . . . . . . .

*Einsatzgruppe D*
Location: Simferopol

## Shootings

An additional 2,910 Jews and 19 Communist officials were shot after summary proceedings. The total number of executions has thus risen to 54,696.

. . . . . . . . . . . .

## Jews

Work with Jews is rendered much more difficult because of the Karaite/Krimchaks and Gypsy problem. The total number of Jews is approximately 40,000. Of these, a quarter live in Simferopol. The Crimean population is anti-Jewish and occasionally brings Jews to the Kommando for liquidation. The village heads ask for permission to liquidate the Jews themselves. Until now, executions were made very difficult because of weather conditions.

## Mood of the population

The population shows a positive attitude towards the German occupation. They expect to be included in the Reich after the final victory of Germany. However, they hope that they will be granted maximum self-administration and independence [autonomy].

The Chief of the Security Police
and Security Service

Berlin,
December 15, 1941

65 copies
(51st copy)

*Operational Situation Report USSR No. 146*

. . . . . . . . . . . .

*Einsatzgruppe B*
Location: Smolensk

## *Executions*
## *Partisans*

At midday in the county of Bolinichi, three armed partisans appeared the residence of the mayor of Stay, who happened to be out,
and read a typed order of the alleged partisan commander, declaring
that all the members of the [mayor's] family were to be removed because he had betrayed the Soviets by cooperating with the Germans.
After one of the partisans had added: "It is because of you that our
Jews were murdered by the Germans," another partisan stabbed the
wife and two children with a dagger, severely injuring them. Then
the partisans set fire to the building. The wife managed to escape and
call for help. Villagers who came to extinguish the fire, after hearing
the calls for help, were shot by the partisans. On the following day,
the local commander in Bolinichi carried out a punitive action in the
course of which seven people were shot whose connection with the
partisans could be established.

. . . . . . . . . . . .

It was also confirmed that Jews increasingly help the partisans and
that they support them in every way. Thus, in the beginning of November, in broad daylight, two Jews armed with guns appeared in the
village of Podgorye, situated some 40 km east of Bobruisk and de-

manded bread which they obtained. Members of the police force from nearby Rosvadov, who heard of the incident, were shot at by the Jews when they arrived in Podgorye. After the Jews were finished off, each of them was found to still have 200 rounds of ammunition in his possession. The night after, three armed Jews came to Podgorye, apparently in order to reconnoitre, and were arrested by the police force. The following day, about 40 armed Jews appeared, arresting and shooting five villagers. The necessary [counter] measures have been taken.

. . . . . . . . . . . .

## Jews

Furthermore, at the time of the report, the flight of Jews towards the east could be observed. Thus, the towns of Orel, Medyn, and Maloyaroslavets were free of Jews when the Kommando entered.

Since the Jewish population interferes repeatedly with the aspired pacification of the occupied areas despite severe punishments for its behavior, now as before the harshest methods must be applied against them.

. . . . . . . . . . . .

## Fight against partisans

During an action against the Jews, 12 partisans were spotted in Nudnya. They were shot.

. . . . . . . . . . . .

The following were shot because they belonged to a partisan group or because they had served the partisans as informants: the Jew Elia Lapitski and the Russians Ivan Matveyev, Nikolai Sepanyenko, Gregor Skobilev, and Semyon Agafanov.

. . . . . . . . . . . .

The Jew ... who resided in Bytchits was convicted of delivering several pigs to the partisans. He was handed over to the German Army at its request and hanged in public.

. . . . . . . . . . . .

Immediately following an engagement between the German Army and the partisans in the congested neighborhood of the town, a Teilkommando arrived in Ordzhonikidzegrad. The tension within the population was heightened by the fires that repeatedly occurred. Immediate investigation led to the arrest of the Russian Serge Rishin who had been a member of the fire brigade and who had taken part in the arson according to his own confession. In connection with the arrest of Rishin, it was possible to seize seven Jews who were convicted of having worked as partisans. These eight people were shot.

The Chief of the Security. Police
and Security Service

Berlin,
December 17, 1941

65 copies
(51st copy)

## Operational Situation Report USSR No. 147

. . . . . . . . . . . .

Location: Smolensk

### Actions against officials, agents, saboteurs, and Jews

After summary proceedings, the following were shot:

A Russian from Ruslichi, near Mogilev, who was convicted of having shot German soldiers and had attempted avoiding arrest by escaping;

A Russian who, as a member of the police force, had agitated against the Reich and had also looted;

A Russian who had arranged to work as a simple laborer in a peat pit in order to cover up his activity as a leading member of the Komsomol, and who agitated against the Reich among the workers of the plant;

Two Russians who had tried to incite the local village youth of Bolshoye-Sabolotye against the German occupying forces;

The kolkhoz representative, two workers, and an accountant who were responsible for the orderly management of Kolkhoz Sukhoy near Shklov. They neglected their work in such a way that their sabotage intentions were quite obvious. Thus, among other things, only three hectares of potatoes were harvested out of thirty, and rye stacks were not covered with straw. They had also illegally manufactured vodka. Partisan weapons and gun powder were found near Bobrov;

A Russian woman who had been an NKVD agent for many years and incited people against the German occupying forces;

The manager of the former glue factory in Mogilev and a Russian who had incited people against the Reich in his position as an NKVD agent;

A Jew who was a Communist Party member since 1920 as well as an NKVD agent. He tried to set fire to the village of Zavadyeyka with gasoline before the German troops entered;

Eight Jews and Jewesses who had been hiding outside the ghetto in Mogilev; 62 Jews and Jewesses who had disobeyed the order relating to the wearing of a Jewish badge;

Two Russians who wandered about for weeks in the surroundings of Mogilev and spread rumors among the population that the Soviet troops would be returning soon;

Three Russians who were convicted of being leading NKVD agents;

Two Russians who attempted to sabotage the orders of the German occupying forces by carrying out work assigned to them unwillingly, as well as inciting their fellow-workers to do inferior work;

Nine Jews who terrorized the population of Mogilev through usury;

A Russian in Vitebsk who was an active leader of the NKVD;

A Russian who had torn down a picture of the Führer that had been affixed to his house, declaring that it was only because of Hitler that the Russians were having such hard times;

In Vyazma a Jew who belonged to the Communist Party since 1928 and held the office of a Politruk in the Red Army;

Two Russians who had been members of the Soviet Army as Politruks;

A Russian who belonged to the Communist Party since 1920 and had been inciting;

The Jew Naychin and his wife and three other Jews who had made derogatory remarks concerning the German Army.

The Chief of the Security Polie
and Security Service

Berlin,
December 19, 1941

65 copies
(51st copy)

*Operational Situation Report USSR No. 148*

. . . . . . . . . . . .

*Einsatzgruppe B*
Location: Smolensk

## Measures against criminals and looters

The following were shot after summary proceedings:

One Russian who was proved to have murdered mayor Nikita Kaslov in Pudavaya near Mogilev;

One second lieutenant who had committed embezzlement in several cases;

A Russian who had hung around as a vagrant for several months and who had made his living as a thief;

Two Jews and two Russians who had looted repeatedly;

Four Russians who had made their living by committing punishable offences, mainly robberies;

The Russian Ivan Gorlov in Gzhatsk, a member of the Communist Party since 1924 who was proved to have participated in setting fire to mills, warehouses, and granaries;

Two Russians who, after the arrival of the German troops, carried out looting of food, and illegal slaughtering in Gzhatsk;

Three Russians in Kursk who had looted;

A Russian in Orel who was caught in the act of setting a fire, and 12 other persons, among them several Jews, who were proved to have helped in starting other fires;

Sidarov, a member of the NKVD, who had a leading part in starting fires and in looting in Orel;

The head of the local Order Police in Rudnia Korochenko, who did not carry out any of the instructions of the German occupation authorities. A considerable amount of loot was found in his apartment;

Three Russian women in Gomel who were involved in prostitution and had infected several German soldiers.

## *Special Operations*

During the purging of the forced labor camp at the Mogilev base, 150 Jews were apprehended who had been rebellious. They were shot.

During the checks along the roads radiating out of Mogilev carried out with the help of the Order Police, 135 people, mostly Jews, were apprehended. The Jews were not wearing the Jewish badge; others were on a "tour" without the prescribed [identification] papers. 127 people were shot.

In agreement with the commander, the transit camp in Mogilev was searched for Jews and officials. 126 people were found and shot.

As was shown by confidential messages, the Jews in Bobruisk became active again immediately after the Teilkommando was withdrawn. Some of them no longer wore their Jewish badges. Refusals to work increased. Connections with partisans were detected, and, finally, provocative conduct towards members of the German occupying forces [was detected]. The strongest measures had to be taken to stop these activities which greatly endangered public security and order. Therefore, by carrying out a special action, a total of 5,281 Jews of both sexes were shot. The town of Bobruisk and its nearby area is free of Jews.

Since the Jews in Partichi near Bobruisk showed a hostile attitude to the Germans and had close connections with the partisans, a special action was carried out in the course of which 1,013 Jews and Jewesses were shot.

A large-scale action against the Jews was necessary in Rudnya near Smolensk because they lent extensive help to the partisans, spread disruptive propaganda, partly refused to work, and did not wear their Jewish badges. Thus, altogether 835 Jews of both sexes were shot.

52 Jews were caught in Gomel without identification papers, trying to pass themselves off as Russians. Among them were also Communist agitators. They were shot.

Confidential agents reported that the still numerous partisans in

Gomel were aided in every way by the Jews. Consequently, a special action had to be carried out in Gomel, Rogachev, and Kormu. Thus, a total of 2,365 Jews and Jewesses were shot.

Following an action against the partisans which was carried out by the 221st Security Division with the aid of a troop of Einsatzkommando 9 in the area of Klinovichi, a reorganization of the township of Klinovichi and Cherikov became necessary because the Jews of these townships proved hostile to the Germans and sympathized with the partisans. Altogether 786 Jews of both sexes were shot.

For the same reasons an action had to be carried out in the township of Lyubavichi, in the course of which 492 Jews of both sexes were shot.

At the request of the local commander, 146 Jews, who were arrested and imprisoned because of loitering and endangering public security, were shot in Borisov.

For reasons of public security and order, several actions had to be carried out in the vicinity of Krichov. A total of 1,213 Jews of both sexes were shot.

For the same reasons, special actions were carried out in Roslavl and Shumyachi near Roslavl. A total of 510 Jews of both sexes were shot.

Sixteen mentally ill Jewish and Russian children were shot in Shumyachi. They had been placed in a children's home which had been left in a totally neglected condition by the Soviet authorities. In part, the children were lying for weeks in their own excrement. All had severe eczema. The German chief military physician from the hospital in Shumyachi who was called in for consultation declared that the children's home and its inmates were an epidemic center of the first degree, sufficient reason for their shooting.

In Vitebsk, the ghetto was evacuated. During this process a total of 4,090 Jews of both sexes were shot.

The Chief of the Security Police
and Security Service

Berlin,
December 22, 1941

65 copies
(51st copy)

*Operational Situation Report USSR No. 149*

. . . . . . . . . . . .

*Einsatzgruppe B*
Location: Smolensk

## Special actions

In the course of a thorough examination in the prisoner-of-war camp in Vitebsk, 207 prisoners were apprehended and shot.

More special actions had to be carried out in Sloboda, Polotsk, Bychitsa, and Biskatovo, since the Jews sabotaged the orders of the German occupying authorities. A total of 286 Jews were shot.

The ghetto in Gorodok had to be evacuated as there was a danger of an outbreak of epidemics. 394 Jews were shot.

During an examination of the prisoner-of-war camp in Vyazma, a total of 117 Jews were caught and shot.

. . . . . . . . . . . .

*Einsatzgruppe D*
Location: Simferopol

. . . . . . . . . . . .

## Jews [in Yerpatoria]

After a Jewish Council was set up, the Jews were registered; 750 persons were counted; they were concentrated [into the ghetto] on November 21, 1941. In connection with the action against the Jews, six localities and several kolkhozes are to be searched in the environs of Yevpatoria where a few Jewish families are still living.

The Chief of the Security Police
and Security Service

Berlin,
January 2, 1942

65 copies
(57th copy)

## Operational Situation Report USSR No. 150

. . . . . . . . . . .

*Einsatzgruppe A*

### Reports

. . . . . . . . . . .

The number of persons checked within the period of the report by the Kommandos of the Einsatzgruppe around Leningrad amounts to several hundred. Altogether 93 people have been executed, among them a gang of Gypsies who caused trouble in the Severskaya region. There is no longer any Jewish civil population.

. . . . . . . . . . .

### Executions

1) In Krasnoyo-Selo ten people out of 70 arrested suspects were shot for partisan activity.

2) Sonderkommando 1b shot eight persons at Slutsk and Tosno for the following reasons: out at night, partisan activities, looting, crimes related to the use of explosives, and on suspicion of espionage.

3) Between November 1 and 22, 1941, the political department of the Police HQ of Reval submitted to Einsatzkommando 1a 282 completed sentences [and discharges], as follows:

79 executions
154 internments in a concentration camp
49 releases.

*Einsatzgruppe D* reports:

## Situation and general mood

General mood is governed, as before, by the food problem. The attitude towards Jews has been confirmed. In general, the shooting of Jews has been positively received after the initial fear of similar treatment for the rest of the population has subsided.

. . . . . . . . . . . .

## Jews

Simferopol, Yevpatoria, Alushta, Krasubasar, Kerch, and Feodosia and other districts of western Crimea are free of Jews. From November 16 to December 15, 1941, 17,645 Jews, 2,504 Krimchaks, 824 Gypsies, and 212 Communists and partisans have been shot. Altogether 75,881 persons have been executed.

Rumors about executions in other areas complicated the action in Simferopol. Reports about actions against Jews gradually filter down from fleeing Jews, Russians, and also from the loose talk of German soldiers.

The Chief of the Security Police
and Security Service

Berlin,
January 5, 1942

65 copies
(65th copy)

*Operational Situation Report USSR No. 151*

. . . . . . . . . . . .

*Situation in Krasnogvardeisk and vicinity*

The population's mood in the town and vicinity depends almost entirely on the food situation. In the town, one is generally glad that the Germans are here and, thus, at least the threat of war is over. Furthermore, the setting up of a labor office has greatly contributed to calming down the atmosphere since the work given out by the labor office has provided a part of the population with the means to acquire food.

As for the general political and military situation, one keeps quiet. Citizens of Marienburg, along with their Russian mayor in the lead, have developed a plan for a uniformed "Russian Volunteer Unit" that is to lead an armed struggle against Bolshevism.

In answer to the concrete question why some people reject Bolshevism, they gave three reasons:

1) Bolshevism has, they claim, destroyed their property and taken away all their land. They claimed that they earned hardly enough for their most essential needs.

2) They said that Bolshevism had destroyed religion.

3) They said that the leading persons in Bolshevism were Jews.

*Overview*

. . . . . . . . . . . .

All the Jews, without exception, in the General Kommissariats

Lithuania and Latvia, are now interned in ghettos. The Jews of the Riga Ghetto who are employed by the German Army and civilian authorities, are no longer permitted to go freely to their places of work. In the morning, they are picked up in closed columns by authorized personnel who then escort them from the ghetto to their workplace. and returning them in the evening in the same way.

In Minsk, as well as in Riga, everything is prepared for the reception of the Jewish transports from Germany. The first transport, composed of Jews from Hamburg, arrived in Minsk on November 10, 1941. On the same day, the Jews were assigned living quarters. It was observed that some of the Jews had a totally mistaken picture about their future. They imagined, for example, that they are pioneers and will be used to colonize the East. The first three transports that were to come to Riga were sent to Kaunas. The Riga camp that is to admit about 25,000 Jews is being built and will be completed very soon.

In the meantime, the Higher SS Police in Riga, SS-Obergruppenführer Jeckeln, started a [mass] shooting action on Sunday, November 30, 1941. He removed about 4,000 Jews from the Riga ghetto and from an evacuation transport of Jews from Germany.[1] The action was originally intended to be carried out with the forces of the Higher SS and Police Chief; however, after a few hours, 20 men of EK 2 who were sent there for security purposes were also employed in the shooting.

---

1. In fact, the action took place on November 30. Of the approximately 10,600 victims, 1000 were from a transport of deportees from Berlin, and the rest from the ghetto (see Report 156). The remaining Jews were killed a week later on December 8 (see Report 155).

## Operational Situation Report USSR No. 152

. . . . . . . . . . . .

*Einsatzgruppe A*
Location: Krasnogvardeisk

. . . . . . . . . . . .

On November 29, 1941, the workers of the meat export main office in Pernau went on strike because they felt that their wages were too low. The necessary inquiries and measures have been initiated.

A constantly growing number of Estonian citizens tries to buy additional food on the black market. Fantastic prices are demanded and paid on the black market. 402 people were shot after summary proceedings in Vilnius on December 22, 1941. Of these, 385 were Jews, the rest Poles who had been active Communists.

A German soldier was found stabbed to death in Kaunas on the night of December 16/17, 1941.

An escaped Russian prisoner-of-war who could be the culprit was arrested on December 22.

The felt factory in Smilovich (Byelorussia) was completely burnt down during the night of November 29-30, 1941. 200 pairs of felt boots and 800 kg. of wool were destroyed.

. . . . . . . . . . . .

Five persons were arrested in Minsk on December 18, among them three Jews who fled from the ghetto, one auxiliary policeman, and an OT man who looted. On the same day, two Jews who had left the ghetto without permission and two looters were shot. The Einsatzkommando in Minsk uncovered plans for an uprising of prisoners-of-war in the camp in Minsk. A general escape from the prison was to take place on the night of January 3/4, 1942. The prisoners had already equipped themselves with maps of the town and issued marching orders. On December 30, two Jews fled from the barracks that was being built near Salaspile where at the time 1,000 Jews from Germany are being used as manpower.

The Chief of the Security Police          Berlin,
and Security Service             January 9, 1942

60 copies
(57th copy)

*Operational Situation Report USSR No. 153*

. . . . . . . . . . . .

*Einsatzgruppe A*
Location: Riga and Krasnogvardeisk

. . . . : . . . . . . . .

*Report on Polish resistance movements in Byelorussia*

. . . . . . . . . . . .

The Catholic priests are the carriers of the Polish resistance movement in western Byelorussia. In several cases one could establish that the leading activists of the Polish resistance movement, among them also Roman Catholic clergymen, have made contact with other enemies. There exists a close relationship between the Communists, former NKVD agents, and the Catholic priests, such as in Tushkiviche in the district of Gorodiche. Even the Jews are not excluded from the fighting community of the Polish resistance movement although, in general, they do not enjoy much sympathy among the Polish population. They are considered as comrades-in-arms on a common defense front and, in particular, as carriers of a propaganda whisper campaign.

. . . . . . . . . . . .

*Einsatzgruppe D*
Location: Simferopol
1) The operational areas of the Teilkommandos, particularly in smaller villages, were made free of Jews. During the period covered

by the report, 3,176 Jews, 85 partisans, 12 looters, and 122 Communist officials were shot. In all: 79,276. In Simferopol, apart from Jews, the Krimchak and Gypsy question was also solved. The population generally welcomed the elimination of these elements.

. . . . . . . . . . . .

## General mood

The attitude towards German occupation continues to be positive. A large part of the population is afraid of a Russian return. 7,000 prisoners from Feodosia on the march via Simferopol-Dznakoy, partly under guard, [made] no attempt to go over to the Russians.

Food supplies already very difficult. Presently attempting to send parts of town population to the countryside.

Tartars are in general positively inclined towards the German occupying forces. They constantly offer active help against partisans, setting up of independent armed units and actively destroying the partisan [units].

The Chief of the Security Police
and Security Service

Berlin,
January 12, 1942

65 copies
(51st copy)

## *Operational Situation Report USSR No. 154*

. . . . . . . . . . . .

Einsatzgruppe A
Location: Krasnogvardeisk

. . . . . . . . . . . .

### *Arrests*

The district chief of Utona, Grebliauskas Pranas, was arrested on November 14, 1941. He failed to hand over Jewish property. He took objects from Jewish homes and did not obey orders of German officials.

The County Chief Antanas Sabaliauskas and the Mayor Wolfas Juodka of Raseinai, were deprived of their functions because of their repeated help to Jews in the course of a special action organized by the Security Police. They were suspected of taking Jewish property for themselves.

. . . . . . . . . . . .

During a special action in Novgorod, 14 Jews, two partisans who had been arrested, one female Communist Party official, and one Russian engineer were shot because of attempted sabotage and setting fire to technical works in Novgorod.

During the action on November 29 in Kaunas, 15 Soviet terrorists as well as 19 Lithuanian Jews were also shot for refusing to live in the ghetto.

. . . . . . . . . . . .

# General situation in the present area of General Kommissariat Byelorussia

. . . . . . . . . . . .

During a punitive expedition, the village of Augrina near Rositten was burned down. The population had given shelter, food, and support to the partisans. In nearly all the houses that were burned down, there were explosions caused by hand-grenades and ammunition. The total population of 250 was taken prisoner. 30 men, the chief participants, were publicly shot in the market square of Rositten. The remainder were shot as well. The population is showing complete understanding of these drastic measures. The Jews who escaped on December 30 from the huts of the Salaspils camp near Riga were retaken in a shelter in Riga. Their execution was carried out in the camp area in the presence of 1,000 Jews from the Reich who are kept in the camp.

. . . . . . . . . . . .

On December 22, 402 people were shot in Vilnius: 385 of them were Jews, the remainder were Poles. On December 20, a Lithuanian was found shot in Kaunas. The person suspected of having committed the crime is a member of a Lithuanian partisan battalion in whose house a pistol was found. The calibre of the pistol coincides with the size of the bullet found at the scene of the crime. For the time being, the suspected person is still denying the deed. Investigations are proceeding. In Vilkoviskis, on January 3, 1942, 50 Jews who were loitering were seized and shot. In the area of Kaunas, 10 Jews were arrested in the last few days because they had strayed from the ghetto. On January 4, there was a fire in a sawmill in Kaunas, probably due to arson. In order to prevent further cases of sabotage, all former Communists working in the plant were arrested.

The Chief of the Security Police
and Security Service

Berlin,
January 11, 1942

65 copies
(51st copy)

## Operational Situation Report USSR No. 155

. . . . . . . . . . . .

*Einsatzgruppe A*
Location: Krasnogvardeisk

. . . . . . . . . . . .

### Communists

All the leading Communist officials, except for one, have now been arrested and rendered harmless in Estonia. The total number of Communists who were arrested in Estonia is about 11,500. Of these, about 1,100 were shot and 5,377 were sent to a concentration camp. 3,785 less important sympathizers were set free.

Since the illegal group organized under the leadership of the top Estonian Communist Party officials was broken up, beginning with the arrest of almost all its officials and members, a revival of extensive Communist agitation in Estonia is not expected.

. . . . . . . . . . . .

### Jews

Efforts are being made to purge the Eastern Territory [German occupied Soviet Union] of Jews as completely as possible. Shootings were carried out in such a way as to attract as little public attention as possible. Up to the present, this method was successful almost everywhere. Even in towns where large-scale shootings have been carried out, the time and place of the killings of the Jews never became known. In the general population and even among the remaining Jews, the impression prevailed that the Jews had been resettled in other parts of the Eastern Territory. Estonia is already free of Jews. In Latvia, Jews remain only in Riga and Daugavpils. The number of Jews left in Riga, 29,500, was reduced to 2,600 by an action carried out by the Higher SS and Police Leader Ostland. In Daugavpils, there are still 962 Jews left who are urgently needed for the labor pool.

In Lithuania, an effort had to be made thoroughly to purge the rural districts and the small towns of Jews. Apart from basic considerations, this was also an urgent necessity because Communist elements, particularly terror groups and parts of the Polish resistance movement, made contact with the Jews, instigating them to carry on sabotage and to offer resistance. The Jews, in turn, repeatedly attempted to work up anti-German feeling in originally loyal and co-operative Lithuanian circles. Several times guards were fired at from the Kaunas Ghetto.

The Jews were particularly active in Zagare. There, on October 2, 1941, 50 Jews escaped from the ghetto which had already been cordoned off. Most of them were recaptured and shot in the course of a large-scale action which was carried out immediately. In course of subsequent preparations for the wholesale execution of the Zagare Jews, at a prearranged signal, they attacked the guards and the men of the Security Police Einsatzkommando while being transported to the place of execution. Several Jews who had not been searched thoroughly enough by the Lithuanian guards drew knives and pistols and, uttering cries like "Long live Stalin!" and "Down with Hitler!" they rushed the police force, seven of whom were wounded. Resistance was broken at once. After 150 Jews were shot on the spot, the transport of the remaining Jews to the place of execution was carried through without further incident.

In several Lithuanian towns, the Jewish quarters have become sources of epidemics owing to bad living conditions and nutritional problems. The spread of the diseases which broke out in the ghettos was prevented by the complete extermination of the Jews.

In Lithuania, there are at present only 15,000 Jews left in Kaunas (who are urgently needed for the manpower pool), 15,000 in Vilnius, and 4,500 in Schaulai.

In Byelorussia, the purge is in progress. The number of the Jews in the area handed over to the civil administration is at present approximately 139,000. 33,210 Jews were shot by Einsatzgruppe A since it took over its official duties in Byelorussia.

. . . . . . . . . . . .

## Retaliatory actions

In the village of Audrini near Rossitten, six Russians had been in hiding for months, according to a prearranged plan. Some time ago, they shot three Latvian Auxiliary Police on duty. On January 2, at the order of Einsatzgruppe A of the Security Police and the Security Service, the village was completely burned down after removal of all foodstuffs, etc., and all the villagers had been shot. 301 men were publicly shot in the market square of the neighboring town, Rossitten. All these actions were carried out without incident.

The Chief of Security Police
and Security Service

Berlin,
January 16, 1942

<u>65 copies</u>
(51st copy)

*Operational Situation Report USSR No. 156*

. . . . . . . . . . . .

*Einsatzgruppe A*
Location: Krasnogvardeisk

. . . . . . . . . . . .

## Situation of Security Police work
### Arrests

The following were arrested:
41 Communist officials or members of Communist organizations
11 escaped prisoners of war
1 person for insulting the German Reich
1 person for manipulating Jewish property
1 person based on information in the secret search file
2 persons for the purpose of examination of personal data
1 Politruk, and
3 Russian prisoners of war were transferred to the camp from the Stalag [prisoner of war camp] for instigating rebellion.

13 foreigners (Russians and Poles) who had entered Latvia after June 17, 1940 were interned.

In the course of the action against the illegal Communist organization in Riga, the number of arrested persons has risen to 115. A hand-grenade was found in the possession of one of the arrested people and secured. No special events were recorded during the inquiries. The action is not yet concluded.

On December 1, 1941, a Russian pilot who had made a forced landing was arrested 40 km from Modohn. He had been ordered to pick out a suitable landing site for [partisans] parachutists.

Another partisan was arrested by the Auxiliary Security Police in Daugavpils.

## Shootings

During the period covered by the report, the following were shot by order of a summary court:

```
in Libau ................................ 20 Communists
........................................... 1 Jew
in Modohn .............................. 28 Communists
in Yakobstadt .............................. 1 Communist
totaling ...................................... 50 persons
```

The total to date in the area of Einsatzkommando 2 comes to 33,970.

On November 30, 1941, 10,600 Jews were shot in Riga. The action was led by the Higher SS and Police Chief. One officer and 20 men of Einsatzkommando 2 took part.

## Libau

In the period November 28 to December 4, 1941, 18 formerly active members of a Communist organization were arrested in the local district. At present, there are 469 political prisoners in the prisons of Libau, of these, 219 in the concentration camp.

Because of political agitation at their place of work, three released Ukrainian prisoners of war were arrested. The Ukrainians work in closed work units. The arrested persons sang Communist songs and gave inciting speeches.

A rumor is being spread among the population that the Americans together with the Swedes are preparing to land troops on the coast of Kurland [Latvia]. This is to occur before Christmas. The rumor obviously stems from Jewish quarters. According to some information, it is assumed that the workers refuse to work for this reason. It is explained that it makes no sense to earn money which will probably be valueless in a short time.

The pamphlet "Latvija" No. 1 has again appeared in the district of Libau. The pamphlet was sent from Riga by mail to the dairy cooperative in Ezere.

*Einsatzgruppe C*
Location: Kiev

## The Jewish question in Kharkov

At the moment discussions are being conducted with a view to the most thorough registration of the Jews. According to experience gained so far, the lines between the saboteurs and the partisans are mainly being kept open by the Jewish segment of the population of Kharkov. The registration of all Jews would seem to indicate a considerable contribution to the solution of the partisan problem in this area. In agreement with the authorized Army HQ[1] and the Field Kommandatur, preliminary steps to a major action against the Jews are to be taken by SK 4a, as soon as arrangements for the accommodation of the Kommando have been made.

## Activity of Teilkommando SK 4a in Poltava

On November 17, 1941, Teilkommando Poltava of SK 4a took over the arrangements of the proceedings left behind by SK 4b. Future cooperation with the Security Service, Secret Military Police, Field Gendarmerie, the German police and local Kommando was outlined in a meeting with the militia organized in Poltava. In this context the so-called political department of the Poltavian Ukrainian militia was dissolved. In the period ending November 20, 1941, quite a number of arrested Communists were interrogated and most of them were shot.

A major Jewish action took place on November 23, 1941, after the Jewish population, on the previous day, had been requested by means of posters to assemble. In all, 1,538 Jews were shot. Their clothing was handed over to the mayor of Poltava who gave special priority to ethnic Germans when distributing it.

## Activity of Teilkommando SK 4a in Lubny

On November 18, 1941, the Teilkommando of SK 4a at Lubny took over the evaluation of the NKVD files left behind by the Vorkommando as well as the handling of current correspondence.

Together with the Ukrainian militia set up in Lubny, it was possi-

---

1. The HQ of the Sixth Army.

ble, with the aid of the acquired files, to arrest a considerable number of NKVD agents and several leading Communists. 34 agents and Communists, and 73 Jews were shot.

The total number of people shot by Sonderkommando 4a as of November 30, 1941, was 59,018.

Einsatzkommando 5 has, up to December 7, 1941, shot 36,147 people. Of this number, during the period November 23 through 30, 1941.

64 political functionaries

46 saboteurs and looters and

2,615 Jews

were shot. During the period December 1 through 7, 1941, EK 5 shot

60 political functionaries

47 saboteurs and looters and

1,471 Jews.

On November 26, 1941, a Teilkommando of EK 5 searched Staraya and Novaya Darnitsa and Nikolska-Slabotka, east of the Dnieper. A surprisingly large number of Communists and political functionaries were taken. In the course of this action, 24 Jews, 20 Communists and partisans, and nine political functionaries, as well as three Politruks, were shot.

. . . . . . . . . . . .

## Sonderkommando 4b

SK 4b had to limit its activity again to work in the places that it passed through during the march toward Kramartorskaya. According to the information gathered so far, active partisan activity has to be counted upon in the new location. While Communist elements appear to exist in respectable numbers, it could generally be noted that the Jews had fled before the arrival of the Kommando. The number of Jews living in towns occupied by SK 4b in the environs of Kramartorskaya is estimated to be no more than 1,500. During the search for suspicious elements, the mayor of Kremenchug, Vershovsky, was arrested and shot: He frequently managed to carry out his duties in gross defiance of German orders and wishes that were well known to him. In his order of September 28, 1941, he succeeded in sabotaging the handling of the Jewish problem by having a great number of Jews baptized in order to remove them from German control.

*Einsatzkommando 6*

During the period November 24 through 30, 1941, EK 6 carried out 274 shootings. This figure includes:
19 political functionaries
29 saboteurs and looters and
226 Jews.

Up to November 12, 1941, EK 6 shot 800 of a total of 1160 mentally deficient patients of the Igrin mental hospital near Dniepropetrovsk.

. . . . . . . . . . . .

*Einsatzgruppe D*

Location: Simferopol

On November 23, 1941, towards 16:00 hours, partisans shot at an army truck convoy, 9 km north-west of Alushta, on its way to Yalta with guns and grenade-throwers. The Army suffered the following casualties: eight dead and six wounded. In addition, three trucks were so badly damaged that they had to be towed away. In reprisal 32 Communists and 30 Jews from Bium-Lambat and Alushta were shot on November 21, 1941.

The Chief of the Security Police
and Security Service

Berlin,
January 19, 1942

65 copies
(57th copy)

*Operational Situation Report USSR No. 157*

. . . . . . . . . . . .

*Einsatzgruppe D*
Location: Simferopol

## General situation and mood

. . . . . . . . . . . .

The mood was also influenced by the deportation of Jews, Gypsies and Krimchàks from the Crimea during the period under report. The unfounded fear that the Germans would exterminate the entire population had subsided entirely a few weeks after the occupation of the Crimea. It was revived when the deportation of 12-13,000 Jews, Krimchaks and Gypsies was started in the beginning of December. It surfaced for the first time due to Bolshevik propaganda spread by Jewish refugees and [German] soldiers' gossip; the Jews were convinced that they would be shot and not deported, while the population was terrified of being deported by the Germans. A few days after the deportations, calm set in. While the population in the towns of Simferopol, Karasubasar, and Mushta were quiet again, the Karaites in Yevpatoria are still convinced that their turn has come now. On December 20, 1941, they even delivered all the gold in their possession to the Teilkommando leader, a large amount, as a sign of their loyalty. Obviously they do so from fear and in hope that this would prevent their deportation.

The deportation of the Jews, Krimchaks, and Gypsies, which is seen almost without exception as the last deportation, is generally welcomed. This again proves the general rejection of Jewry on the

-284-

part of the population, in the countryside as well as in the towns. The identical treatment for Jews and Krimchaks is looked upon as natural because the Krimchaks are generally regarded as Jews.

According to experiences reported to date, the majority of the population knows, even if only vaguely, about recent developments in the war situation in the Crimea and the rest of the eastern front. In recent days, from time to time, there was a rumor that the Russians are advancing toward Moscow and Rostov and that the German troops in the Crimea are in danger. The effect, however, is not so much of joy as fear that with the return of the Russians, a new wave of liquidations and deportations could occur. The Tartars, who freely offered their services to the Germans, declared that they can only accept existence under German protection. They rightly assume that they would be totally exterminated if the Reds returned.

The fact that 7,000 Russian prisoners of war, taken during the occupation of Feodosia, broke out and did not flee towards the landed Russian troops but rather started marching almost unguarded towards the German troops in order to reach Simferopol indicates the extent of the rejection of Bolshevism as well as indifference and rejection of the war among other sectors of the population.

. . . . . . . . . . . .

## *Executions*

The Security and SD-work was intensified during the time covered by report, the aim being the final elimination of unreliable elements. With special regard to the utilization of Tartars, the confidential agents' network at Simferopol is ready for action. Individual results are already at hand. Among others that were caught during the last few days were Ivanov Ivanovich, friend and assistant to Mokrousov, partisan-leader of the Crimea, at present employee of the town administration, and Petchenko, one of the partisan leaders, who was staying in the town.

Katchura, generally known throughout the Crimea to be a notorious NKVD agent, having thousands of lives on his conscience, was last seen in Simferopol.

Hazanov, party organizer and commander of an extermination battalion.

Vera Sergevner and her sister Maria, liaison agents between Simferopol and Mokrousov.

Exdorf, head of police district 6, a Jew with false papers, a member of an extermination battalion.

685 Jews, 1,639 partisans and Communists were shot between January 1 and 15, for a total of 80,160. The fight against partisans was primarily conducted by intelligence work during the time covered by the report. Where troops and armed Tartars were available, actions were undertaken, the Kommandos supplying data and leadership. Tdraktash near Sudak was attacked by 80-90 partisans and isolated Soviet soldiers. The Tartar Self-Defense Company which had already been organized was mobilized by Sonderkommando 10b. The results: 50 prisoners, 10 dead, one heavy machine-gun, five rifles, ammunition, and other material were captured. One Tartar was wounded. The Tartar Self-Defense Company stood the test very well. Four partisans were killed and one taken prisoner by Kommando 11b in the course of reconnoitering near Alushta.

65 copies
(51st copy)

## Operational Situation Report USSR No. 163

. . . . . . . . . . . .

*Einsatzgruppe A*
Location: Krasnogvardeisk

### Executions
### Jews and Church

The priest Brock, who has Polish sympathies and who influences all of the Catholic population of Lettgalen, was arrested in Daugavpils [Latvia].

Two Jews from the Reich who had escaped from the ghetto in Riga were arrested.

. . . . . . . . . . . .

### Executions

All told six people, among them one Jewess, were shot for Communist activities. 136 were released from the Riga prison after having been screened. Accordingly, the total result up to date of people shot within the area of Einsatzkommando 2 amounts to 34,193.

The Chief of the Security Police
and Security Service

Berlin,
February 4, 1942

65 copies
(51st copy)

## Operational Situation Report USSR No. 164

. . . . . . . . . . . .

*Einsatzgruppe A*
Location: Krasnogvardeisk
1) In Vilnius, 14 Poles were arrested because of extensive passport forgeries. They had sold the passports at high prices, particularly to fleeing Jews. In agreement with the General Kommissar and the German Army Commander in Lithuania, a new arrangement for the handling of passports and certificates will be set up in the near future.

. . . . . . . . . . . .

*Einsatzgruppe C*
Location: Kiev

. . . . . . . . . . . .

Contrary to expectations, the Christmas days passed quietly everywhere. One could note only increased Communist leaflet propaganda. In the course of the investigations, a raid was carried out in a suburb of Kramatorskaya. With the assistance of 230 German soldiers, a part of the town was closed and 350 people were arrested without any outside help. Of these, 60 people were shot as active members or officials of the Communist Party, partisans, etc. The others were released after a severe warning. This action has deeply impressed the population. A noticeable deterioration of the mood in the population could be felt, not only with respect to the Communists but also in national Ukrainian organizations. The original East Ukrainian population is visibly united against the newly-arrived West Ukrainians who are seen as the main carriers of the idea of nationalism. Just like the Communists, the members of the national Ukrainian movement use various false documents, cover names, secret codes, etc. Lately Communists hung up posters that falsified the original text in a Communist sense. They also hung next to the German posters so-called translations that had the same number of lines but was nothing but Communist propaganda.

. . . . . . . . . . . .

## Arrest of the Jews in Kharkov

The extensive preparations that became necessary in the matter of the arrest of the Kharkov Jews were speeded up within the framework of SK 4a responsibilities. First of all, it was necessary to find a suitable area for the evacuation of the Jews. This was accomplished with the closest understanding of the municipality's housing department. An area was chosen where the Jews could be housed in the barracks of a factory district. Then, on December 14, 1941, a summons was issued from the city commander in which they (the Jews) were told to move to the area by December 16, 1941. The evacuation of the Jews went off without a hitch except for some robberies during the march of the Jews in the direction of their new quarters. Almost without exception, only Ukrainians participated in these robberies. So far, no report is available on the number of Jews that were arrested during the evacuation. At the same time, preparation for the shooting of the Jews is underway. 305 Jews who have spread rumors against the German Army were shot immediately.

The Chief of the Security Police
and Security Service

Berlin,
February 6, 1942

65 copies
(57th copy)

*Operational Situation Report USSR No. 165*

. . . . . . . . . . . .

*Einsatzgruppe A*
Location: Krasnogvardeisk

. . . . . . . . . . . .

## General

. . . . . . . . . . . .

5) A total of 125 people were arrested in Minsk during the period January 20 to 31, 1942; five of these people were arrested for sabotage, 30 for their partisan activities, 17 for being NKVD agents, one parachutist, three for suspicion of being spies, and 35 for their participation in riots. Three Auxiliary Police were arrested because they helped prisoners escape.

6) In order to clean the prison of the typhus epidemic, 311 people were shot in Minsk during the period January 23 to 29, 1942.

7) On February 1, 1942, the last 38 Jews and Gypsies were executed in Loknia.

8) On January 20, 1942, two German railway guards were shot at by partisans on the Minsk-Baranovich railway line. One sentry at the Minsk airport was also shot.

9) On January 26, 1942, Peteris Junge, a teacher at an elementary school, was arrested. He was a member of the Highest Council of the Latvian Soviet Republic. He had formerly been taken prisoner by the Germans as a Russian soldier under the name of "Peter Jugin."

10) In the central prison of Riga, 11 more prisoners fell ill with typhus so that on February 4, 1942, the number of sick persons numbered 87.

*Einsatzgruppe D*
Location: Simferopol

## Executions

During the period covered by this report, thanks to searches for Communists and other untrustworthy elements in the areas of Simferopol, Krausbasar, Alushta, and Yevpatoria, made by a network of special secret agents, it was possible to arrest and shoot in Simferopol alone, besides Jews, more than 100 Communist NKVD agents and saboteurs. Among others, the chief of the militia, Granovski, was found guilty of being a Communist propagandist. In Yevpatoria, members of the Red Army who were separated from their units and had formed partisan groups were found and annihilated. During search operations for NKVD agents, a woman among others was arrested, her task being to spy on German units. She was supplied with arsenic to poison German soldiers. Kommando Feodosia combed the city and, on January 28, was able to kill in combat 36 Communists and partisans in hiding. Sixteen were captured. The Teilkommando in Dshankoy cleaned up urban and rural districts and, during the last two weeks, arrested 141 suspicious people. 76 have already been shot after having been interrogated. Among others, a Russian has been arrested who, as a Party official and a liaison officer with the partisans, destroyed several factories in Kerch. Another arrested person who had been appointed village head by the German Army and who [in fact] served under the Soviets as a "revolutionary and military People's Commissar," had connections with the partisans and laid plans for sabotage. A certain Sara Plett had pretended to be an ethnic German. When she was arrested, papers and drawings stolen from the offices of the railroad were secured.

. . . . . . . . . . . .

Six hundred suspect persons were registered on card indexes and some groups have already been removed. Yefilov was arrested as a Communist agitator together with five Communists during a secret meeting. Kantor, a Jewish physician, was arrested as a leader of a group of arsonists and saboteurs.

. . . . . . . . . . . .

From January 15 to 31, 1942, 3,601 people were shot. 3,286 of these were Jews, 152 Communists and NKVD agents, 84 partisans, and 79 looters, saboteurs, and asocial elements. In all, to date: 85,201.

The Chief of the Security Police
and Security Service

Berlin,
February 11, 1942

<u>65 copies</u>
(57th copy)

## Operational Situation Report USSR No. 167

. . . . . . . . . . . .

*Einsatzgruppe D*
Location: Simferopol

### Work of the Security Police in the Crimea

. . . . . . . . . . . .

A large-scale cleansing action against Communist elements was carried out in the area of Orchankov. 92 persons were arrested and brought under heavy guard to prison camp by the Tartar Self-Defense Company. At the same time, other places were mopped up in that area and the arrested persons, 49 in all, were taken to Dzhankoy.

After the conclusion of the investigations, 75 of the arrested were shot, mainly party members and members of sabotage units who had arrived a short while before the retreat of the Soviets.

### Situation and general mood in the Yalta area

. . . . . . . . . . . .

The majority of the population welcomed the German Army in November with joy and expectation. Even now, the Army is regarded and appreciated as the deliverer from the Jewish Communist yoke. Particularly the small segment of the old intelligentsia that remained in Yalta, firmly believes in them.

The Chief of the Security Police
and Security Service

Berlin,
February 13, 1942

<u>65 copies</u>
(57th copy)

## Operational Situation Report USSR No. 168

. . . . . . . . . . . .

*Einsatzgruppe A*
Location: Krasnogvardeisk

. . . . . . . . . . . .

### From Byelorussia

In Minsk, during the period February 1 to 4, a total of 123 people were arrested, 80 of them for refusing to work. Lately, the number of those refusing to work has increased, especially at the railroad offices. Five people who had refused to work were shot by a summary court in the presence of the whole crew of an industrial plant. In each case, the person refusing to work was handed over to a labor camp for a term of 3-5 months. Insufficient pay was given most of the time as the reason for this refusal to work.

On February 3, 1942, the so-called Minsk black market was raided, the entire Kommando being deployed for this purpose. Nearly 2,000 persons were searched and large quantities of black-market goods were confiscated, chiefly German tobacco, cigarettes, and saccharine. Since large amounts of German money were also found, it must be concluded that Germans have largely participated in these barter transactions and that German railroad men have played a major role in this.

On February 4, 1942, the Rakov Ghetto, 35 km from Minsk, with roughly a hundred people in it was liquidated. The Jews had begun to entice the population to rebel.

63 copies

## Operational Situation Report USSR No. 170

. . . . . . . . . . . .

*Einsatzgruppe A reports:*

### On the development of the situation in Leningrad

. . . . . . . . . . . .

Evacuation mainly of Jews, experts, and high officials of the Soviet regime is carried out continuously from Rzhevka airport. For this purpose they had daily about 15 transport planes at their disposal with a capacity of 30 persons each. They made three daily flights of 150 km in the direction of Vologda.

These evacuations have propaganda value in the first place. They are actually important only for the families of higher civil and military officials, or Jews. Nor, as the Soviets had hoped, can any relief be expected in the food situation. This is so since the number of evacuees does not make an impact on the entire population of more than four million.

More than half of the Jews who had lived in Leningrad before the war are said to have been evacuated. There are at present about 150,000 Jews in Leningrad.

. . . . . . . . . . . .

The hatred of Jews has become obvious under the stress of an increasingly unbearable situation. There are reports of excesses that have occurred on several occasions. Thus, in December, a crowd killed several Jewesses after having stood in line in vain while the Jewesses were given preferential treatment as they shopped for food.

Besides, Jews in whose possession food supplies were found were killed by their neighbors. The militia is unable to do anything against these outbreaks of hatred, particularly since, in most of the cases, the population takes the side of the aggressors. With malicious joy, they point out to the Jews what their fate will be when the Germans will march in.

. . . . . . . . . . . .

*Einsatzgruppe D* reports:

## Work of the Security Police

In the northern parts of the Crimea particularly, the territory of Security Police work, four Teilkommandos are engaged in combing the area village by village. These are for the most part villages with 15 to 300 inhabitants, mainly Russians and Ukrainians. Apart from carrying out executions, the Teilkommandos set up advance message centers in the villages. From time to time secret agents were questioned about everyone who had moved into this territory and about related events. On the whole it can be said that comparatively few unreliable elements exist in the rural territories of the northern sector. Important officials etc. have not been apprehended as yet, mainly Jews in hiding and, in isolated cases, partisans. By the end of February, the search missions in occupied Crimea will be completed; certain important areas, towns in particular, are being rechecked regularly.

The search for isolated Jews who, up to now, have avoided being shot, by hiding or giving false personal data, was continued. From January 9 to February 15, more than 300 Jews were arrested in Simferopol and executed. With this the number of persons executed in Simferopol increased to almost 10,000 Jews, about 300 more than the number of Jews registered. In the other Kommando territories, 100-200 Jews were also disposed of.

. . . . . . . . . . . .

Between February 1 and 15, 1,451 people were executed, of which 920 were Jews, 468 Communists, 45 partisans, and 12 looters, saboteurs and asocial elements. The total to date: 86,632.

65 copies
(51st copy)

## *Operational Situation Report USSR No. 172*

. . . . . . . . . . . .

*Einsatzgruppe* A reports:

. . . . . . . . . . . .

### *From Byelorussia*

. . . . . . . . . . . .

It was possible to arrest in Minsk a partisan who had been employed as a courier between a partisan camp near Minsk numbering 500 men and an advance contact post run by the partisans.

A Jew living outside the ghetto maintaining such a partisan post in the ghetto and who was supposed to recruit partisans, was arrested in Minsk. Furthermore, one former prisoner-of-war who worked for the partisans as a forger was caught, as well as a member of the Polish resistance and two Russian women who had helped twelve Russian prisoners-of-war escape.

On February 17, 1942, due to the insufficient number of guards, fifteen prisoners-of-war broke out just from camps in Minsk.

It was discovered that there exists a partisan camp numbering 400-500 men in the forest area of Durch-Klinek, east of Minsk. Weaponry included: carbines, automatic pistols, light and heavy machine guns, and anti-tank rifles. Large reserves of ammunition and food were also found. According to the statement made by a captured partisan, ammunition had been brought to the camp on sleds in the course of seven days.

Within 30 km of the Cherven-Bugovitche district, there are five similar camps. The partisans have strict orders not to start any action, only to attack and destroy German search parties.

Partisans arranged a dance in the village of Rypkhosvolna east of Minsk where there are about 150 partisans. A three-man German patrol and a translator were lured into the village by false information. They were held up with pistols and fortuitously set free.

Eleven more Jews and Jewesses, as well as two Russians, were arrested for transmitting partisan mail. This occurred in connection with the arrest of a partisan courier who established contact between a partisan group consisting of 500 men and their relatives from Minsk.

111 more executions were carried out, among them 40 Jews and 15 women.

The Chief of the Security Police
and Security Service

Berlin,
February 25, 1942

<u>65 copies</u>
(51st copy)

## *Operational Situation Report USSR No. 173*

. . . . . . . . . . . .

*Einsatzgruppe A*
Location: Krasnogvardeisk

. . . . . . . . . . . .

In the course of a routine Security Police screening of an additional part of the civilian population around Leningrad, 140 more people had to be shot. The reasons for this were as follows:

a) Active participation in the Communist Party before the arrival of the German troops;

b) Seditious and provocative activity since the arrival of the German Army;

c) Partisan activity;

d) Espionage;

e) Belonging to the Jewish race.

. . . . . . . . . . . .

*Einsatzgruppe C*
Location: Kiev

During the period January 14 to February 12, 1942, 861 people were shot by order of the Summary Court by Sonderkommando 4b. Of this number, 649 were political officials, 52 saboteurs and partisans, and 139 Jews.

The number of Summary Court shootings carried out by Einsatzkommando 5 during the period January 12 to January 24, 1942, totalled 104 political officials, 75 saboteurs and looters, and about 8,000 Jews. In the past weeks, Einsatzkommando 6 shot 173 political officials, 56 saboteurs and looters, and 149 Jews.

In Dniepropetrovsk particular importance has recently been attached to combatting the numerous habitual criminals. On February 14, 1942, it was possible, in collaboration with the Ukrainian militia, to arrest 25 capital offenders, some of whom were escaped prisoners. Among those arrested were two of the main perpetrators of a mass murder, and a document forger who was particularly skilled in the art of making German and Ukrainian official seals.

During the period January 10 to February 6, 1942, in Dniepropetrovsk, 17 habitual criminals, 103 Communist officials, 16 partisans, and about 350 Jews were shot by order of the Summary Court.

In addition, 400 inmates of the Igrin mental hospital and 320 inmates of the Vasilkovska mental hospital were disposed of.

The Chief of the Security Police
and Security Service

Berlin,
March 2, 1942

65 copies
(51st copy)

## Operational Situation Report USSR No. 175

. . . . . . . . . . . .

*Einsatzgruppe A*
Location: Krasnogvardeisk

. . . . . . . . . . . .

## Byelorussia

. . . . . . . . . . . .

Increased partisan activity in the area of Slutsk and Baranovichi continues. Several arrests for holding arms without permit. Locomotives collided in Baranovichi due to an act of sabotage by Polish railway workers. Two electricians were arrested in Minsk. They are suspected of having cut the telegraph cable of the military airport three times during the last eight days.

A Jew was shot in public in the Baranovichi Ghetto because he refused to work. In Minsk, four Jewesses and six Jews were arrested for being outside the ghetto without a permit and because they did not wear the Jewish badge. The Polish district mayor of Chukin in the district of Baranovichi was shot by a Sonderführer of the German Army for resistance activity. A secret agent obtained a wireless receiver for partisans through an agent from the factory for telecommunication equipment. Distribution of land that had been announced in the Rear Army Area was interpreted as a sign of weakness by the Communist adversary. Part of the population expressed considerable joy as its first reaction [to the announcement].

The mood continues to be low within the population because of rumors of increased partisan activity, air attacks, etc. In the towns, the food situation gets worse from day to day. More and more places of work are abandoned.

Emigration, even by Jews, to the west has been noticed for the first time in the rural communities. The peasants hide part of their last reserves of grain and fodder.

The Chief of the Security Police
and Security Service

Berlin,
March 4, 1942

65 copies
(51st copy)

## Operational Situation Report USSR No. 176

. . . . . . . . . . . .

*Einsatzgruppe A*
Location: Krasnogvardeisk

. . . . . . . . . . . .

### Byelorussia

1) On the night of February 24/25, the Lithuanian guard posted near the Minsk waterworks was attacked and shot at by several partisans on skis. A search action against the partisans had no result.

2) During the last few days, telephone wires and cables belonging to the German Army were destroyed by partisan sabotage units.

3) The Jew Brasser was arrested on February 27 because he is highly suspect of being a spy. Brasser is one of the best known sculptors and painters in Russia and has worked for many political and military leaders in the Soviet Union. After the German occupation of Minsk, Brasser managed to gain access to almost all [German] units in Minsk. He made drawings of many officers and soldiers and thus succeeded in entering the private homes of officers and soldiers.

4) The arrest of two Russian Jews led to the disclosure of extensive bribery in the communal kitchen of Minsk run by the municipal administration for the Byelorussian population. Food that was to be distributed to the people was sold on the black market. About fifteen arrests are pending.

65 copies
(51st copy)

## Operational Situation Report USSR No. 177

. . . . . . . . . . . .

*Einsatzgruppe C*
Location: Kiev

### General situation in regard to basic views

The strong measures taken by the Einsatzgruppe against the Jews and former Communist Party members had good results with respect to the feelings of the general public. Not only the treatment of the Jews but also the actions against persons causing unrest are accepted with [sympathetic] understanding.

. . . . . . . . . . . .

In general, cooperation with Ukrainian offices and with the militia is good. The fact that Senitsa, the mayor of Kremenchug, was arrested for sabotaging orders, demonstrates that responsible officials are not always selected with the necessary care and attention. Only after the Einsatzkommandos had interrogated the official could it be established that he had purposely sabotaged the handling of the Jewish problem. He used false data and authorized the chief priest Protyorey Romansky to baptize the Jews whom he himself had selected, giving them Christian or Russian first names. His immediate arrest prevented a larger number of Jews from evading German control. Senitsa was executed.

. . . . . . . . . . . .

## Executions

After the advance of the front had come to a standstill, the long stay of the Kommandos resulted in a considerable accumulation of cases. Police activity suffered very much from the cold temperature and the obliteration of tracks by the snow.

Sonderkommando 4b executed 1,317 people (among them 63 political agitators, 30 saboteurs and partisans, and 1,224 Jews). With this action, the district of Artemovsk was also freed of Jews.

As a result of the activity of Einsatzkommando 5, a number of political agitators, 114 saboteurs and looters, as well as 1,580 Jews were shot, in all 1,880 people. This Kommando also carried out an action against the Bandera group.

As a result of the measures carried out by Einsatzkommando 6, both the Gorlovka and Makeyevka districts are free now of Jews. A small number who remained in Stalino will be moved as soon as weather conditions permit. A total of 493 people were executed here, among them 80 political agitators, 44 saboteurs and looters, and 369 Jews.

The number of arrested old members of the Communist Party remaining here is striking. This suggests specific intentions of the enemy in this zone. Also, four armed parachutists were liquidated here.

The Chief of the Security Police
and Security Service

Berlin,
March 9, 1942

65 copies
(51st copy)

## Operational Situation Report USSR No. 178

. . . . . . . . . . . .

*Einsatzgruppe A*
Location: Krasnogvardeisk

### From Lithuania

A large number of partisans was reported in several villages west of Babtai in which the population is predominantly Russian and Polish. The police measures to combat this group of partisans were completely successful on the third of this month. Altogether, 102 people, including 11 women, were brought in for investigation. Besides that, six Russian prisoners of war were found as well as 12 Russian and one Polish peasant. It was determined that they helped partisans and had connections with Soviet terrorists. They were shot. The prisoners of war were temporarily taken into custody for a thorough investigation.

On February 27, four more persons who had participated in acts of sabotage on railroad installations were arrested in Pabrado and Butiai and transferred to Vilnius. Among the people arrested is also the organizer of sabotage, Stanislaus Szklenik, from Pabrado. During the arrest of two criminals in the village of Guzili, five inhabitants of the village were found in possession of firearms and ammunition; two revolvers, one rifle, and one crate of rifle ammunition were found and seized. All five people were shot on the spot.

. . . . . . . . . . . .

## From Latvia

Within the last few days, three Jews deported from the Reich to Riga were caught after escaping from the ghetto or their work quarters. The Jews were shot or hanged in the presence of the ghetto or camp inmates.

. . . . . . . . . . . .

## From Byelorussia

On March 2, three young fellows who worked for the partisans as informers in the environs of Minsk were arrested.

The Jew Bronstein who ran a partisan recruiting office was also arrested. Inquiries revealed that the partisans in the Minsk area are constantly receiving reinforcements of manpower and materials from Minsk. Thus, a transport of 13 partisans was sent from Minsk in the direction of Lagoisk.

. . . . . . . . . . . .

During an action against the Jews, carried out on March 2 and 3, 3,412 Jews were executed in Minsk, 302 in Vileyka, and 2,007 in Baranovichi. In all, a total of 5,721 Jews were executed.

The partisan question is increasingly discussed in German circles. From the Byelorussian side it was stated that the partisan movement has grown stronger since the beginning of the winter and that the situation is indeed serious.

The execution of the Jews of Minsk on March 3 has raised the conjecture in the minds of the town population that further large-scale actions will take place in all of Byelorussia within the next few weeks. The population welcomed the actions taken for they had grown angry that the Jews are relatively well-supplied with respect to food. This was determined again and again while searching through empty Jewish apartments. At the suggestion of the commander of the Security Police and the Security Service, a discussion took place at the General Kommissariat on questions concerning ethnic Germans.

Generous and extensive care for ethnic Germans [due to the harsh winter] is to be introduced immediately.

On the basis of a confidential report, it was possible to arrest the former manager of the accounts department on the civilian prison in Minsk. A Soviet Russian was also arrested on suspicion of Communist activity. There were frequent irregularities on the part of the Schutzmannschaft against civilians, such as pillaging, thefts, and physical ill-treatment during house searches.

In connection with the arrest of two Russian Jews in Minsk, it was determined that a widespread gold trade is still going on among them.

. . . . . . . . . . . .

*Einsatzgruppe B*
Location: Smolensk
The situation and the mood in the Vitebsk district have considerably deteriorated. This is due to two factors: the deputy mayor of Vitebsk was murdered on the night of January 29/30. This incident naturally elicited a feeling of unrest and insecurity among the population. On the one hand, the town's population views this murder as an act of revenge by the Jews, on the other, the work of the partisans.

. . . . . . . . . . . .

*Einsatzgruppe D*
Location: Simferopol

. . . . . . . . . . . .

## Activity of the Security Police

During the period under report, the areas north of Simferopol in the Crimea were searched again. The western part as far as the Yevpatoria Ak-Sheih line, the eastern part as far as the railway line Simferopol-Dzankoy, as well as the rural area in the north as far as Dzankoy heights, have now been worked over. The Teilkommando that has been posted in the central region is greatly handicapped by the bad conditions of the roads. A one-time survey of the entire Crimea is almost complete. Thus the southern territories of Kommandos 10b, 11a, and 11b, particularly the larger localities, are frequently, some even constantly, under surveillance. Due to the severe cold and snowstorms, as well as the impassable roads, Kommando 12 was forced to limit its activity in the period under report to places closer to the territory in which the Teilkommando was deployed. For the time being, its location is being changed to the area south of Stalino. In the period under report, further success was achieved concerning the arrest and the disposal of unreliable elements thanks to the extended network of secret informants. Besides, more than 1,000 Jews and Gypsies, many of them politically suspect persons, were caught.

. . . . . . . . . . . .

From February 16 to 28, 1942, 1,515 people were shot, 729 of them Jews, 271 Com munists, 74 partisans, 421 Gypsies and asocial elements, and saboteurs.

The Chief of the Security Police
and Security Service

Berlin,
March 11, 1942

65 copies
(51st copy)

*Operational Situation Report USSR No. 179*

. . . . . . . . . . .

*Einsatzgruppe B*
Location: Smolensk

. . . . . . . . . . .

## Enemy propaganda

Because of the proximity of the front, increased enemy propaganda, particularly the dropping of leaflets, was observed in Vitebsk and vicinity. Contrary to earlier occasions when such leaflets were generally ignored, it is now observed for the first time how they are passed from hand to hand. This might be explained in terms of interest in events on the front and the lack of relevant German propaganda. Next to leaflet propaganda, whisper campaigns have considerably increased. The originators are, without exception, the Jews who are still living scattered throughout the villages.

The following report is available on Gomel: because of the present situation at the front, increased anti-German tendencies are noted, finding expression in Gomel on posters, calling upon the population to come out and fight against the German Army. These calls are enhanced by vivid whisper propaganda, transmitted by partisans in transit and Jews who are still on the move in the area.

The Chief of the Security Police
and Security Service

Berlin,
March 13, 1942

65 copies
(51st copy)

## Operational Situation Report USSR No. 120

. . . . . . . . . . . .

*Einsatzgruppe A*
Location: Krasnogvardeisk

### Byelorussia

A Russian was arrested in Minsk for having obtained food belonging to the municipality from the municipal kitchen and sold it on a large scale. Seventeen suspicious Russians were arrested. They had been in hiding 28 km from Minsk.

According to reports from the Army Field Post Office, for some time field-post parcels have been stolen. Inquiries conducted by the Security Police revealed that 25 prisoners of war who are employed there have robbed the mailbags.

Eight Latvian Auxiliary Policemen were arrested for looting in the ghetto and stealing from comrades.

*Einsatzgruppe B*
Location: Smolensk

. . . . . . . . . . . .

### Executions
### General

. . . . . . . . . . . .

As can be learned from the report of EK 9, the partisans receive considerable reinforcement from the Communist Party and from Jews who even now live scattered throughout the countryside.

65 copies
(51st copy)

## Operational Situation Report USSR No. 181

. . . . . . . . . . . .

*Einsatzgruppe A*
Location: Krasnogvardeisk

. . . . . . . . . . . .

The arrest of the mayor and five other people from Yavni, 8 km north of Fekino, and the seizure of a partisan ammunition hoard, prove the existence of organized partisan gangs in the area around the Loknya-Khelm road.

38 Jews and 1 Gypsy were shot in Loknya.

The population in the neighborhood of Loknya consisting largely of peasants and agricultural workers is generally friendly towards the Germans.

The Chief of the Security Police
and Security Service

Berlin,
March 18, 1942

65 copies
(51st copy)

*Operational Situation Report USSR No. 182*

. . . . . . . . . . . .

*Einsatzgruppe A*
Location: Krasnogvardeisk

. . . . . . . . . . . .

## Latvia

Twenty-one sick Jews no longer fit for work and twelve incurable mental patients were executed in Daugavpils on February 28. Russian planes dropped leaflets with Communist propaganda in the region of Avrene; more than 1,000 such leaflets were picked up.

Metropolitan[1] Augustin has left for a three-month leave of absence. Bishop Alexander von Odohn replaces him and is in charge of church matters.

## Byelorussia

Fourteen persons were arrested for supporting the partisan movement, including one Jewess who did not wear the yellow badge, and political Kommissars who ran a partisan recruiting station in the Minsk POW camp.

Fifty partisans on horseback arrived in Moroch and removed the Byelorussian Auxiliary Police. Three policemen fell; the rest were taken prisoner and moved to another place. About ten Jewish inhab-

---

1. Greek Orthodox ecclesiastical rank above an archbishop; the equivalent of a cardinal.

itants of the local ghetto in Uroche, in Slutsk county, escaped and joined the partisans in the area.

On March 8, 28 Byelorussian Auxiliary Policemen were shot by partisans in Vinosno, Kolki county.

. . . . . . . . . . . .

Because of the growing danger from partisans, the Army has started to re-arrest the prisoners of war that had been released during the summer, returning them to the POW camps. In response to these re-arrests of prisoners of war, the partisans, on their part, recruit into the partisan movement all the former prisoners of war who work on collective farms. There are increased accounts about partisan gangs. Lately there have appeared gangs who rob the civilian population and plunder cattle stock in the smaller localities.

In the course of various searches during the period March 5 to 8, 1942, in the area of the 707th Infantry Division, a total of fifty people were arrested. Of these, 30 were shot on the spot.

The deeper the propaganda regarding land reform penetrates, the better the mood of the rural population becomes, although counter-propaganda has the reverse effect. On the other hand, the mood in the towns is deteriorating. A rather large meeting of all the community leaders and collective farm elders, chaired by the district commissioner, was held in Rudiensk (Minsk province) concerning the question of agrarian reform. The resulting mood was very good.

In Byelorussia, the propaganda of the Polish resistance movement continues without respite. It becomes more and more evident that the resistance movement has systematically planned its organization.

The Chief of the Security Police
and Security Service

Berlin,
March 20, 1942

65 copies
(51st copy)

## Operational Situation Report USSR No. 183

. . . . . . . . . . . .

*Einsatzgruppe A*
Location: Krasnogvardeisk

. . . . . . . . . . . .

### From Lithuania:

On March 12, 1942, ten Soviet parachutists landed near Labilish in the district of Birshai. During the chase, all ten were shot. The parachutists were equipped with weapons, hand grenades, maps, documents, German and Russian money, and a radio transmitter. All the equipment was seized.

### From Byelorussia:

In the period February 5 to 28, the main SD office in Vileyka shot 29 Jews, four Communists, five partisans, five public enemies, and four persons for sabotage. Another 16 people were arrested.

During a round-up in Minsk of persons refusing to work, eleven people were arrested and sent to the SS labor camp.

The Chief of the Security Police
and the Security Service

Berlin,
March 23, 1942

65 copies
(51st copy)

## Operational Situation Report USSR No. 184

. . . . . . . . . . . .

*Einsatzgruppe A*
Location: Krasnogvardeisk

### Lithuania

1) On March 14, 1942, 22 Poles were arrested in Vilnius for having falsified large numbers of food ration cards and for offering faked cards for sale. Armed prisoners of war were arrested recently near Yanova.

2) The Security Kommando, deployed for the pacification of that area, arrested armed prisoners of war on the Santakai farm. One Russian prisoner of war and one Jew were killed during a fire fight. The search has not yet been completed.

3) On March 13-14, 1942, four more Poles belonging to a large partisan organization were arrested in the area of Pabrado. A teacher, Peter Schmirski from a factory in Drushiany, is among those arrested; he is a leading member of the above-mentioned [partisan] organization.

. . . . . . . . . . . .

### Byelorussia

1) On March 17, in Ilya, east of Vileika, 520 Jews were shot.

2) During street checks, 11 people were arrested in Minsk for refusing to work and brought to the SS work camp.

3) The General Commissioner has announced a salary raise as of

May 1. This is because of the continuing deteriorating mood within Bylorussian intellectual circles and the present salaries which are below the minimum living wage; a teacher receives a monthly pay of 500 rubles, a physician 300 rubles.

. . . . . . . . . . . .

7) On March 18, 1942, 23 people were arrested in Minsk. Among them were five Jews with forged passports, one NKVD agent, one former NKVD official, and one Soviet-Russian first lieutenant who had escaped from a POW camp some time ago.

. . . . . . . . . . . .

*Einsatzgruppe D*
Location: Simferopol

. . . . . . . . . . . .


## Executions

. . . . . . . . . . . .

1) In the area of Dzankoy alone, 241 Jews who had recently come there were arrested. 437 more were shot in other parts of the Crimea. In these activities the system has shown itself very effective. The village elders etc. constantly report to the Kommandos or Teilkommandos about strangers.

. . . . . . . . . . . .

III) Because of the special situation, Feodosia was searched three times. A quarter of the town is to be searched within the coming days. The searches, conducted on March 5, 19 and 23, 1942, with the help of 350 soldiers were more successful compared to the [all-encompassing] large-scale actions carried out in the towns.

Arrested were:

66 Jews, 28 members of the NKVD (among them two judges and three political commissars), and 27 partisans (among them a battalion commissar and several officers of the NKVD).

. . . . . . . . . . . .

During the time under report, 2,010 people were shot, of them 678 were Jews, 359 Communist officials, 153 partisans, and 810 asocial elements, Gypsies, mentally ill, and saboteurs.

In addition, a number of Jews and Jewesses were arrested and shot in Orel. They had engaged in Communist propaganda in a particularly impertinent way and incited against the German Army in an ugly manner. In the course of the searches, German canned food provisions were found that originated from Army supplies and, according to our understanding, were given to the Jews by soldiers.

The Chief of the Security Police
and Security Service

Berlin,
March 27, 1942

65 copies
(51st copy)

## Operational Situation Report USSR No. 186

. . . . . . . . . . . .

*Einsatzgruppe A*
Location: Krasnogvardeisk

. . . . . . . . . . . .

## Byelorussia
## Mood and behavior of the population

. . . . . . . . . . . .

Further large-scale actions against Jews, for instance, in Rakov and Cherven (15,000 Jews were shot in Cherven) caused insecurity, even some anxiety among the Byelorussian population, whose educated circles remarked that they are not used to such actions since the time of the Soviets and [worried] that there might be unforeseen consequences to such measures.

. . . . . . . . . . . .

*Einsatzgruppe B*
Location: Smolensk

## Fight against partisans

On March 8, 1942, at a meeting in the office of the commander of the Rear Army Group Area Center, a large-scale action was discussed, to be carried out by the German Army in the area around Bobruisk and Bryansk.

The commander, General von Schenkendorff, expressed his gratitude to Einsatzgruppe B for their Security Police and Security Service activity. He remarked that the Army would not have been able to act successfully without their cooperation. He pointed out that the Security Police and Security Service were indispensable to the Army because of their experience gained in the campaign in the east. He added that he expected the officers participating in the meeting (commanders of Divisions Ia, Ib, etc.) to work in closest contact with the Security Police forces and the Security Service, particularly in the planned action.

The Chief of the Security Police
and Security Service

Berlin,
March 30, 1942

<u>65 copies</u>
(51st copy)

*Operational Situation Report USSR No. 187*

. . . . . . . . . . . .

*EInsatzgruppe A*
Location: Krasnogvardeisk

## *Latvia*

. . . . . . . . . . . .

Until March 20, about 8,000 men have volunteered for the newly [re]organized Auxiliary Police. However, recruiting has, for the time being, come to a complete standstill ever since the population of Latvia has learned that the volunteers who were previously recruited were not satisfied. This is because they were given faulty weapons and are to be employed for guard duty in the Ukraine, even though at the time of their recruitment they were promised to be used to fight Bolshevism at the front.

. . . . . . . . . . . .

*Einsatzgruppe C*
Location: Kiev

## *Situation and mood*

The mood of the population in the area of EK 6 can still be regarded as satisfactory. The frequent troop movements and retreats of German troops on some fronts caused a certain tension and insecurity among the ethnic Germans and [other] segments of the population who were friendly towards the Germans. Hostile propaganda and agitation have increased during the last weeks. The Reds drop leaflets announcing their forthcoming return. They threaten to shoot that part of the population which is friendly to the Germans. The Jews are called upon to remain in hiding for the time being. Their rescue is said to be imminent. The bad food situation also has an unfavorable influence.

. . . . . . . . . . . .

Police actions were taken against members of the Communist Party. This is within the framework of defense measures ordered for Kharkov to prevent increased Bolshevik influences in the area that is particularly vulnerable to it here. On this occasion, 236 people were arrested and interrogated. 193 were found to be agitators and dangerous. Seditious elements were shot. The same applied to 64 Jews who possessed forged passports, kept hiding, or were convicted for spreading seditious rumors in connection with enemy propaganda.

EK 6 purged Jews out of Avdeyevka, Berdyansk, Gorlovka, Grishino, and Makeyevka. It also arrested and executed several forgers of passports as well as two spies.

In retribution for cutting an Army telephone line, eight people were hanged and eight were shot in Konstantinovka. In Kiev, three people were publicly hanged for sabotage.

The Chief of the Security Police
and Security Service

Berlin,
April 3, 1942

<u>65 copies</u>
(51st copy)

## *Operational Situation Report USSR No. 189*

. . . . . . . . . . .

*Einsatzgruppe A*
Location: Krasnogvardeisk

### *The situation in Ingermanland[1]*

. . . . . . . . . . .

At present, the number of Jews is unknown. In general, it is assumed that there were only a few Jewish settlers who managed to escape.

The county of Pskov, including Porshov, Luga, and Krasnoye Selo, are free of Jews.

. . . . . . . . . . .

### *From Byelorussia*

. . . . . . . . . . .

In the Security Police building in Minsk, there was a Jewish furnace attendant. In the building of the General Commissioner, two Jewish building custodians and a servant girl worked for the partisans.

---

1. Area to the southwest of Leningrad.

. . . . . . . . . . .

Besides the partisan units, there is also the Party in Minsk which exerts a certain degree of supervision. A Georgian Jew Mustafa Delikurdgly who runs the Party apparatus, was arrested. The Party leadership was in the hands of a committee of seven. An illegal group of 60 ghetto Jews financed the work of the Party, bought weapons, and constantly augmented ranks of the partisans. 60-80 Jews joined the partisans from the ghetto. In the apartment of the Jew Delikurdgly a number of weapons, bandages, and medicines were confiscated, as well as a functioning printing press and eight typewriters.

*Einsatzgruppe C*
Location: Kiev

. . . . . . . . . . . ʼ

In the period March 28 to 31, a total of 434 people were given special treatment. Among them were:
33 political officials
48 saboteurs and looters
352 Jews and
1 mentally sick person.

The Chief of the Security Police
and the Security Service

Berlin,
April 8, 1942

65 copies
(51st copy)

## *Operational Situation Report USSR No. 190*

. . . . . . . . . . . .

*Einsatzgruppe C*
Location: Kiev
Within the area of the Commander of the Security Police and of the Security Service for the Ukraine, 1,315 people were given special treatment during the period March 1 to April 3, 1942; 85 of them were political officials, 121 saboteurs, and 1,009 looters.

. . . . . . . . . . . .

*Einsatzgruppe D*
Location: Simferopol

. . . . . . . . . . . .

### *Security Police measures*

. . . . . . . . . . . .

Except for small units which occasionally show up in the northern Crimea, there are no more Jews, Krimchaks or Gypsies. As experiences of the past weeks have proven, wherever they have been able to hide their identity with false documents, etc., they will be recognized anyway sooner or later.

. . . . . . . . . . . .

In the second half of March, a total of 1,501 people were executed.
Among these were:
588 Jews
405 Communists
247 partisans
261 asocial elements, including Gypsies.
To date, 91,678 have been shot.

The Chief of the Security Police
and Security Service

Berlin,
April 10, 1942

77 copies

*Operational Situation Report USSR No. 191*

. . . . . . . . . . . .

*Einsatzgruppe A*
Location: Krasnogvardeisk

. . . . . . . . . . . .

**Separate reports**

. . . . . . . . . . . .

**From Lithuania**

. . . . . . . . . . . .

Within the framework of the Security Police actions, the following
arrests were made in the period February 16 to March 21, 1942:

**Arrests**

in Kaunas: 9 Communists
37 Jews
4 Poles
11 saboteurs
In all: 61
in Vilnius: 94 Communists
24 Jews
192 Poles
9 counter-intelligence agents and saboteurs

In all: 319
in Siauliai: 21 Communists
3 Jews
In all: 24
Total: 404
The following were shot:
in Kaunas: 38 terrorists (among them 7 women)
6 spies (among them 1 woman)
18 NKVD agents and professional criminals
(among them one Catholic priest)
19 active Communists (among them 12 Russian and
one Polish farmer)
1 Russian prisoner of war
24 Jews (among them 1 Jewess)
total: 106
in Siauliai 2 Russian prisoners of war hanged
1 Russian peasant (active Communist)
total: 3
in Vilnius: 23 active Communists (among them 24 women)
73 Jews (among them 23 women and 2 children)
14 Poles (resistance movement)
20 Poles (forgers of passports and others, among
them 4 women)
7 spies
total: 137
*Einsatzgruppe C*
Location: Kiev

## Situation and mood in the Ukraine; Situation and mood in the western Ukraine

. . . . . . . . . . . .

## Jews

As always, the Jews constitute the busiest and most active part of the population in the General District Volhynia/Podolia and in the localities from where they have as yet not been resettled. Not only trade, but handicrafts are controlled by them.

So far in Volhynia/Podolia, 40,000 Jews have been resettled [deported]. The Jews in the town are at present concentrated in so-called Jewish quarters which are, however, not completely isolated. Therefore, a very active black market flourished in the Jewish quarters: peasants who came to town exchange clothing and household articles (which they needed urgently) for agricultural products. This nuisance was eliminated through strict police measures. The Jews are servile and subjugated to German officers. Most of them are, for the time being, indispensable as skilled workers and craftsmen. The present mood of the Jews which is, of course, not at all identical with their submissive and servile behavior, is best characterized by the following remark made by a Jew: "It would be enough for us if the Bolshevik regime would return even for two hours so that we could take revenge for what is done to us."

The Jews have disappeared from Kharkov ever since they were removed. Nevertheless, there are still some Jews in hiding in the rural districts as well as in town. This occurred with the help of the Ukrainians who, after adequate indoctrination, have recognized the destructive nature of the Jews. They have reported Jews in hiding, or families who housed them; these are being arrested each day. With a few exceptions, the attitude of the population of Kharkov to the Jews is absolutely negative.

. . . . . . . . . . . .

### Resistance movements

There are no indications of the remains of an organized Bolshevik organization in the General District Volhynia/Podolia. However, there are individual members and agents of the NKVD all over, who engage in whisper campaigns and seditious activities. In some cases, Jews were also caught for spreading biased reports.

The Chief of the Security Police
and Security Service

Berlin,
April 17, 1942

75 copies
(51st copy)

## Operational Situation Report USSR No. 193

. . . . . . . . . . . .

*Einsatzgruppe A*
Location: Krasnogvardeisk

### Individual reports

. . . . . . . . . . . .

### Lithuania

On April 7, 1942, in Olita, 22 people were shot because of Communist activities and connections with partisan groups. Russian hand-grenades and explosives were found on several of the Communists and were then seized.

The same day, in Kaunas, 22 people, among them 14 Jews who had purportedly recently spread Communist propaganda, were shot.

. . . . . . . . . . . .

*Einsatzgruppe D*
Location: Simferopol

### Report concerning searches in Feodosia

. . . . . . . . . . . .

## Execution of the operation

. . . . . . . . . . . .

For the first raid, 380 soldiers were [made] available [to the EG] to man street blocks and carry out screening operations. Search units arrested 351 people and brought them to headquarters via assembly points. Of these people, 64 were able-bodied men fit for military duty. They were transferred to the prisoner-of-war camp in Feodosia because they were loitering in the city without work. Thirteen people, among them four women, were sent to prison. The remainder were discharged on the same day.

Among the 13 arrested were:

four Jews, two of whom had forged passports (they allegedly forged them themselves);

three Jewesses, two of whom had forged passports (allegedly forged by their husbands);

1 partisan;

1 member of the NKVD;

1 man who hid partisans;

1 woman who hid and fed partisans;

1 member of the Communist Party who refused to accept work;

1 man who, being a civilian and a long-time fugitive, killed and plundered German soldiers at the time Feodosia was occupied.

Later, all 13 people were executed. The man who had killed soldiers was publicly hanged in the market place.

During the raid, a large amount of different German Army supplies were confiscated. At 18.30, the action was completed.

For the second raid about 360 members of the German Army were placed at the disposal [of the EG] by the troop commander. 447 people were arrested and handed over to investigators to be thoroughly interrogated. 57 people, all able-bodied men fit for military duty, were sent to the prisoner-of-war camp because they were unemployed. Fifteen people, among them five women, were sent to prison for further special treatment. All other people who were arrested were discharged on the same day.

The 15 people comprised:

6 Jews, three of whom had passports forged by the NKVD;

3 Jewesses;

1 woman who had looted German Army goods in large quantities;

1 1st lieutenant of the Russian Army in civilian clothing (separated from his unit, but presumably a partisan);

1 member of the NKVD;

1 19-year-old spy who had come through the front lines with his orders and who had been sought for several days;

1 member of the Communist Party who was formerly very active and now refused to work.

After a thorough examination, all 15 were shot.

During this raid, we were also able to confiscate different German Army supplies that had been hoarded or looted.

At 17:00 hours the action which began at 8:00 hours was completed.

The third raid also started at 8.00 hours. Approximately 350 German soldiers were [made] available [to the EG].

In the course of this action, 257 people were sent to the investigators. 23 of them who were able-bodied and fit for military duty were transferred to the prisoner of war camp since they were without work. 17 people were transferred to prison, the rest were discharged on the same day.

Among these 17 people, there were:

3 Jews

3 members of the NKVD

8 Jewesses and children

2 men who had looted

1 Politruk (in civilian clothing) separated from his unit.

Later, 15 of these 17 people were executed. Two were discharged because the looting could not be proved.

Once again, various amounts of hoarded and looted goods were seized. The raid was completed at 18.00 hours.

In the course of the fourth raid, for which 350 German soldiers were made available, 54 people were turned over to the investigators. Eleven of them were transferred to the prisoner-of-war camp because they were without work. Seven people were sent to prison:

3 Jews;

3 Communists and people who refused to accept work;

1 leading member of the NKVD.

After a thorough interrogation all seven people were later executed.

In the course of this action, which was completed at 13:00 hours, only a small amount of hoarded goods were seized.

The Chief of the Security Police
and Security Service

Berlin,
April 21, 1942

<u>75 copies</u>
(51st copy)

*Operational Situation Report USSR No. 194*

. . . . . . . . . . . .

*Einsatzgruppe B*
Location: Smolensk

. . . . . . . . . . . .

*Police activity*

. . . . . . . . . . . .

In the period between March 6 and 30, 1942, the following were given special treatment in the area of the Einsatzgruppe:

By Sk 7a: 1,657 people, among them:
27 for belonging to partisan units and members of the former Communist Party;
45 Gypsies;
1,585 Jews.

By Sk 7b: 82 people, among them:
19 for cooperating with partisans;
22 for Communist propaganda activity and proven Communist Party membership;
14 for inflammatory remarks;
27 Jews.

Sk M[1] 52 people, among them:
41 Russians for belonging to partisan units;

---

1. Sonderkommando Moskau.

4 people for thefts or attempts to poison;

7 Jews.

EK 8 1,609 people, among them:

20 Russians for Communist activities, sabotage, and membership in the NKVD;

5 Russians for theft, burglary, and embezzlement;

33 Gypsies;

1,551 Jews.

EK 9 273 people, among them:

85 Russians for belonging to partisan units;

18 people for Communist propaganda and criminal offences;

170 Jews.

Smolensk unit 60 people, among them:

29 Russians for assisting partisans;

13 for thefts, looting, intelligence activity, and sabotage;

18 Jews.

The Chief of the Security Police
and Security Service

Berlin,
April 24, 1942

75 copies
(51st copy)

## Operational Situation Report USSR No. 195

. . . . . . . . . . . .

*Einsatzgruppe A*
Location: Krasnogvardeisk

### General situation and mood

. . . . . . . . . . . .

The major activities of the Latvian people are:
1) The fight against the Red Army and partisans in Latvia;
2) Removal of Jews and freemasons;
3) The positive outcome of the recruiting action for the Reichsarbeitsdienst;
4) The extremely successful result of the collection of winter clothes for the front;
5) The enlistment of volunteers for the police forces;
6) Teaching the Latvians to understand national-socialism and to recognize the task of the German people as renewers of Europe.

. . . . . . . . . . . .

### Institute for Anti-Semitism

The Latvian Institute for Anti-Semitism, together with the Propaganda Department of the General Commissariat, is preparing an anti-Bolshevik exhibition to take place in Riga on July 1, 1942. The director-general for education, Celms, who has repeatedly tried to sabotage the Institute for Anti-Semitism, has entrusted Professor Schwalbe with the production of a similar exhibition to take place May 1. Celms, as well as Schwalbe, is known all over Latvia to be veteran Ulmanis followers. Celms has participated in many decrees aimed against the cultural life of the German ethnic minority. Professor Schwalbe used to try through pseudo-scientific papers to lower the value of German cultural work in the Baltic countries.

. . . . . . . . . . . .

## Situation of Security Police Work

1) *Arrests*
The following were arrested:
83 people for Communist activities;
4 escaped Russian prisoners of war;
4 people for communicating with prisoners of war;
3 people for listening to transmissions of foreign countries;
5 Jews, among them three for theft during the collection of wool and fur clothing; two Jews for living outside the ghetto without permission; ·
1 person suspected of spying.
In all: 100 people.

. . . . . . . . . . .

In Daugavpils, seven Communists who took part in the shooting of German pilots after they had made a forced landing in the summer of 1941 were executed, as well as two sick Jews who were no longer fit for work.

. . . . . . . . . . . .

## Miscellaneous

Within the period of the report, a total of 1,272 people were executed, 983 of them Jews with infectious diseases or who were so old and infirm that they were no longer fit for work, 71 Gypsies, 204 Communists, and 14 more Jews who were guilty of different offences and crimes.

The Chief of the Security Police
and Security Service
— Headquarters

Berlin,
May 1, 1942

*Reports from the Occupied Eastern Territories, No. 1*

. . . . . . . . . . . .

*Einsatzgruppe A*
Location: Krasnogvardeisk

. . . . . . . . . . . .

## *Lithuania*

1) During the investigation of the fire in the government fur factory Kailis in Kaunas at the beginning of February this year, it was established that all the employees of the factory regularly stole army goods. A total of 16 people were arrested; 13 of them were shot and the rest given long prison terms. Some of the stolen goods were retrieved. It was also found that the economic manager of the factory who posed as an ethnic German is a full Jew[1] also involved in the disclosed thefts.

Finally, a Polish department manager and his mistress were shot. It was established that they were not merely involved in the fur thefts but were connected to the Polish resistance movement in the General Gouvernement.

2) On April 15, five people were arrested in Vilnius because they were suspected of having been involved in passport and other identity document forgeries. One of those arrested was convicted of helping Jews from Vilnius to travel to the General Gouvernement by supplying them with forged travel passes.[2] Up to 1,000 rubles were paid for one pass. The investigations continue.

---

1. "Volljude," as opposed to "Mischling," one of mixed parentage.
2. Laissez-passer.

## *Byelorussia*

. . . . . . . . . . . .

3) Nine more Jews were shot in Minsk for belonging to a partisan unit in Minsk.

. . . . . . . . . . . .

*Einsatzgruppe D*
Location: Simferopol

. . . . . . . . . . . .

## *Jews*

Only a small number of Jews who had been in hiding were resettled [deported]. Three Jews were in possession of passports that had been forged by the NKVD.

The Chief of the Security Police       Berlin,
   and Security Service        May 8, 1942
    —Headquarters


*Reports from the Occupied Eastern Territories, No. 2*

. . . . . . . . . . . .

### *Enemies and Executions*

Summing up the single reports on partisan movements in Byelorussia up to March 23, 1942, the following was disclosed:

Since the defeat of the Soviet forces, particularly near Vyasma and Bryansk, many Russian officers from the Soviet Army who managed to obtain civilian clothing and false passports settled in Minsk. It is they who provide the chief source of leadership and manpower replacements for the partisans.

In August/September 1941, a Jew tried to organize these units and consolidate them. He was the oil engineer Isay Kosinyets who assumed the name Mustafa Delikurdogly and possessed false papers in this name. Although Kosinyets was an officer in the reserve, he was not called up when the war broke out. In the beginning, Kosinyets limited himself mainly to listening to foreign broadcasts. He did so together with some close acquaintances in the home of a certain individual, Georgy, with the cover name Shorsh. He spread information by word of mouth.

Kosinyets and his colleagues gained new initiative in December/January 1942, when the Russian offensive began and the German advance came to a standstill. More people were recruited and obligated to cooperate. Thus, the organization of an illegal Communist Party and party movement was in place by mid-March 1942.

The leadership of the Communist Party consisted of a committee of seven, each of whom was responsible for a special task.

1) Kosinjets was the chairman of the committee and worked in matters concerning the ghetto. In this function, his job was to maintain

connections with the Jews in Minsk in order to recruit for the partisans and to collect clothing, as well as to see to it that the ranks of the partisans were kept full.

. . . . . . . . . . . .

Although the partisans had not carried out any acts of sabotage and terror in Minsk, new partisans were constantly recruited and assigned to the various partisan units in Byelorussia. They were brought in groups of 10-15 men to the partisan units by liaison people. They were brought from one location to the next by guides who were only familiar with the route to the next location and the liaison person there, thus minimizing the danger of betrayal. It was impossible to establish the number of people who had joined the partisans. So far, about 100 Jews were brought to the partisans from the ghetto. It is worth noting that the unit commanders of the partisans and the military council itself reject Jews as partisans because they are too cowardly and cannot be used in action. The main interest of the Jews in the partisan movement is to leave the ghetto; however, they avoid any other activity. Therefore, it was decided by the [partisan military council] to dispatch the Jews with incorrect orders and wrong marching routes so that these groups would wander about aimlessly. Part of them were picked up by the German Army.

. . . . . . . . . . . .

Kosinyets transmitted his information to the members of the committee through an agent who has also been arrested. In addition, whenever several news items were collected, they were printed in a secret printing shop and distributed by leaflet. The printing workshop was in an apartment building near the ghetto and was managed by a Jew called Chipchin who lived outside the ghetto. The printing shop was fully equipped to print leaflets as well as brochures. At the time of its discovery, the proof sheets of a brochure were found containing one of the most recent speeches by Stalin. The entire printing material, like matrixes, etc., had been stolen by Ivanov from the printing workshop Durchbruch in Minsk. Ivanov had received the types from the ghetto. The printing shop regularly fulfilled printing assignments given by outside partisan units. According to investigations carried out so far, about 3,000 propaganda leaflets were produced by the partisans.

The partisan movement was mainly financed by donations from the ghetto. Investigations have revealed that practically the entire ghetto is organized and divided into units and sub-units. Investigations in this direction have been limited for the time being since there are plans to dissolve the ghetto.

Ever since the beginning of March 1942, the [partisan] committee or military council maintains communications with Moscow via a group of parachutists.

. . . . . . . . . . . .

The partisans were informed by the Jews employed in the office of the General Kommissariat that a map of Minsk had been produced at the cartographic office of the German army. It listed all its units, the offices of the civil administration, the police, including the security police, as well as all factories, indicating at the same time whether they served the civil administration or the army. The head of the [partisan] reconnaissance unit commissioned a Jew who worked in the General Kommissariat to steal the map that was lying open in the office. The Jew, who, by the way, was in possession of a certificate made out by the General Kommissariat to the effect that he was of mixed origin, carried out the mission. He delivered the map to the head of the reconnaissance unit. Later on, the map was given to the group of parachutists who, on their part, evaluated the map and sent it on to Moscow.

The chief of the military council, Rokov, also recruited a man who was employed as a furnace tender at the local office and who had been a former officer. He was soon to blast the building housing the Security Police in Riga. The head of the parachute units was assigned to obtaining from Moscow the explosives needed for this project. Two more Jews employed in the workshops of local [German] offices were arrested as members of the partisan unit. Their task was to investigate matters concerning the activity of the Security Police and the Security Service.

In the course of the investigations conducted so far, a total of 404 people were arrested, including the partisans who had been organized in the ghetto. Of these, 212 had already been shot. A large quantity of weapons and ammunition was seized.

The Chief of the Security Police
and Security Service
— Headquarters

Berlin,
May 15, 1942

*Reports from the Occupied Eastern Territories, No. 3*

. . . . . . . . . . . .

Lately, it was possible to render harmless a number of people in the vicinity of Orel who were trained as terrorists in so-called espionage and saboteur courses given by the NKVD on the Lisosky farm near Orel. These courses usually lasted five days and were conducted by the chief of the special unit of the NKVD, Belyak (a Jew).

The Chief of the Security Police
and Security Service
— Headquarters

Berlin,
May 22, 1942


*Reports from the Occupied Eastern Territories, No. 4*
*Resistance movements in the Ukraine*
*The Bandera movement*

. . . . . . . . . . . .

Great weight was attached to the training of the participants of the course in the handling of weapons. They were told that a free and independent Ukrainian state can be achieved only by force. It should be pointed out that before captured arms and ammunition were delivered to the German Army, pursuant to a secret order issued to the militia leaders, the arms were hidden in their offices. Weapons were also collected by the Jews. When several depots of ammunition were seized in the district of Kostopol the militia leaders tried to cast the blame on the Jews.

. . . . . . . . . . . .

The Bandera group was financed mainly from Galicia. Some of the members make regular contributions while some are in charge of food supplies. In many cases, business managers of cooperatives are also Bandera followers. One could find even Jews who were contributors, although in many cases they were blackmailed. So far, however, Jews were not found to cooperate voluntarily. No cooperation between the Bandera movement and the NKVD could be found.

. . . . . . . . . . . .

### Jews in the Crimea[1]

The first notable Jewish settlements in the Crimea can be traced back to the end of the 18th century when the Crimea, except for Sevastopol and the Imperial summer residence, was allotted to the Jews as an area for settlement.

---

1. Editor's Note: This passage is seriously inaccurate both factually and historically and it is filled with willful misinterpretations.

The Jews tried to create for themselves in Asian Russia the autonomous Jewish province Birobidzhan. This attempt was made, with strong financial support from Jewish organizations in America, to provide in the European part of the USSR, in the Crimea, a Jewish province that was to be as secluded as possible. The general influence exerted by the Jews at that time is delineated by the fact that the "Kosed,"[2] a supervisory body especially created by the Reds, a unit of the NKVD, was totally governed by the Jews within a short time. The settling of the Jews, mainly during the period of intense collectivization (around 1928) in the Crimea, was made possible almost exclusively at the expense of the ethnic Germans and Tartars. Entire German villages in the western and central parts of the steppe were evacuated and handed over to the Jews. However, in the Crimea, as in Birobidzhan, the attempts to make a farming people of the Jews failed. Already in 1939, out of the 65,000 Jews in the Crimea, 44,000 (i.e. almost 70%) lived exclusively in the towns of Simferopol, Sevastopol, Kerch, Yevpatoria, Yalta, and Feodosia. In the countryside they were active mainly as administrators of large depots and distribution offices. There they were busy with their usurious trade as they bought and sold household articles and other goods that were hard to obtain.

Very soon, all walks of life in the towns of the Crimea were dominated exclusively by the Jews. If a chairman of some commissariat was not Jewish, then his deputy or first secretary was sure to be a Jew.

Of the Krimchaks (about 6,000) who were usually counted as part of the Jewish population, well over half lived in Simferopol (2,500) and in Karasubatsar. Their extermination, together with that of the Jews and the Gypsies in the Crimea, was accomplished for the most part by the beginning of December, 1941.

The population did not show any particular anxiety about the fact that Krimchaks and Gypsies were made to share the fate of the Jews.

. . . . . . . . . . . .

The particularly positive attitude of the Crimean Tartars towards Germany again became clear on the occasion of the Führer's birthday. Thus, the Tartars are said to have conducted services with prayers for the Führer. Furthermore, their influence on public life has grown.

---

2. Probably "Komset" — the committee for agricultural settlement of the working Jews.

## The Ethnic Situation in the Crimea (%)

. . . . . . . . . . . .

| Year | Russians | Ukrainians | Tartars | Germans | Jews and Krimchaks | Greeks | Bulgarians | Armenians | Others |
|------|------|------|------|------|------|------|------|------|------|
| 1897 |  | 43.3 | 34.1 | 5.8 | 5.2 | 3.1 | 1.1 | 1.6 | 3.9 |
| 1921 |  | 51.5 | 25.7 | 5.9 | 7.0 | 3.3 | 1.7 | 1.5 | 3.4 |
| 1926 |  | 53.6 | 25.1 | 6.1 | 6.4 | 2.3 | 1.6 | 1.6 | 3.3 |
| 1939 | 49.6 | 1.37 | 19.4 | 4.6 | 6.3 | 1.8 | 1.4 | 1.1 | 2.1 |
|  | 63.3 |  |  |  |  |  |  |  |  |

. . . . . . . . . . . .

The Karaites are people that are dispersed and on the verge of dying out. In many cases their religion is considered as belonging to the Jewish faith, but with respect to their language and ancestry, they belong to the Turko-Tartarian peoples.

The Karaites, themselves, estimate their number at approximately 15,000; about 8,000 of them live in the Soviet Union, 4,000 in the Crimea proper. They reject the Talmud [Biblical Commentaries] and are also in many other respects opposed to Judaism although they have some Jewish blood. During the Tsarist period, they frequently held higher positions in the economy and the administration. In 1917, the year of the revolution, they were closely connected with the White Guard and were, accordingly, persecuted and decimated by the Bolsheviks. A partial rapprochement with the Tartars of the Crimea has taken place prompted considerably by a common anti-Bolshevik attitude. In contrast to the Karaites, the Krimchaks are only found in the Crimea. Their number is estimated at about 6,000. According to their religion, they are genuine Jews. They speak the Tartar language with a touch of Hebrew. As for their origins, they are without any doubt a tribe that derives mainly from Jewish ancestors. Under the Tsarist regime, they were given the same treatment as the Jews (prohibition of land-ownership, etc.) However, in contrast to other Jews, their attitude towards Bolshevism was passive. The Krimchaks are violently rejected by the Tartars and the Karaites.

Settling Jews in the Crimea was primarily promoted by the Bolsheviks. Here as elsewhere, it proved impossible to make farmers out of the Jews.

In 1939, of the 65,000 Jews who lived in the Crimea (5.8%), 44,000 lived in the six largest towns. As elsewhere in the Soviet Union, the Jews in the Crimea held the most important positions in the economy, in cultural life, as in the Party and state administration.

The Chief of the Security Police
and Security Service (SD)
— Headquarters

Berlin,
May 29, 1942

*Reports from the Occupied Eastern Territories, No. 5*

. . . . . . . . . . . .

On May 5, 1942, 28 members of the Byelorussian partisan organization were hanged in public in Minsk. 251 people were shot on the same day, most of them partisans and Jews. An action against a railroad saboteur unit has been carried out. 126 people were arrested.

The Chief of the Security Police
and Security Service (SD)
— Headquarters

Berlin,
June 5, 1942

*Reports from the Occupied Eastern Territories, No. 6*

. . . . . . . . . . . .

## *The Jews in Estonia*

As Estonia was closed to Jewish immigration during the time of Tsarist rule until about the middle of the last century, Jews remained numerically unimportant, amounting to only 1.38% (4,500).

Their influence, however, in all spheres of life, was much stronger. Through their connection with the NKVD in particular, the Jews managed to carve out a strong position for themselves.

When the German troops marched in, most of the Jews had left Estonia. Only some 2,000 Jews remained, about half of them in Tallinn. The Jews were gradually apprehended by the Security Police in order to avoid unnecessary disruption of Estonia's economic life.

Today, there are no more Jews in Estonia.

The Chief of the Security Police
and Security Service (SD)
— Headquarters

Berlin,
June 12, 1942

*Reports from the Occupied Eastern Territories, No. 7*

\* \* \*

### The Jews in Latvia

In 1935, there were 93,479 Jews in Latvia, 4.79% of the total population. While prior to 1940, the year of the occupation of Latvia by the Soviet Union, no Jews were employed in the Latvian civil administration, a short time later they held influential positions. For instance, about 50% of the judges were Jews. In the superior courts, particularly the high court of justice, the number of Jews even reached 80%. The same applies to economic and cultural life.

Following the entry of the German Army, about 70,000 Jews remained in Latvia, the rest having escaped together with the retreating Bolshevik Army.

Most of the cases of sabotage and arson that occurred shortly after the entry of the German troops were instigated or actually carried out by Jews.

Thus, for instance in Daugavpils, so many fires were started that a large part of the town was destroyed. Furthermore, the deportation of 33,038 Latvians is due to Jewish influence.[1]

At present, there are only a few Jews left in the ghettos who are employed as skilled laborers.

---

1. This assertion, of course, is rank nonsense. Thousands of Jews were deported along with ethnic Latvians by the Communist rulers. Just as Jewish and Latvian "bourgeois capitalists" were victimized by the class war, so were Jewish nationalists (Zionists) and their Latvian nationalist counterparts who opposed annexation to the Soviet Union.

The following numbers of Jews are employed:

in Riga ....................................about 2,500[2]

In Daugavpils: .............................about 950

In Libau: ..................................about 300.

Apart from these Jews, Latvia has become free of Jews in the meantime.

---

2. This report is somewhat out of date. By June, 1942, there were in the Riga ghetto, besides the 2500 Latvian Jews, an additional 10-11,000 Jews deported from Germany, Austria, and Czechoslovakia.

The Chief of the Security Police
and Security Service (SD)
— Headquarters

Berlin,
June 19, 1942

## Reports from the Occupied Eastern Territories, No. 8

. . . . . . . . . . . .

### The Jews in Lithuania

According to a census taken in 1923, the number of Jews living in Lithuania was 153,743, i.e., 7.58% of the population at that time.

While the influence of the Jews had originally been limited mainly to economic matters, after the Soviet Union's occupation of Lithuania in 1940, they soon gained influence on every aspect of public life. It is characteristic that, above all, the Jews were active in the NKVD.

Because of their influence, 40,000 Lithuanians were deported to Siberia.[1]

Although the Lithuanian population expressed its hatred of the Jews in various pogroms, the Jewish problem as such had to be solved by the Security Police and the Security Service.

Those Jews who had not left Lithuania together with the retreating Bolshevik Army were interned in ghettos. As a first stage, prisons were combed in order to ferret out Jews.

At present, ghettos exist only in Kaunas, Vilnius and Siauliai. The distribution of the population in the ghettos is as follows:

Kaunas about 15,000 Jews
Vilnius about 15,000 Jews
Siauliai about 4,000 Jews

At present, these Jews are being used as skilled laborers, mainly for work essential to the army. Some of them work in three shifts.

Apart from these Jews, Lithuania is now free of Jews.

---

1. This assertion, too, is false. See note for Report No. 7.

### The Jews in Latvia

During a raid carried out in Liepaja [Libau] a short time ago, several Jews were arrested while trying to escape to Sweden.

The Chief of the Security Police
and Security Service
— Headquarters

Berlin,
June 26, 1942

*Reports from the Occupied Eastern Territories, No. 9*

. . . . . . . . . . . .

## The Jews in Byelorussia

More than 400,000 Jews lived in Byelorussia in 1926. In 1931, an additional 500,000 Jews were counted in the western areas that had once belonged to Poland. Jewish influence grew, particularly in trade, in the economy at large, as well as directly in the government administration and the Party leadership.

The measures taken by the Security Police and the Security Service have produced a fundamental change. Jewish Councils were established, and a general registration and concentration in ghettos was carried out. The Jews were identified [with a yellow patch]. In order to assure a high level of productivity, Jews arrive at their place of work under guard.

. . . . . . . . . . . .

Since the beginning of 1942, there has been information to the effect that the Soviet resistance movement and the Polish resistance movement are increasingly finding common cause ideologically. There are the organized beginnings of a joint fighting force partly assisted by the Jews who serve as messengers, smugglers of ammunition, and propagandists. Increasing numbers of Jews have also joined partisan groups. Until the late autumn of 1941, partisan-style sniping was very rare in the former east-Polish areas. Since March 1942, there are just as many reports concerning recruitment, attacks, and successes of the partisans as from the entire old Soviet territories. Regularly issued reports of the commander of the Security Police and the Security Service in Byelorussia during the last two months, especially in the last three weeks, reveal that partisan disturbances have assumed grave proportions.

. . . . . . . . . . . .

Kommando Baranovichi of the Security Police and the Security Service for Byelorussia, consisting of eight German officers and petty-officers, two members of the district Kommissariat Novogrudok, one lieutenant, and one sergeant of the Gendarmerie, and 15 Lithuanians and Russians set out for an action against the Jews[1] and arrived in the vicinity of Naliboki,[2] north of Stolpce. Naliboki is situated in an area covered by dense forest and in front of the forest there is a vast plain. As the cars and the vans of the Kommando emerged from the forest, machine-gun fire opened up on them from two sides. They tried to take the village by storm, but the plain offers no cover. Besides, the Kommando was not as well equipped with fire-arms as the partisans.

In the unequal fight, members of the Kommando fell one by one, with the exception of the SS sergeant, one SS-man, and four interpreters or drivers who were able to retreat. Some of them were wounded.

On June 10, the commander of the Security Police and the Security Service in Byelorussia, supported by motorized Gendarmerie and local police, advanced with almost all the forces under his command in the direction of Baranovichi. Fifteen members of the Kommando of the previous day were found dead in Naliboki. The boots of all the fallen had been taken off. The SS-men were stripped to their underwear and robbed of their documents and identity marks. One SS first lieutenant had a swastika and a Soviet star burned onto his chest.

Interrogation of the villagers revealed that four members of the Kommando, probably two junior officers and two members of the Gendarmerie were taken prisoner and led through Naliboki. They had red flags stuck into their tied hands. The partisans explained jeeringly to the population: "Look! These are your masters."

Further investigations revealed that on June 6 the four abducted men were shot in a forest near Naliboki.

---

1. Judenaktion.
2. In the original, wrongly, Walibokie.

## The Jews in Byelorussia

Of all the areas in Ostland, Byelorussia had always been most densely permeated by Jews. According to a census taken in 1926, more than 400,000 Jews lived in the former Byelorussian Soviet Socialist Republic (BSSR). According to the last census in 1931, more than 500,000 Jews were living in the western areas that formerly belonged to Poland alongside a majority of Byelorussians. Only part of the Jews admit to being Jews, as we know from experience, in order to hide their real identity. Thus, only a part of the Jews is included in the number of Jews listed who actually live in Byelorussia. Thus, the actual total is much higher.

At the time of the outbreak of war more than half of the Jews of Byelorussia lived in the larger cities, particularly in Minsk, where of about 238,000 inhabitants, 100,000-120,000 were Jews. Although the larger part of the Byelorussian Jews were poor, they had, nevertheless, in the course of years, become influential in all spheres of life in the former Polish as well as the originally Soviet Russian areas. In the former Polish area, the influence exerted by the Jews was mainly due to their strong economic position. In the Soviet part of Byelorussia, they held positions within the state apparatus, in the first place within the Communist Party, especially its power-centers, the Central Committee and the Politbureau.

The measures taken by the Security Police and the Security Service have created a fundamental change in Byelorussia as far as the Jewish question is concerned. Jewish Councils were set up in order to keep the Jews effectively under control, irrespective of the measures to be taken later on. These councils were responsible for the behavior of the members of their race. Moreover, Jews were registered and concentrated into ghettos. Finally, the Jews were identified with a yellow badge to be worn on the chest and on the back, like the Jew-star that has been introduced in the Reich. In order to make full use of the work potential of the Jews, they are generally used in groups for cleaning jobs.

These measures have created the basis for the planned Final Solution of the European Jewish question specifically with respect to Byelorussia.

The Chief of the Security Police
and Security Service
— Headquarters

Berlin,
July 17, 1942

*Reports from the Occupied Eastern Territories, No. 12*

. . . . . . . . . . . .

### *Jews (Ukraine)*

It was possible to render harmless a group of partisans in the district of Vladimir-Volynsk who had planned an uprising in the town. They also planned to set free from the local prisoner camp 8,000 Soviet Russian officers. The action was to be carried out with the assistance of the ghetto (about 15,000 Jews) and a significant number of Bolshevik agents who were in town at the time. Most of the imprisoned officers had alrady made themselves pointed knives out of broken steel helmets for this event. In the course of the security measures that were taken, 36 Communist officials as well as 76 Jewish-Bolshevik officers, among them a number of political commissars, were found to be the main organizers. The Communist agents as well as the 76 Jewish officers were given special treatment.

The attitude and mood of the population were favorably disposed to the fact that this partisan group had been rendered harmless.

A Jewish woman physician was arrested in Uman. She had been active with the Red Army and was taken prisoner by German troops. After her escape from the prisoner-of-war camp, she took work under an assumed name as a physician in a children's home in Uman. She exploited the chance to commit espionage by gaining occasional access to a prisoner-of-war camp.

In the area of Shatsk, a cleansing action took place following a recent attack on a police Kommando in the course of which 340 Jews and Communists were shot.

In a forest camp near Slatopol, 14 Jews and Jewesses were shot after they were hunted down and then tried to escape.

The Chief of the Security Police
and Security Service
— Headquarters

Berlin,
July 24, 1942

*Reports from the Occupied Eastern Territories, No. 13*

. . . . . . . . . . . .

The ongoing war of Germany against the Soviets is, in the first place, an ideological war. Thus, all those elements left behind who had supported the international Communist movement in the areas that the German Army liberated now no longer enjoy sufficient room to function. Therefore, the major part of the Communist and the Soviet activists, as well as the Jews who failed to escape with the Bolsheviks, went into the forests where they joined the partisans.

The Chief of the Security Police
and Security Service (SD)
— Headquarters

Berlin,
August 7, 1942

*Reports from the Occupied Eastern Territories, No. 15*

. . . . . . . . . . . .

## *Lithuania*

In the vast forest areas of the northern part of the Kedainiai district
and the adjoining areas of the districts Panevezys and Siauliai, bands
numbering up to 100 men were reported, [partisan units] which,
lately, had upset the population with acts of terror, constantly at-
tacking smaller groups of police and civilians. The major part of these
bands consisted of escaped Soviet Russian prisoners-of-war, and of
Jews who had evaded being placed into ghettos ...

In the area of Kharkov, cleansing operations continued and several
hundred people were seized for special treatment.

An action against Communist bandits and Jews carried out in the
town of Korocha brought no results as almost all the Jews and Communists who lived there had already been evacuated. It was learned
that there are bigger groups of scattered Soviet Russian Army units
in the forests and orchards south of Korocha where they were joined
by local bandits. A security division will be dispatched to fight against
these bands.

The Chief of the Security Police
and Security Service (SD)
— Headquarters

Berlin,
August 14, 1942

## Reports from the Occupied Eastern Territories, No. 16

. . . . . . . . . . . .

The number of inhabitants who remained in Rostov [on the Don] comes to approximately 200,000-300,000. Most of the Armenians, mainly men aged 17-50, were evacuated by the Soviet Russians. The ethnic Germans in the zone of the present action were also taken to the eastern areas of Soviet Russia.[1] The influence of Soviet propaganda on the rest of the population can still be felt; however, the fear that the Soviets might return is clearly subsiding.

Following the departure [retreat] of the German troops in November 1941, the administration of Rostov was placed in the hands of the NKVD. In order to carry out an extensive political purge, it mobilized the Jews of Rostov, some of whom enrolled in the NKVD. Citizens who had maintained close contact with the Germans were shot. The number of people shot reached about 800.

During the winter and thereafter, almost the entire population was forced to work on the construction of defense works outside and inside the city. An attempted uprising in one of the suburbs was cruelly suppressed. Besides, many persons froze to death, died of exhaustion, and perished as a result of severe punishments.

Until November 1941, the number of Jews in Rostov is said to have amounted to 50,000. All professions were occupied by Jews. A high percentage of them were physicians and pharmacists, and many held various professions connected with the law; more than half the judges in Rostov were Jewish.

On August 1, 1942,[2] a Jewish Council was installed by order of the Sonderkommando stationed in Rostov; so far, 2,000 Jews have been registered. Further necessary measures [for their extermination] have been started.

---

1. This is a reference to the Volga Germans whom Stalin had deported en masse for security reasons to the Soviet Republics in Central Asia.
2. Following the return of the German occupation forces.

The Chief of the Security Police
and Security Service
— Headquarters

Berlin,
August 20, 1942

*Reports from the Occupied Eastern Territories, No. 17*

. . . . . . . . . . . .

Activity by [partisan] gangs in the eastern territories, particularly northwest of Vyazma, has increased considerably. Especially in the vicinity of Vladimirskoye strong gangs have appeared who hold the road to Kholm and attack nearby villages. A total of 102 attacks occurred in one week.

The majority of the gang-members are recruited from the scattered Red troops who, led by officers and Jews, roam and loot in the neighboring countryside. Some of them stay with the frightened population overnight; others try to make their way to the Russian front.

There are also many prisoners-of-war who wander through the area begging until they are admitted into the gangs.

. . . . . . . . . . . .

In Selidovka, in the area of Kommando Kharkov, one Jewess and one Russian were arrested for possession of poison, probably in order to poison wells.[1]

---

1. This is an old anti-Semitic canard dating back to the Middle Ages when Jews were frequently accused of poisoning wells, usually in times when the plague raged through Europe.

The Chief of the Security Police
and Security Service
— Headquarters

Berlin,
September 4, 1942

*Reports from the Occupied Eastern Territories, No. 19*

. . . . . . . . . . .

## Byelorussia

On August 22, relying on reports of the Security Service's reconnoitering services from Baranovichi, the forces of the Security Police
carried out a partial action against the gangs [partisans] northwest of
Slonim.

The forces of the Security Police continued their reconnoitering
activity during the action and frequently clashed with the enemy.
Among other things they succeeded in taking captive groups of
armed Jews. Interrogation on the spot produced important information on their numbers, their arms, and the movements of the gangs.

According to information received to date, in the course of an
armed fight lasting about six hours, 200 bandits, half of them Jews,
were shot.

Except for a few wounded soldiers, the German side lost four gendarmerie employees and one member of the Latvian police force.

Two larger gang camps which were camouflaged and difficult to attack because of their location were eradicated.

. . . . . . . . . . .

The Konotap county, near Glukhov, as well as the area around
Putivl, are almost entirely under the rule of robber gangs [partisan
units]. A band of robbers numbering 800, among them Jews, women
and children, was found in the forest area of Doborichi and Tyligova.
The robbers were in possession of machine guns and rocket launch-
ers.

. . . . . . . . . . . .

On August 11, 1942, in order to test the population in the band-infested area around Ratno, a Security Police force [composed of Ukrainian SS Auxiliaries] wearing Soviet Russian uniforms and equipped with various weapons was sent to the villages of Staroseim and Konishe.

The population behaved in a servile manner towards the "gang." They addressed the leader as "comrade lieutenant," asked with concern if sentries were posted. An Ukrainian arrogantly offered his help, supplied information as to the numbers of the police force and offered to provide information in the future. A woman told that her people were kept informed of the conditions in Ratno through the collaboration of two members of the militia there. The mayor declared that he had repeatedly sheltered gangs before.

Three persons, the above-mentioned woman as well as seven Jews, were given special treatment.

After the action was completed, the population was unequivocally told to offer resistance to the gangs. This action obviously had a very strong psychological and propaganda effect.

The Chief of the Security Police
and Security Service
— Headquarters

Berlin,
September 18, 1942

*Reports from the Occupied Eastern Territories, No. 21*

. . . . . . . . . . . .

Fifteen people belonging to an illegal Communist organization under the leadership of a Jew were arrested in Berdichev (Ukraine). Besides spreading Communist propaganda, they intended to set the grain harvest on fire and to derail trains.

The Chief of the Security Police
and Security Service
Headquarters

Berlin,
October 9, 1942

*Reports from the Occupied Eastern Territories, No. 24*

. . . . . . . . . . . .

Most of the population, particularly in the gang-infested territories, is kept informed about events on the front and other matters only through the eyes of enemy propaganda. As always, rumors spread wildly. In the area of Berdichev, there was a rumor that after the Jews, all the Poles in the camp would be shot.

The Chief of the Security Police
and Security Service
— Headquarters

Berlin,
November 6, 1942

*Report from the Occupied Eastern Territories, No. 28*

. . . . . . . . . . . .

The commander of the Security Police and Security Service in Kiev arrested a Jew who wore a German Army uniform. He was a Soviet prisoner-of-war. After his release from prison he was used as a driver for a German military unit. Inquiries revealed that he had been a secretary of the Komsomol and an NKVD agent.

The Chief of the Security Police                    Berlin,
     and Security Service                    November 13, 1942
       — Headquarters


*Reports from the Occupied Eastern Territories, No. 29*

. . . . . . . . . . . .

In the territory of the Security Police and the Security Service Command in Latvia, several [Soviet] parachute units were observed as they jumped. Until now, it was possible to arrest three of the parachutists. Apart from this, a Jewish female parachutist was shot during an armed battle. She was in possession of a Nagan revolver and a flashlight.

. . . . . . . . . . . .

In the eyes of the local population, the Labor Office in Riga has taken over the functions of the Jewish NKVD. Thus, the people call this office the Cheka. They say, "The Jews (Communists) have deported us to Russia, the Germans to the Reich." The Russians have similarly used the word-play "voluntary deportation" coined by the Germans.

The Chief of the Security Police
and Security Service
— Headquarters

Berlin,
December 4, 1942

*Reports from the Occupied Eastern Territories, No. 32*

. . . . . . . . . . . .

According to reports, there has been a rapid decrease in black marketeering in the places that are free of Jews.

The Chief of the Security Police           Berlin,
and Security Service              December 11, 1942
— Headquarters


*Reports from the Occupied Eastern Territories, No. 33*

. . . . . . . . . . . .

## *Gang [partisan] disturbances*
## *Latvia*

Intensive intelligence work has revealed that Jews intend to escape from Riga together with escaped Russian prisoners-of-war in order to join up with bandits in east Latvia. Through reliable sources it was learned that relevant discussions were held in a private house. At that meeting, all details were confirmed concerning ammunition, route of flight, and linking up with the gangs. At night, nine Jews who had fled the ghetto met in an empty apartment together with a Soviet Russian lieutenant, Pismanov, called "Borka," who had escaped from the POW camp. Pismanov is a Jew and he escaped from the prison camp in Riga on September 5. He was the leader and organizer of the Jews who escaped [from the ghetto] and the [Soviet] prisoners-of-war. Ever since his flight, Pismanov had been staying illegally in Riga and had established contact with the ghetto through Sandel, the Jewish leader of a workers' marching group.[1] A man who maintained contact with the Jews arranged for a van and driver to be supplied to the members of the group. The van was to transport the escaped Jews to Anspils in the area of the gang's activities. Here they were to be met by a liaison officer of the gangs.

The van was stopped by a Kommando of the Security Police on the Riga-Modohn road. Immediately, all the passengers in the van opened fire. In the course of the battle that lasted for about 1½ hours,

---

1. Jewish slave workers would march out of the ghetto in groups, each one composed of workers assigned to the same work location (Dienststelle).

seven Jews were shot [and killed] and two were arrested. On the side of the Security Police, one man was wounded. The Jews carried the following weapons:

Two German army pistols 0.8, five drum-revolvers, and one Russian machine pistol with two magazines. The Jews wore winter clothing, padded trousers, and jackets. In the course of the action, the leader of the organization as well as 16 people, among them five Soviet Russian officers, were arrested. If all had gone according to plan, in case the first trip was successful, further transports would be brought to the territory controlled by the gangs.

The Chief of the Security Police
and Security Service
— Headquarters

Berlin,
December 18, 1942

*Reports from the Occupied Eastern Territories, No. 34*

. . . . . . . . . . . .

## *Gang [partisan] Disturbances*

On December 4, an auxiliary policeman on a reconnoitering mission succeeded in locating a fortified bunker in a forest. The man, who is a local inhabitant, did not hesitate to organize a small shock troop [team of soldiers] with which to attack the bunker on December 6. The unit was armed with five rifles and six hand-grenades. [On the way] at a distance of about 300 meters, they met a bandit in the forest who was armed with a machine gun. He was finished off immediately. Then, the unit proceeded towards the bunker, overpowering three bandits who were standing nearby. Three other men and two women who offered resistance were rendered harmless with a hand-grenade. One bandit managed to escape, but was caught and finished off later in the next village. Most of the bandits were Jews who had escaped from the Radun Ghetto.

. . . . . . . . . . . .

## *Ethnic Germans in the Caucasus operational area*

Social help related mostly to providing clothing which was found in Jewish homes. A preferential food supply was arranged in cooperation with welfare leaders. Ethnic Germans can find work easily if they speak both languages. The others are treated preferentially when it comes to employment. In this way, wherever possible, social and economic improvement was achieved. Assignment of better living quarters lead to improved and more hygienic living conditions.

The Chief of the Security Police
and Security Service
— Headquarters

Berlin,
January 22, 1943

*Reports from the Occupied Eastern Territories, No. 38*

. . . . . . . . . . . .

## Operation "Hamburg" in the area of Slonim

So far, this has been the greatest success in the Byelorussian area. Information provided by the intelligence unit of the Security Police and Security Service was so exact that every single [partisan] camp could be pinpointed. 1,676 bandits [partisans] were killed in numerous battles. Furthermore, 1,510 people were shot on grounds that they belonged to the gangs. A rich hoard of captured loot included four armored cars and eight guns. The number of cattle and amounts of grain can barely be calculated. Furthermore, 2,658 Jews and 30 Gypsies were arrested in the communities inside the area of the action. German losses: seven dead and 18 wounded.

## Operation "Altona" in the area of Kossov-Byten

This action was aimed at a larger group of gangs who had escaped southwards during Operation "Hamburg." Reconnoitering was done by the Security Police units. The band lost 97 dead during the fighting. Furthermore, 785 persons were shot on suspicion of belonging to gangs. 126 Jews and 58 Gypsies were arrested. The amount of cattle and food was considerable, but [the quantity of] ammunition was not very large. No losses on our side.

The Chief of the Security Police
and Security Service
— Headquarters

Berlin,
January 29, 1943

*Reports from the Occupied Eastern Territories, No. 39*

. . . . . . . . . . . .

*Gang [partisan] activity in the operational area of Einsatzgruppe B*

. . . . . . . . . . . .

In some cases, gang members want to resign from the gangs. This desire is intensified as a result of the winter weather conditions and the food situation. The reasonable treatment of the prisoners-of-war now under discussion among the members of the gangs does not fail to produce its effect. The main body of the bands still adheres firmly to Bolshevism and consists mostly of paratroopers, Communist Party functionaries, officers, and Jews. It has its own strict system [of discipline] to have all orders carried out promptly, without hesitation. This system makes it difficult for the gang's rank and file to leave the gangs of their own free will. This fact, with the aid of leaflets, is used for propaganda purposes and for driving a wedge between the leadership of the gang and its members. The leaflets point out that the gangs' nuisance value merely worsens the poverty of the civilian population, which is already poor enough, and intensifies the misery of the Russian people.

# Index

Karatchev, 254
Karyago, Feodor, 232
Kaslov, Nikita, 262
Katchura, 285
Katjucko, 95
Katzman, Ber, 233
Katzman, Salomon, 233
Kaunas, 1, 4, 6, 7, 10, 11, 17, 18, 47, 82, 88, 89, 90, 91, 269, 270, 274, 275, 277, 328, 330, 337, 350
Kedainiai, 90
Kerch, 267, 291, 344
Kharkov, 238, 239, 240, 281, 289, 322, 329, 357
Kherson, 142, 143, 161, 168, 175, 176, 189
Khmielnik, 102, 103, 136
Khorostov, 60
Khoslavichi, 149, 178, 179
Khotin, 19, 25, 63, 110, 118
Kieper, Judge, 97
Kiev, 38, 47, 83, 93, 102, 164-165, 168, 172, 173, 184-186, 187, 196, 199, 211, 214, 217, 228, 229, 236, 238, 239, 249, 251-252, 281, 288, 299, 304, 321, 322, 324, 325, 328, 364
Kikerino, 133, 156, 157, 160
Kikorino, 142
Kirnychny, Dr., 20
Kirovo, 129, 136
Kirovograd, 101, 159, 215
Kishinev, 76, 107
Klimaitis, 7
Klimov, 150
Klinovichi, 264
Klintsy, 171, 180
Klusk, 112, 113
Kobrin, 13
Kodyma, 76, 109-110
Kolkhoz, 43
Kolkhoz Voroshilov, 117
Komarovka, 123
Königsberg, 17
Konishe, 361
Kopie, 84, 85
Kopis, 70
Koreliche, 45
Kormu, 264
Korosten, 99, 102, 129, 135, 198
Korostyschev, 79
Koryukov, 139
Koseletz, 179, 180, 238
Koshevatoye, 199

Kosinyets, Isay, 339-340
Koskull, Stürmbanführer, 107
Kossov-Byten, 370
Kostopol, 114
Kotelnia, 134
Kotovsk, 109
Koziatyn, 103
Kraljovo, 200
Kramartorskaya, 282, 288
Krasnogvardeisk, 191, 222, 224, 230, 237, 245, 268, 270, 272, 274, 276, 279, 287, 288, 290, 294, 299, 301, 303, 306, 311, 312, 313, 315, 316, 319, 321, 323, 327, 330, 335, 337
Krasnoyo-Selo, 243, 266, 323
Krassnyje, 101
Krasubasar, 267, 291
Krause, 84
Kremenchug, 139, 186, 282, 304
Kremenets, 39, 57, 67, 127
Kribishevno, 247
Krichov, 264
Krimchaks, 250, 345
Krivoy-Rog, 131, 136, 215, 228
Krointnichi, 70
Kropka, 70, 72
Krottingen, 10, 16
Krugloye, 180
Krupka, 53, 54, 206
Kube, Gauleiter, 205
Kupreyev, Dr., 51
Kurland, 47
Kursk, 262
Kuyachiche, 205
Kvasinitse, 121

Labilish, 315
Lachoviche, 37, 70
Lakhoviche, 45, 46, 84
Lapitski, Elia, 258
Latgale, 61
Leikina, Fania, 233
Lemberg, 40
Lemnitsa, 203
Leningrad, 245, 266, 295, 299
Lepel, 206
Lettgalen, 287
Libau, 6, 225-226, 280, 349, 351
Lida, 5, 9, 14, 23, 45, 70, 71, 92
Liepaja, 163
Linden, Abraham, 233
Lishovishi, 129
Lisunova, Nina, 232